DANGEROUS SISTERS OF THE HEBREW BIBLE

DANGEROUS SISTERS OF THE HEBREW BIBLE

AMY KALMANOFSKY

Fortress Press
Minneapolis

DANGEROUS SISTERS OF THE HEBREW BIBLE

Cover image: © RMN-Grand Palais/Art Resources, NY Picasso, Pablo (1881-1973) ARS, NY

Cover design: Laurie Ingram

Library of Congress Cataloging-in-Publication Data

Kalmanofsky, Amy.

Dangerous sisters of the Hebrew Bible / Amy Kalmanofsky.

pages cm

Includes bibliographical references.

ISBN 978-1-4514-6995-0 (pbk. : alk. paper) — ISBN 978-1-4514-7969-0 (ebook)

1. Sisters in the Bible. 2. Bible. Old Testament–Criticism, interpretation, etc. I. Title.

BS579.S57K35 2014

221.9'22082–dc23

2013034857

The paper used in this publication meets the minimum requirements of American National Standard for Information Sciences — Permanence of Paper for Printed Library Materials, ANSI Z329.48-1984.

Manufactured in the U.S.A.

This book was produced using PressBooks.com, and PDF rendering was done by PrinceXML.

CONTENTS

Acknowledgments

This is a book about relationships. I am grateful to have many relationships with people that shape me intellectually and support me emotionally.

I thank my teachers and colleagues at the Jewish Theological Seminary of America who model how to apply a critical eye to beloved material, and who create a stimulating and respectful learning community. I especially am privileged to work with gifted and learned Bible scholars: Stephen A. Geller, Stephen Garfinkel, Robert A. Harris, Walter Herzberg, David Marcus, and Benjamin D. Sommer. In particular, I thank Alan Cooper and Edward L. Greenstein, whose guidance and expertise I depend upon. I also thank David Hoffman, Barry W. Holtz, Daniel Nevins, and Seth Schwartz for your generous and good humored encouragement.

My first Bible teacher was Tikva Frymer-Kensky of blessed memory. She opened my eyes to the beauty of the Bible and to its complications. In many ways, her questions are my questions and her readings are my readings. I will always be grateful to her.

I thank my students at JTS and in the communities in which I have taught. Over and over again, I have the pleasure of engaging with people who are committed to and who love learning. Consciously and unconsciously, your ideas are in this book.

I thank the women in my life, my sisterhoods. Because this is a book, I single out my sisters in the academy who understand what it takes to write one while teaching full time and living fully. I thank you for your critiques and for your support along the way: Shira D. Epstein, Deborah Glanzberg-Krainin, Esther J. Hamori, Karina Martin Hogan, Carol K. Ingall, Marjorie Lehman, Adriane Leveen, Stephanie Oppenheim, Nicole J. Ruane, Shuly Rubin Schwartz, Nancy Sinkoff, and Andrea L. Weiss. I also thank Leslie Rubin for her calm demeanor and expert editing.

Above all, I thank Jeremy Kalmanofsky, who every day and in every way is my משיב נפש.

This book is dedicated to sisters Hadas and Odelya and to their brothers Yedidya and Shaya. I offer you all a sister's blessing and hope that you grow into multitudes.

Ideal and Dangerous Sisters in the Bible

Family narratives are among the most well known and beloved stories of the Bible. Fathers, sons, brothers, and mothers take center stage in the Bible's grand narratives, which relate how God selects and sustains one family—and ultimately one nation—to participate in a covenantal relationship. The efforts to secure land and progeny, central concerns for any family in the ancient world, create tension within the biblical narrative as characters position themselves and betray one another to achieve those goals. Will Sarah have a son, and will Abraham kill him? Will Ishmael and Esau be granted their rightful inheritances? Will the descendents of Jacob make it out of Egypt and the wilderness and to the land of Canaan? Once in the land, can they remain there?

Within the context of the Bible's greater narrative, sisters are often overlooked as significant players in these family dramas. For good reasons, sisters and their stories seem superfluous to the Bible's central story and to the world it reflects. Family, referred to in the Bible as the *bet av*, the house of the father, was the essential social unit of ancient Israel. A typical *bet av* would include an elder patriarch and his wife or wives, their sons and their wives and children, unmarried daughters, and, if the family was affluent, slaves, who lived together in a family compound.[1] Sisters and daughters maintained a precarious position within the Israelite family, which privileged its males and preserved their authority.[2]

Scholars debate whether to apply the value-laden label "patriarchal" to ancient Israel, arguing that women were no less valued in their homes and were as essential to the household's survival as men were.[3] Scholars also argue that the term "patriarchal" is anachronistic and does not accurately describe ancient Israel's society.[4] Whether Israelite society was patriarchal is beyond the scope of this study. I do not attempt to describe family life in ancient Israel. Rather, I am concerned with the Bible's ideological orientation as reflected in its family narratives, in particular its portrayal of sisters. Although I recognize its anachronistic assumptions, for want of a better term, I use "patriarchal" to describe the Bible's ideology that privileges men over women. I also use the term "patriarch" to refer to the privileged males in any household and the term "designated patriarch" to refer to the privileged males in Abraham's line.

1

Two customs ensured a young woman's marginal position within her natal family. First, as long as there were sons, daughters could not inherit their father's property, that is, property was based on patrilineal descent passed.[5] Second, once married, young women would leave their natal homes and join their husbands' families; that is, families lived patrilocally.[6] Given the patrilineal and patrilocal nature of the Israelite family, it is not surprising that sisters play minor roles within the biblical narratives that are primarily concerned with securing Israel's inheritance. Esther Fuchs observes that in general, women are central figures in the Bible only when they help or hinder the overall goals of providing an heir and securing the inheritance.[7] Therefore they appear in the family narratives mostly in the roles of wives—or potential wives—and mothers.[8] Rebecca, a prominent figure, is an excellent example of how a woman typically functions in the context of the family narratives. She appears as a powerful wife in Genesis 25, who provides an heir for her husband, and as a powerful mother in Genesis 27, who secures her son's inheritance. Few readers recognize that she also appears as an ideal sister in Genesis 24, which I discuss below.

In particular, sisters seem extraneous to the Bible's family narratives. As transient figures in their natal homes without inheritance rights—with the notable exception of Zelophehad's daughters who inherit their father's property in Numbers 27—sisters have no natural place in the biblical story about heirs and property. In contrast, brothers dominate the Bible's family narratives. Beginning with the story of Cain and Abel, fraternal rivalry is among its most common tropes. After killing his brother Abel in a jealous rage, Cain's question to God ("Am I my brother's keeper?"[9]) introduces the family narratives and sets their tone. Apparently the answer to Cain's question must be *no* because from then on, biblical brothers deceive, threaten, and betray one another as they vie for their fathers' legacies.

In these family narratives rarely does the Bible seem to focus on sisters. And when it does, sisters could be seen, as Frederick E. Greenspahn sees them, to be pale reflections of the more dominant male characters in the family narratives. In Greenspahn's reading, Rachel and Leah, the Bible's most prominent sisters, function as little more than as stand-ins for the brothers Jacob and Esau. The narrative of sororal rivalry serves as a reminder of Jacob's betrayal of his father and of his older brother.[10] Jacob's marriage to Leah is his just come-uppance for having tricked his father and stolen his brother's blessing.

Yet this conventional reading can overlook the Bible's significant sisters. Their narratives reflect a sister's unique place within the Israelite family and serve a distinct purpose within the context of the Bible's family narratives. At particular moments of familial crisis and vulnerability within the patrilineal narratives, the Bible assigns sisters crucial roles. Lot's daughters (two sisters), Sarah, Rebecca, Dinah, Rachel, Leah, Miriam, the daughters of Zelophehad, Tamar, Michal, Merav, and the metaphorical sisters of Judah and Israel are sisters whose stories scholars too often have overlooked. This study shines a light on sisters and their stories.

My goal is to understand how the Bible represents sisters and sisterhoods—women's networks not defined by immediate kinship ties—and to consider how they function within their discrete narratives as well as within the Bible at large. My analysis of the Bible's sister and sisterhood stories draws upon recent social and historical scholarship about ancient Israel's families and society, but my argument here is a literary analysis rather than a historical one, though it may have implications for understanding the roles sisters and sisterhoods played in ancient Israelite families. I am interested in how sisters and sisterhoods are portrayed and how they function in the biblical narratives. To understand how the Bible represents sisters and sisterhoods, I provide a close literary reading of each narrative, considering its rhetorical strategies, themes, and function within the greater biblical narrative. All translations of the biblical texts that I include are my own. I rely upon the resources of contemporary biblical scholarship to enrich my understanding of these narratives, as well as to offer points of comparison to my own readings. When brought together, these readings reveal common themes and narrative strategies that provide a coherent image of the biblical representation of sisters and sisterhoods.

The texts I address in this study come from a variety of biblical books and cross genres such as narratives, poetry, and law. As such, they certainly reflect different periods in Israel's history and in the composition of its texts. Despite this range, I believe it is possible to discuss the *biblical* representation of sisters even as it relates to the structure of the family in the ancient world because, as Jon L. Berquist observes, the structure of the family remains consistent through much of Israel's history.[11] Studies like this one that consider the literary representation of particular figures are crucial to the study of the Bible.[12]

By bringing together a number of texts that focus on a particular figure, we can observe literary patterns within the Bible and can identify underlying ideologies.[13] Tikva Frymer-Kensky states this to be her intention in *Reading the Women of the Bible*. By reading the biblical stories of women collectively, Frymer-Kensky is able to identify common themes and concerns that shape these narratives.[14] A study of the Bible's sisters sheds light on its family narratives, with their implicit gender dynamics and ideologies. Through the sister and sisterhood narratives, the biblical authors reveal pressing anxieties raised by women's roles in a patrilineal ideology. In narratives about property, the sisters are critical figures in ensuring the passage of the patrimony to the proper heirs. In stories about progeny, the sisters—especially regarding the consequent possibility of incest—play important roles in the generation of new heirs. In stories about exogamy, the sisterhoods serve to deter intermarriage and thus maintain the community's firm boundaries.

By analyzing the Bible's sister and sisterhood stories, I identify a heretofore overlooked common narrative concern and function. Just as there is a typical brother story about rivalry and inheritance, there is a typical sister story concerned with the vulnerability of the natal household and a typical sisterhood story concerned with the vulnerability of Israelite society. Although many of these stories function as cautionary tales, protecting the Bible's patriarchal structures, they should not be seen only as patriarchal propaganda, as Fuchs sees them, designed to limit the roles women play in the Bible. For Fuchs, the Bible not only marginalizes its women, it "advocates their marginality," to support a "politics of male domination."[15] My readings of the Bible's sister and sisterhood stories seeks to expand our perception of the roles women play beyond that of mother, daughter, and wife and reveals their narrative and rhetorical power.

The Bible's sisters and sisterhoods are powerful figures, and their stories are essential to the greater biblical narrative. Analyzing their significance sheds light on women in the Bible and perhaps in ancient Israel. My analysis suggests insight into the nature of actual interpersonal relationships within families and society and the particular anxieties sisters induce. Sisters and sisterhoods may be marginal and, at times, destabilizing figures, but they are crucial players in the biblical drama. As we will see, sisters ensure the success of the designated patriarch; and sisterhood provides a potent model for the divine-human relationship.

I divide this study into three parts and begin with the stories—two narratives and one parable—of the paired sisters Rachel and Leah, Michal and Merav, and Rebel Israel and Faithless Judah, whom the prophets Jeremiah and Ezekiel portray as sisters married to God. Next, I examine the role sisters play in the Bible's incest narratives and consider the stories of Lot's daughters, Sarah as Abraham's wife-sister, and Tamar, who is raped by her half-brother. Although I identify the women I study as sisters, I recognize that they also play other roles such as mothers, wives, and daughters within their narratives. In my analysis, I offer reasons for identifying them as sisters and their narratives as sister stories, but I do not argue that they must be seen exclusively as sisters. Rather, I argue that seeing them as sisters illuminates their role in their specific narratives and provides insight into the overall role sisters play in the biblical narrative.

In the final section of my study, I examine sisterhoods and begin with the daughters of Adam, Moab, the land, and Israel. I then consider the daughters of Jerusalem in the Song of Songs. In the final chapter, I examine the relationship between Ruth and Naomi, which I argue is the Bible's most positive sisterhood. I conclude by reflecting on the role of sisters and sisterhood in the Bible and consider its narrative and theological implications.

Throughout this study, I identify two paradigms of sisters and sisterhoods—which I call the "ideal" and the "dangerous"—that shape these passages and determine their broader narrative function. I believe these paradigms reflect the Bible's implicit gender ideology and provide general insight into the biblical representation of women. At no point does the Bible explicitly present its gender ideology or these paradigms. It is the role of the reader, and specifically the role of the feminist Bible scholar, to extract the gender ideology that is encoded in the text. Gale A. Yee models this in her book *Poor Banished Children of Eve: Woman as Evil in the Hebrew Bible* in which she states that it is the critic's role to decode the text and consider the often conflicted relationship of the text to the ideology or ideologies it embodies.[16] Following Yee's example, I strive to extract the Bible's gender ideology through its depictions of sisters and sisterhoods. My paradigms of the ideal and dangerous sister offer an illustrative distillation of the Bible's gender ideology that works to preserve the power, property, and honor of the family's patriarchs, often at the expense of its females.[17]

Claudia V. Camp adopts a similar rhetoric to my own when addressing the specific roles sisters play within the Bible's priestly texts. Camp argues that sister stories serve the priestly ideology that is concerned with protecting the priests' ascribed status and their unique identity within Israel. Camp describes sisters as "a dangerous anomaly in a system of male descent—both closest kin in the 'right' lineage, yet, as not-male, altogether Other."[18] Since they share a blood line with their brothers, sisters are dangerous because they pose a threat to priestly identity. The texts work to "estrange" sisters in order to secure the power and status only afforded to *male* priests.[19] Addressing many of the texts that Camp does and relying on her insights, my analysis of the Bible's sister stories offers a broader perspective. I agree with Camp that patrilineal ideology is a central concern of the sister stories. However, I argue that these stories are also concerned more broadly with patriarchal authority and the stability of household.

Within their narratives, ideal sisters serve the needs of their patriarchs and strengthen their patriarchal, most often natal, households. In contrast, dangerous sisters are destabilizing figures who assert an independent agency that challenges patriarchal authority and threatens the stability of the natal household. At heart, both of these paradigms reflect a sister's marginal status, and reveal her potential to be destructive within the narratives. Like Miriam, an ideal sister—who protected her baby brother when he floated down the Nile—can turn dangerous when she challenges his leadership in the desert.

The majority of sister stories fit the dangerous-sister paradigm, in which an independent sister destabilizes a natal household in distress, though implicit in this dangerous depiction is its ideal counterpart. One can discern desired values and the parameters of appropriate behavior from stories in which those values and parameters are breached. At one level, simply identifying the Bible's dangerous sisters supports feminist biblical scholars like Fuchs who argue that the Bible depicts women negatively to define their roles and limit their power.[20] Sisters, like women in the Bible in general, are destabilizing figures. However, my study, which considers the function of dangerous sisters within the broader biblical narrative, offers a more complex picture—one that may impact our understanding of the roles women generally play in the Bible.

My study reveals that although they are destabilizing figures within their narratives, these dangerous sisters serve a crucial narrative purpose. The Bible employs dangerous sisters when it seeks to weaken certain households, like those of Lot, Laban, and Saul. In this way, dangerous sisters are *narratively* powerful figures that serve the interests of the Bible's grand story. They help solidify the power of the text's designated patriarch (Abraham, Jacob, and David, respectively) by working to remove a rival family from the narrative. Yet even though the Bible needs dangerous sisters and invests in them, these characters defy patriarchal authority and come to unhappy ends. The Bible does not embrace or reward its dangerous sisters. Their narratives function as cautionary tales that support patriarchal ideology and warn young women, either directly or indirectly, to curb their desires and serve the needs of their patriarchs.[21] In this way, dangerous sisters are *rhetorically* powerful figures.

Surprisingly, my study shows that sisterhoods fare better than sisters in the Bible. To address the broader framework of sisterhood, I look at narratives that mention groups of young women most often identified as "daughters," who form sisterhoods or women's networks. The scattered references to these sisterhoods throughout the Bible conform to archaeological and ethnographic evidence that social networks existed and extended beyond women's families; these references provide a valuable lens into the interpersonal relationship among women.[22] Although scholars like Carol Meyers consider the roles that women's networks served in ancient Israel, few consider, or even notice, the roles they play within the biblical narratives.

Like sisters, sisterhoods conform to the paradigms of the ideal and the dangerous. Just as ideal sisters serve the needs of the patriarchal household, ideal sisterhoods serve the broader needs of patriarchal society. Just as dangerous sisters threaten households, dangerous sisterhoods threaten society. The Bible's dangerous-sisterhood stories function as cautionary tales that encourage appropriate marriages and that warn Israelite men against intermarriage with foreign women. Although the Bible does portray many dangerous sisterhoods, it offers several significant portraits of ideal ones, suggesting that collective sisterhoods raise fewer anxieties than do individual sisters. As a reflection of the Bible's implicit gender ideology, this suggests that women's collective networks were an accepted and valued part of Israelite society. Most surprising in the Bible's patriarchal context is that sisterhood offers an alternative model of family that privileges love and loyalty over lineage and legacy. As we will see, Naomi and Ruth's ideal sisterhood reflects this model and serves as a remarkable paradigm for God's relationship with Israel.

Before beginning my analysis of the Bible's sister and sisterhood narratives, I illustrate the two paradigms and sketch some defining elements of the Bible's sister stories through brief portraits of two ideal and two dangerous sisters. Since all sisters are daughters, it is fair to ask what differentiates sister stories from daughter stories or from any of the Bible's stories that feature women. Indeed they have much in common and, as I suggest, may have a similar overall narrative function. Yet I think there are defining elements of the Bible's sister and sisterhood stories. Following these portraits, I comment on the unique focus and characteristics that mark the Bible's sister and, by extension, its sisterhood stories.

IDEAL SISTER MIRIAM

Miriam functions as an ideal sister in Exodus 2. We first encounter her among the many women in the early chapters of Exodus who represent a variety of professional and familial roles. The lack of personal names given to these women identifies each character with her role. Professionally, there are midwives,[23] attendants, and a wet nurse. The familial roles are wife, mother, daughter, and sister. In one way or another, all of these women act to save baby Moses, whose life is endangered by Pharaoh's command to drown the infant boys of the Israelites. Yet it is the baby's sister Miriam who not only protects the child by guarding him as he makes his way down the Nile River in a basket, but who also ensures the thriving of her natal family. After the baby is discovered by Pharaoh's daughter, Miriam bravely approaches the princess and suggests bringing a Hebrew wet nurse to nurture the child.[24] Thus the sister enables the mother to reconnect with her child and thereby helps preserve her natal household.

By protecting her brother Moses and by ensuring his connection with his family, Miriam functions as an ideal sister who serves the needs of her natal family. She has no identity apart from her role of serving Moses, and she functions in this narrative only as a sister.[25] She is one of the few biblical characters who functions in the role of the sister throughout her narratives. Exodus 15:20 identifies Miriam as a prophet and as Aaron's sister. Numbers 26:59 records her birth along with Aaron and Moses and identifies Miriam as "their sister." Remarkably, Miriam is never portrayed as a mother or a wife, though as we see below, her role as a sister does develop and grows more complicated. In Numbers 12, Miriam, the ideal sister, becomes Miriam, the dangerous sister.

IDEAL SISTER REBECCA

As I mentioned above, Rebecca functions as a powerful wife and mother in most of her narratives, yet she first appears in Genesis 24 as an ideal sister. Genesis 24 tells the story of how Abraham, through the agency of his servant, finds a bride for his son Isaac. Having traveled to Mesopotamia to find a suitable bride, the servant meets Rebecca and discovers that she would be an appropriate wife for Isaac because she is the daughter of Betuel, Abraham's nephew.[26] Yet Betuel plays no meaningful role in the narrative.[27] Instead, his son Laban, Rebecca's brother, is front and center and negotiates the marriage on behalf of his sister. Laban's central role in the narrative renders Rebecca primarily as a sister whose betrothal benefits and enriches her brother and her natal household and, only by implication, the household of her father. In exchange for Rebecca, the servant gives Laban and his mother silver, gold, cloth, and other precious objects (Gen 24:53). The specific mention of Rebecca's mother in this verse makes Betuel's absence in the marriage negotiations even more noticeable, providing support to scholars like Meyers who suggest that mothers took an active role in their children's marriage negotiations.[28]

As an ideal sister, Rebecca directs her independent will and desire in service to her natal household. This is made clear when the servant is ready to leave and Laban and his mother ask Rebecca if she is willing to go. Rebecca replies: "I will go."[29] Happily, mother and son send her forth as their *sister*,[30]

וישלחו את-רבקה אחתם, and Rebecca leaves bearing the specific blessings of, and marked as, a good sister as Gen 24:60 relates:

They blessed Rebecca and said to her: "Our sister, may you grow into multitudes. May your offspring inherit the gates of their enemies."[31]

DANGEROUS SISTER DINAH

In many ways, Dinah is the antithesis of Rebecca. Genesis 24 tells the story of a sister's appropriate marriage, which is sanctioned by a brother and strengthens a natal household. Genesis 34 tells the story of an inappropriate marriage, unsanctioned by brotherly consent and demanding violent revenge. At the start of the narrative, Dinah leaves home [ותצא דינה] to see the daughters of the land.[32] Dinah's independence as well as her desire for female companionship mark her as a dangerous sister and, as we see later, mark the daughters of the land as a dangerous sisterhood. In the narrative's patriarchal ideology, the dangerous sister gets what she deserves for independently leaving the protection of her natal home. Instead of seeing [לראות], Dinah is seen by Shechem [וירא אתה שכם], taken by him—perhaps into his home [ויקח אתה]—and sexually violated [וישכב אתה ויענה]. By the close of the narrative, the independent, once active sister, becomes a dependent and completely passive figure. Mirroring or mocking Shechem and Dinah's initial audacious acts, the brothers *take* their sister and *bring her out* of Shechem's house [ויקחו את דינה מבית שכם ויצאו].

Although Dinah returns tamed to her natal home, irrevocable damage has been done to her and to Jacob's household due to Simeon and Levi's vigilante slaughter of the Hivites as Jacob's reproach to his sons reveals: "You have brought trouble on me, making me odious among the inhabitants of the land."[33] At the end of Genesis 34, Jacob's house is vulnerable. Although Jacob blames his sons for the state of his household, his sons blame their sister. They did what they had to do. Whatever the consequent damage to their household, they could not allow their sister to be treated like a whore.

DANGEROUS SISTER MIRIAM

As mentioned above, Miriam functions in Exodus 2 as an ideal sister who protects and sustains her natal household. Yet in Numbers 12, Miriam becomes a dangerous sister who asserts her independence by speaking against Moses' choice of a Cushite wife and by challenging his status as a prophet. Although their brother Aaron also challenges Moses, only Miriam, the sister, is punished. God strikes Miriam with leprosy and banishes her from the camp. Her punishment fits both her crime and her marginal status as a sister within the patriarchal household. Her challenge against Moses' status results in her being shunned by God and removed from the camp.

Miriam's assertion that Moses introduced an inappropriate bride into the family results in Miriam being removed from her family. When appealing to Moses to heal their sister, Aaron compares her leprous body to a fetus ejected from its mother's womb.[34] With this image, Aaron suggests that Miriam has been aborted from her family.[35] Moses prays on Miriam's behalf. Once punished and healed, Miriam returns to the camp, yet it remains unclear whether she is ever fully reintegrated into her family. The verb used to describe her reintegration into the community, אסף, typically appears in the expression "gathered to one's kin," connoting death. Both Aaron and Moses are said to be gathered to their kin upon their deaths.[36] Yet the expression is noticeably absent in Num 20:1, which is the next mention of Miriam and records her death. The absence of this expression at her burial suggests that dangerous sister Miriam had been accepted back into the Israelite community, but not into her natal family.

These brief portraits of ideal and dangerous sisters illustrate the expectations and the anxieties associated with sisters in the Bible and reflect a fear of female agency. Their focus is on the natal household that sisters, as temporary members, can either strengthen or weaken. Ideal sisters, like Rebecca and Miriam in Exodus 2, support their natal homes whereas dangerous sisters, like Dinah and Miriam in Numbers 12, assert an independent agency that threatens their natal families. As we see when we discuss the incest narratives, sisters do not have to be agents pursuing their individual desires to be dangerous. They can threaten their homes by being objects of desire as well.

Of course, fears of female agency and desire are not directed only against sisters in the Bible. Whether mothers, daughters, sisters, or sisterhoods, all women provoke these fears within the patriarchal context of the biblical narrative. Honor and shame were essential values that shaped ancient Israelite society, and a woman's honor was associated with the qualities and behaviors of submission. According to Yee, a woman must be timid, deferential, submissive to male authority, passive, and sexually pure.[37] A woman who does not embody these qualities elicits anxieties and is a destabilizing figure in the biblical narratives.

Yet a woman's particular role in the narratives shapes the way fears are manifest, and her specific role raises particular anxieties. A mother asserts agency differently than a sister or a wife does; her narratives reflect anxieties related to children as opposed to siblings or spouses. As mothers, Sarah and Rebecca choose one child over another, and their stories reflect anxieties concerned with securing heirs and not husbands. As sisters, the Sarah and Rebecca stories reflect anxieties concerned with supporting brothers and securing their natal households.

Since sisters are also daughters, their stories share common elements with daughter stories. Yet, they introduce unique elements, challenges, and anxieties related to a sister's sibling status in relation to brothers or to other sisters. As the paired sister stories show, the interpersonal relationship among sisters is a complicating factor. The interpersonal relationship among women is naturally a factor in the sisterhood stories as well. The portraits offered above reveal the centrality and particular complexities of the brother–sister relationship. In these portraits, the brother, and not the father, appears to be the primary patriarch in the sister's life. Miriam saves her brother's life. Laban negotiates Rebecca's marriage. Dinah's brothers avenge her sexual violation.

These stories, along with those I examine in greater detail, may reflect the reality or at least the biblical author's ideology that a brother could play a significant role in securing a husband for a sister.[38] They also portray an intimacy between a brother and sister that may have exceeded the intimacy felt between a father and a daughter.[39] Since brothers and sisters grew up together and participated together in household tasks,[40] it is logical that a less hierarchical, more intimate relationship formed between them than between a parent and a child.[41] Siblings could care for each other in practical ways, such as when Tamar tends to her brother's (feigned) illness. Brothers also took care of their sisters. Although legal texts in the Bible suggest that it was a father's responsibility to protect his daughter's sexual purity[42] and a husband's responsibility to protect his wife's,[43] Genesis 34 shows Dinah's brothers assuming responsibility for her sexual purity and responding to its violation.

The brothers' outrage at Dinah's violation is striking when compared to Jacob's passive response. At least as a reflection of the narrative ideology, and perhaps reflecting ancient norms, this tale indicates that a brother responds differently to a sister's sexual violation than a father does to his daughter's. It may be that Dinah is redeemable from Jacob's perspective because a raped daughter can become a legitimate wife according to the law of Deut 22:28-29. Yet a raped sister, as a sexualized sister, cannot be redeemed; she must be avenged. As the incest prohibitions show, the brother-sister relationship ideally is asexual. It is logical to assume then that brothers do not relate comfortably to a sexualized sister—whether as an object of unconsummated desire, as in the Song of Songs or, as in Dinah's case, as a sexually violated, unmarried woman. Even if married, brothers do not have to engage regularly with their sexualized sisters. Following patrilocal custom, married, sexualized sisters move away and into their husbands' homes and function narratively as wives or mothers. As we will see, a brother's discomfort with his sexualized sister is even more apparent in the Bible's incest narratives.

These brief portraits and the more detailed analyses that follow reveal defining features of the Bible's sister stories, which remain evident even when they are adapted to stories about collective sisterhoods. Sister stories focus on the patriarchal natal household, manifest fears of female agency and desire, and are concerned with, or framed by, the sibling relationship. As marginal figures, sisters both cause and reflect the vulnerability of their homes.

Sisterhood stories manifest a similar dynamic with a broader focus on patriarchal Israelite society in general. Here, too, these narratives reflect the fears of the biblical text of female agency and desire; and the stories are concerned with the interpersonal relationship among women. Given biblical anxieties about exogamy, sisterhoods are crucial in responding to this vulnerability and in maintaining the boundaries of Israelite society. The sisterhood narratives also reveal the positive ways in which women's networks contribute to Israelite society. Sisterhoods supported women socially and emotionally by marking their lives ritually and by providing an appropriate outlet for the expression of women's desire and agency.

Scholars have often failed to notice that sisters and sisterhoods are critical figures in the biblical narrative, precisely in those narratives of families and society that are facing crises of stability. They play an essential role in the Bible's grand narrative of how God selects one family for a covenantal relationship. Crucial to the stability of the house of the father, sisters, not unlike brothers, help designate the right family to maintain God's covenant. They build the house of Jacob and establish the house of David. Sisterhoods ensure the stability of the house of Israel by making sure that Israel preserves its purity and its relationship with God. Most remarkably, it is a sisterhood that establishes the Davidic dynasty and provides a paradigm for the divine–human relationship.

Sisters and sisterhoods are not superfluous figures in the Bible. They have their own stories, and they play an integral part in Israel's story. Through their narratives, the Bible recounts the threats and vulnerabilities, but also the building, sustenance, and redemption of the house of Israel.

Notes

1. For a description of the *bet av*, see J. David Schloen, *The House of the Father as Fact and Symbol: Patrimonialism in Ugarit and the Ancient Near East* (Winona Lake, IN: Eisenbrauns, 2001), 147–55.

2. Gale A. Yee describes the patrilineal kinship ideology that privileged ancient Israel's males. See Yee, *Poor Banished Children of Eve: Woman as Evil in the Hebrew Bible* (Minneapolis: Fortress Press, 2003), 37.

3. Carol Meyers discusses the difficulties of using the term patriarchal in *Discovering Eve: Ancient Israelite Women in Context* (New York: Oxford University Press, 1988), 24–46.

4. In his analysis of the Israelite family, Daniel I. Block prefers the term "patricentrism" over patriarchy, arguing that patriarchy carries negative and inaccurate assumptions about the despotic role the father played in the family. See Daniel I. Block, "Marriage and Family in Ancient Israel," in *Marriage and Family in the Biblical World*, ed. Ken M. Campbell (Downers Grove, IL: InterVarsity, 2003), 41.

5. According to Num 27:1-11, a daughter could inherit her father's property if there were no sons and if she married within the paternal clan.

6. Block describes the family in ancient Israel as patrilineal, patrilocal, and patriarchal. See Block, "Marriage and Family in Ancient Israel," 40.

7. See Esther Fuchs, *Sexual Politics in the Biblical Narrative: Reading the Hebrew Bible as a Woman* (Sheffield: Sheffield Academic, 2003), 14.

8. In the Bible, daughters must have husbands, and wives must have children, not for personal fulfillment but, as Fuchs observes, to ensure patrilineal continuity. See ibid., 44.

9. Gen 4:9.

10. In his book examining the ubiquitous plot of a younger sibling usurping an elder, notably entitled *When Brothers Dwell Together*, Frederick E. Greenspahn observes: "Before turning to the details of these issues, a comment is in order about the male orientation that pervades so much of the language used throughout this study. . . . The few exceptions (Rachel and Leah or Michal and Merab) merely confirm the Bible's androcentric focus, for the narratives that do include females invariably function as adjuncts to those dealing with males in one way or another. Thus Rachel and Leah echo Jacob's relation with Esau, and Michal and Merab epitomize the conflict between David and Saul." See Frederick E. Greenspahn, *When Brothers Dwell Together: The Preeminence of Younger Siblings in the Hebrew Bible* (Oxford: Oxford University Press, 1994), 7.

11. See Jon L. Berquist, *Controlling Corporeality: The Body and the Household in Ancient Israel* (New Brunswick, NJ: Rutgers University Press, 2002), 13.

12. Leila Leah Bronner conducts a similar study in her examination of the representation of mothers in the Bible in *Stories of Biblical Mothers: Maternal Power in the Hebrew Bible* (Dallas: University Press of America: 2004).

13. Introducing his study on the representation of disability in the Bible, Saul M. Olyan remarks on the importance of such studies; he writes: "However, representations are central to our enterprise nonetheless because they are ideologically charged and function themselves to mold patterns of thought among those for whom they are intended." See Saul M. Olyan, *Disability in the Hebrew Bible: Interpreting Mental and Physical Differences* (Cambridge: Cambridge University Press, 2008), 4.

14. See Tikva Frymer-Kensky, *Reading the Women of the Bible: A New Interpretation of Their Stories* (New York: Schocken, 2002), xvii.

15. See Fuchs, *Sexual Politics in the Biblical Narrative*, 11.

16. See Yee, *Poor Banished Children of Eve*, 24.

17. This supports Yee who observes that ancient Israel's patrilineal ideology "disenfranchised the female in a hierarchy of gender." See ibid., 38.

18. Claudia V. Camp, *Wise, Strange and Holy: The Strange Woman and the Making of the Bible* (Sheffield: Sheffield Academic, 2000), 228.

19. Camp uses Miriam's punishment after having challenged Moses' authority to illustrate her point; she writes: "Her affliction with leprosy, a form of impurity, merely dramatizes the point. . . . Aaron is clean no matter what he does—his status is ascribed, not achieved—and the primary importance of his relationship with his brother is established. Miriam's (female) impurity, her irrevocable difference, is simply made manifest, the reality of her strangeness to the patrilineage exposing the illusion of her insider blood." See ibid., 231.

20. See Fuchs, *Sexual Politics*, 14.

21. Perceiving the sister stories as cautionary tales raises the question of the Bible's intended audience. Current scholarship views the Bible as a product of, and for, the ruling male elite. See Karel van der Toorn, *Scribal Culture and the Making of the Hebrew Bible* (Cambridge, MA: Harvard University Press, 2007). Although women might not have had direct access to Israel's national literature, they could still be influenced by its stories and ideology. I will consider this argument in my analysis of the portrayals by Jeremiah and Ezekiel of Israel and Judah as sisters married to God.

22. See Carol Meyers, "'Women of the Neighborhood' (Ruth 4.17): Informal Female Networks in Ancient Israel," in *Ruth and Esther: A Feminist Companion to the Bible (Second Series)*, ed. Athalya Brenner (Sheffield: Sheffield Academic, 1991), 110–27 and Aubrey Baadsgaard, "A Taste of Women's Sociality: Cooking as Cooperative Labor in Iron Age Syro-Palestine," in *The World of Women in the Ancient and Classical Near East*, ed. Beth Alpert Nakhai (Newcastle upon Tyne: Cambridge Scholars Press, 2008), 13–44.

23. The midwives are first identified professionally as midwives before their names are mentioned.

24. Exod 2:7.

25. Although I identify Miriam as the sister, it is possible that Exodus 2 could be referring to another sister. Among Moses' female saviors, the only women named are the midwives Shiphrah and Puah. Perhaps being named indicates that they are not as selfless as the other women saviors and do not work solely for the good of the patriarchal household. After all, God rewards their actions by granting them their own households.

26. As I will discuss further, the family narratives reflect a preference for endogamous marriage to an individual who is closely related to the nuclear family without defying the laws of incest. See Joseph Blenkinsopp, "The Family in First Temple Israel," in *Families in Ancient Israel*, ed. Leo G. Perdue, Joseph Blenkinsopp, John J. Collins, and Carol Meyers (Louisville: Westminster John Knox, 1997), 59.

27. Betuel is mentioned in Gen 24:15, 24.

28. See Meyers, "'To Her Mother's House': Considering a Counterpart to the Israelite Bêt 'āb," in *The Bible and the Politics of Exegesis: Essays in Honor of Norman K. Gottwald on his Sixty-Fifth Birthday*, ed David Jobling, Peggy L. Day, and Gerald T. Sheppard (Cleveland: Pilgrim, 1991), 50–51.

29. Gen 24:58.

30. Gen 24:59.

31. As stated above, all biblical translations are my own.

32. The expression ותצא דינה marks an independent action. Like Dinah, other women independently "go forth" and by doing so initiate irrevocable, significant, and often deadly events. In Gen 30:16, Leah goes out to meet Jacob and informs him that she has purchased him for the evening with Reuben's mandrakes. In Judg 4:18 and 22, Yael goes out to meet Sisera to lure him into her tent and then to kill him. In Judg 11:34, Jephthah's daughter goes forth to greet her father and seals her death. In 2 Sam 6:20, Michal goes out to criticize David for revealing himself before his maidservants.

33. Gen 34:30.

34. Num 12:12.

35. The French commentator Rashbam (1085–1158) understands the image of the aborted fetus as a powerful appeal to Moses as Miriam's *brother*; he writes: "For your sake, may you yourself not be like one dead, in as much as all born from the same mother's womb partly die, that is to say

after Miriam was born from Moses' mother's womb dead, it is as if Moses' flesh is half-consumed."

36. Num 20:24 and 27:13.

37. See Yee, *Poor Banished Children of Eve*, 41.

38. Basing himself on Genesis 24 and 34, as well as on the prominent role of the brothers in the Song of Songs, Ingo Kottsieper argues that brothers negotiated the marriages of their sisters. See Kottsieper, "'We Have a Little Sister': Aspects of the Brother-Sister Relationship in Ancient Israel," in *Families and Family Relations as Represented in Early Judaisms and Early Christianities: Texts and Fictions*, ed. Jan Willem Van Henten and Athalya Brenner (Leiden: Deo, 2000), 73–74.

39. Kottsieper writes: "In contrast to the father, the full brothers have a closer relationship to their sister, based not on legal terms but on an emotional proximity. They take care of her fate and represent her interests regarding an outsider." See ibid., 73.

40. According to Block, gender distinctions in labor began during adolescence, and children spent their earliest years working together at household tasks. See Block, "Marriage and Family in Ancient Israel," 93.

41. Other biblical passages convey brother-sister emotional intimacy. In the Song of Songs, the male lover's favored term of endearment for the female lover is "my sister, my bride." As I discuss in chapter 8, the term "sister" does not always indicate kinship but can indicate a non-kindred feeling of fellowship.

42. Deut 22:13-21.

43. Num 5:11-31.

PART I

Sister Pairs

1

Rachel and Leah

Like brother stories, a sister story is a narrative paradigm that construes the family primarily upon its horizontal axis. In a sister story, identity is determined and the narrative is defined by the sibling bond, as opposed to the more hierarchical parent-child relationship. As I note in my introduction, brother stories dominate the Bible. By the time we meet sisters Rachel and Leah in Genesis 29, Cain has killed Abel, Isaac has usurped Ishmael, and Jacob has deceived Esau. At the conclusion of Rachel and Leah's sister story, brothers return to the spotlight as Joseph and his brothers become the focus of the narrative. The Bible's prevailing trope of fraternal rivalry is essentially about patrilineal descent in which paired brothers fight for their father's and for God's blessing. Pairing the brothers helps focus the rivalry and makes clear who is the elder and who is the younger and who, therefore, should have the legitimate claim to their father's property.[1] There can be only one winner, one blessed heir in the patrilineal narratives.

Naturally, a good story defies cultural expectations, and younger brothers, more often than not, claim their father's and God's blessings. Examining this motif in separate works, both Frederick E. Greenspahn and Jon D. Levenson observe how the status of the Bible's younger sons reflects Israel's status, and how their stories reflect Israel's national story.[2] Like Israel, younger sons have no inherent right to the status they acquire in the course of their narratives.[3] And like Israel, younger sons must experience exile and humiliation to acquire their blessings.[4] Isaac faces his father's knife. Jacob is sent to Paddan-aram to serve and fall victim to his uncle Laban. Joseph is sold into servitude in Egypt. For Greenspahn and Levenson, brothers are not only essential figures in Israel's story; they are Israel's story.

Without the right to inheritance, it is logical that biblical sisters play little part in the patrilineal narratives. Their stories, therefore, cannot reflect, and arguably are even inessential to, Israel's national story. For Levenson, sisters

Rachel and Leah are part of the humiliation Jacob must suffer to assume his position as designated heir.[5] Unlike for brothers, it does not formally matter which sister was born first. Not granted the rights of primogeniture, sisters are essentially interchangeable within their families. Although Rachel and Leah's father Laban insists that custom prevents a younger sister from marrying before the elder (Jacob is not bothered by this custom),[6] he blithely exchanges this one for that [ונתנה לך גם-את-זאת], one sister for another.[7] Similarly, Saul promises first one daughter, then the other to David, and indicates that either daughter could serve as an effective trap for David. Even when the sister narrative is about inheritance, as in the story of Zelophehad's daughters, birth order is not significant or even mentioned. In this remarkable story, five sisters appear before Moses as equal claimants to their father's property after their father died without leaving sons or heirs.[8] The sisters' names appear in a different order in Num 27:1 and Num 36:11, which makes it impossible even to speculate on their birth order.

Like brothers, sisters appear in pairs throughout the Bible. Lot's two daughters,[9] Rachel and Leah, Michal and Merav, and Rebel Israel and Faithless Judah are paired sisters. The appearance of paired sisters suggests that they share a narrative function similar to paired brothers. For Greenspahn, sibling pairs become "the locus of competition."[10] He understands the pairing of siblings, along with other paired biblical characters like wives, to be a literary convention that highlights differences and emphasizes the hero's virtue. Isaac and Jacob appear calm and thoughtful next to their wild and impetuous brothers Ishmael and Esau. According to Greenspahn, God values these highlighted qualities.[11] As with brothers, the pairing of sisters pits one sister against another and focuses their rivalry, though without implications for inheritance and blessing.[12]

My reading reveals a more complex picture in which the convention of pairing sisters at times highlights distinct characteristics of each sister and induces conflict, while at other times, it brings the sisters in relation to each other and enables them to cooperate. The relationships between paired sisters are depicted with a greater emotional range than those of paired brothers, who are invariably defined by rivalry. Their stories serve as excellent resources for understanding the ways in which the Bible depicts interpersonal relationships among women and the anxieties these relationships evoke. Not competing for blessing and property, paired sisters are free to relate to each other either as peers or as rivals. Although both sororal competition and solidarity advance the biblical narrative, the Bible is as suspicious of sororal solidarity as it is of sororal agency and desire, which are also evident in these narratives. When sisters conspire and when they assert agency to fulfill their desires, they threaten patriarchal authority and destabilize their homes. In these moments, they become dangerous sisters who, as I show, play a significant role in the patrilineal narratives.

My analysis of the Bible's paired sisters begins with Rachel and Leah. In the course of their narrative, each functions as a wife and mother, as well, and are most often seen by scholars in these roles.[13] When viewed as wives and mothers, their story focuses primarily on Jacob and Rachel and Leah's relationship to him. Seeing them as sisters provides a different focus to their narrative. As sisters, their story focuses upon the interpersonal relationship between them, as well as on their relationship with Laban, their father. Rachel and Leah are first shown to us in their roles as sisters. Even though they also are daughters, wives, and mothers in the course of their narrative, I contend that they function primarily as sisters. Their story concerns the welfare of their natal household, and their relationship to one another determines the course of its narrative. These features, I argue, support reading their story as a sister story.

As mentioned above, Rachel and Leah's relationship reflects the emotional range available to paired sisters. In the course of their narrative, they compete against and conspire with one another. Sororal competition builds the house of Jacob, while sororal solidarity destroys the house of Laban. Although Rachel and Leah are instrumental in establishing Jacob's house, in effect, they never leave their father's house. Once they establish Jacob and his household at their father's expense, their narrative ends. Rachel and Leah are never portrayed as wives and mothers in Jacob's house. Instead, they function in their narratives as dangerous sisters who betray their father and weaken his home, while enabling Jacob to acquire his status as a designated patriarch.

With Jacob on the run from his brother after he deceived Esau, Rachel and Leah provide a fresh focus to, if not a detour in, the biblical narrative. Extending across several chapters in Genesis, their narrative is arguably the Bible's most developed sister story. Yet Rachel's story does not begin as a paradigmatic sister story. In Gen 29:6, Jacob speaks with the shepherds beside a well in Paddan-aram and inquires after the well-being of his uncle Laban. The shepherds respond: "He is well and there is his daughter Rachel coming with the flock." As Robert Alter demonstrates, a biblical narrative about a young woman at a well is really a story about a bride.[14]

Rachel's relationship with her future husband, like Rebecca's before her and Zipporah's after her, begins while drawing water. As the scene unfolds, it becomes clear that Jacob is, in fact, an appropriate suitor for Rachel. Genesis 29:10 mentions three times that Laban is אחי אמו, his mother's brother. Genesis 29:12 refers to Jacob as Rebecca's son, and Gen 29:13 calls him בן-אחתו, the son of his [Laban's] sister. So far, the only sister that matters in this story is Rebecca, Jacob's mother. Again and again, the text makes clear that Rachel is Jacob's first cousin through his mother's line. Cross-cousin marriage, particularly through the maternal line, was the preferred type of marriage in the biblical world because it enabled a family to expand appropriately while protecting its property by keeping it as close as possible within the family.[15] Thus, Genesis 29 shows that Rebecca still functions as an ideal sister to Laban.[16] As she did in Genesis 24, she continues to protect Laban's patriline, now into the next generation. At this point in the narrative, Rachel behaves like an ideal *daughter* to Laban, who should become an ideal *wife* to Jacob.

Yet with the introduction of Leah in Gen 29:16-18, the Bible shifts focus from Rachel the daughter to Rachel the sister, and the narrative takes on a more complicated dimension:

> Laban had two daughters. The name of the elder was Leah, and the name of the younger was Rachel. Leah's eyes were weak while Rachel was beautiful in form and appearance. Jacob loved Rachel and said: "Let me work seven years for you for Rachel, your youngest daughter."

From this passage it is clear that the sisters are distinct from one another and that their distinctions are accentuated by the convention of pairing them. Leah is older [גדלה], while Rachel is younger[17] [קטנה]. Leah has weak eyes, while Rachel is beautiful. However one understands the meaning of רכות, weak eyes, it indicates a physical contrast between the sisters.[18] Unlike Esau and Jacob who are marked by both physical, as well as temperamental differences,[19] physical qualities alone differentiate the sisters, who appear otherwise aligned with one another at the start of their story.

Until Jacob's arrival, the sisters are without narrative strife or, for that matter, narrative at all. In contrast to brothers Jacob and Esau who wage a prenatal battle, there is no sororal race from the womb to the well. By loving Rachel, Jacob introduces tension within the sisters' relationship and the narrative. Certainly love is a divisive factor in the brothers' story as well. Yet it is parental love and not a potential spouse's love that impacts the brothers' relationship. Isaac loves Esau, while Rebecca loves Jacob.[20] Also, parental favoritism exacerbates, but does not create the strife among the brothers. Jacob and Esau's battle begins in utero even before their parents could pick favorites. Unlike sisters, brothers are born to settle the patrimony.

The intervention of a suitor's love as opposed to parental love is one of the features that marks Rachel and Leah's story as a sister story. Since a brother story is about inheritance, parental love is a crucial factor. Genesis 22:2 designates Isaac, and by implication not his brother Ishmael, as Abraham's beloved son. Isaac's parental love compels him to bless Esau, while Rebecca's love compels her to secure Isaac's blessing for Jacob. In the next generation, Jacob's love for Joseph initiates its own devastating cycle of sibling rivalry among Joseph's brothers.[21] Yet a sister story is about the security of the natal household. Naturally, a suitor's love is a crucial factor in a sister story because a sister must find an appropriate husband who does not threaten, but supports, her home.

Whereas brothers fight for property, sisters fight for husbands. Yet, whereas there can be only one designated *bekhor*, one firstborn male heir, sisters are essentially interchangeable.[22] One sister is not, by law, more entitled to a husband than the other. And to make matters more complicated, they can share a husband and share the status of being his wife. In ancient Israel, a husband could marry more than one primary wife—women of equal status—as well as take secondary wives that have a lower status than the primary wife.[23] Although a man can marry two women in the Bible, there is debate whether a man can marry two sisters because Lev 18:18 states: "Do not marry a woman as a rival to her sister [אשה אל-אחותה] and uncover her nakedness during her lifetime." Scholars continue to consider the meaning of "sister" in this prohibition and the relationship of the prohibition to the family narratives. Angelo Tosato argues that Lev 18:18 does not prohibit sororal polygyny specifically. Rather, he understands "sister" to refer to a "female fellow-citizen."[24] Tosato contends that Lev. 18:18 prohibits general polygyny and reflects a later stage in Israel's history than is reflected in the family narratives.[25] Indeed, sororal polygyny appears to be an accepted form of marriage in the family narratives. Both Jacob and, as we will see, God marry two sisters. Naomi Steinberg argues that sororal polygyny is a desirable marriage construct when the objective is to produce multiple heirs. According to Steinberg, the Rachel-Leah cycle shifts the focus from "lineal/vertical heirship" to a "horizontal/segmented genealogy." Being sisters, Rachel and Leah have equal status as wives. Either sister could produce a viable heir.[26] Noticeably, it takes a sister story, not a brother story, to construe the narrative along this horizontal axis.

Once married, Rachel and Leah's sororal competition and their story should be over. They should now become wives and mothers in narratives that are concerned mainly with husbands and producing sons. Yet, by keeping the narrative focused on the relationship between Rachel and Leah, the Bible extends the sister story. Jacob's love for Rachel remains a complicating factor in the sisters' story since, as Gen 29:30 notes, Jacob loves Rachel more than Leah. In response to Jacob's favoritism, God intervenes and introduces another factor that differentiates the sisters as Gen 29:31 relates: "YHWH saw that Leah was unloved and opened her womb while Rachel was barren." Rachel may be beautiful and loved, but Leah is now fertile. Beauty and fertility, two desired qualities, are split between the paired sisters as if to pit one quality and the sister who possesses it against the other.[27] In the Bible, there is no contest between beauty and fertility. Beauty often creates problems. Characters marked as beautiful, like Sarah in Gen 12:11, Joseph in Gen 39:6, Tamar in 2 Sam 13:1, and Esther in Est 2:7 are vulnerable because of their beauty.[28] Fertility, on the other hand, ensures patrilineal descent and secures the inheritance.[29] Unless Rachel (or God) reverses the situation, fertile Leah should win the sororal competition over beautiful Rachel hands down.[30]

By opening Leah's womb, God creates further discord among the sisters and tips the scale in favor of Leah, yet God's motivation remains unclear. Either God supports the underdog as he does throughout the Bible and effectively chooses weak-eyed, unloved Leah over beautiful, beloved Rachel, or God wants increased sororal strife. In the case of these sisters, the second explanation seems more likely since God has no independent plan for Leah such that he would choose her over her sister. In fact, Leah does not exist narratively except when paired with her sister. This is not true of Rachel who acts alone when she steals her father's idols in Genesis 31. Unlike the favored brothers Isaac, Jacob, and even Joseph, Leah does not experience a private moment of revelation and has no specific mission to fulfill. It seems, then, that God wants to increase sororal strife more than he wants to vindicate Leah. By opening Leah's womb and keeping Rachel's closed, God intentionally sows discord and pits sister against sister.

Of course, God has opened wombs before. In Gen 21:1, God remembers barren Sarah and enables her to conceive. In Gen 25:21, God enables barren Rebecca to conceive. In each of these stories, God's will determines when a woman conceives, which enables the birth of the next generation's designated patriarch. With Rachel and Leah, God employs a different strategy and relies on sororal strife to spur fertility. As Esther Fuchs observes, Genesis 30 illustrates that sororal rivalry serves the Bible's central concern of having sons to secure the patrilineal inheritance. Each sister wants what the other one has, and their jealousy results in a good-for-patriarchy battle for babies. Fuchs describes the sisters' competition to be "the necessary instrumental mechanism that presents Jacob with 12 sons who will constitute the foundation of the Israelite nation."[31]

Although God starts the fight, self-interest motivates both sisters, who whole-heartedly engage in the battle. Fertile Leah desires Jacob's love and hopes that each child born will help her get it. The names she gives her children, such as Reuben—"YHWH has seen my degradation, and now my husband will love me," Levi—"Now my husband will be joined to me for I have born him three sons," and Zebulun—"Now my husband will exalt me for I have given him six sons," make clear that Leah wants Jacob—or at least his love.[32]

Infertile Rachel wants to become pregnant but in contrast to her sister, her desire to be pregnant seems to have nothing to do with Jacob. Rachel exhibits a selfish desire that seeks to secure her own status, particularly in relation to her sister.[33] In fact Rachel views Jacob as an impediment to her fertility, perhaps because he refuses to beseech God on her behalf as her confrontation with Jacob in Gen 30:1-2 indicates:

> When Rachel saw that she had not conceived for Jacob, she grew jealous of her sister and said to Jacob, "Give me sons. If not, I will die." Jacob was angry at Rachel and said: "Do I stand in the place of God who has prevented you from conceiving?"

This angry exchange reveals that God is directly responsible for Rachel's barrenness and not just for Leah's fertility. It also reveals that it is Rachel's jealousy of Leah, and not her love of Jacob, that fuels her desire to have children.[34] One imagines that if Rachel could have a son at this point, she would use the name she gives later to her maidservant Bilhah's second son in Gen 30:8: "Rachel said: 'I have struggled mightily with my sister and have succeeded.' [נפתולי אלהים נפתלתי עם-אחתי גם-יכלתי] She named him Naphtali."

Because this is not a brother story in which God identifies, protects, and rewards the chosen brother, the sister Rachel must become the mistress of her own fate.[35] She offers Bilhah to Jacob as a secondary wife who would bear children for Rachel. The introduction of a secondary wife links Rachel's story to Sarah's in Genesis 16. Like Rachel, infertile Sarah offers her maidservant Hagar to Abraham in order to be built up through her [אבנה ממנה]. Echoing Sarah, Rachel says in Gen 30:3: "Indeed, I will be built up through her [ואבנה גם-אנכי ממנה]." Yet whereas Sarah and Hagar function as rival wives in their narratives, Rachel does not compete with Bilhah who gives birth to two sons. Instead, the focus remains on the relationship between the sisters. Seemingly no longer fertile and still longing for her husband's love, Leah offers her maidservant Zilpah to Jacob as another secondary wife. Like Bilhah, Zilpah gives birth to two sons. Neither Bilhah nor Zilpah introduce tension within the narrative. Instead, they seem to create symmetry by further pairing the sisters as well as their children. Each sister has a maidservant who bears two children.

Without conflict between the primary and secondary wives, the narrative remains a sister story in which *sisters* provide the narrative's tension and determine its progress. Rachel continues to compete with Leah as the name Naphtali indicates. Rachel's struggle with her sister inscribed in Naphtali's name, and her expressed triumph over her, evokes the famous episode in Genesis 32 in which Jacob wrestles a mysterious man and, like Rachel, prevails [ותוכל]. Yet whereas it is unclear whether the man Jacob wrestles is divine or human, Rachel clearly wrestles with her sister. As Fuchs notes, female rivals like Rachel and Leah do not formally reconcile in the Bible.[36] In contrast, the Bible does enable rival brothers to reconcile and provides closure to their narratives. Jacob wrestles with the stranger in Genesis 32, perhaps the specter of his brother, on the eve of reconciling with Esau. Their struggle could be seen as a healing moment in which fraternal rivalry is finally laid to rest. Having wrestled in the night, Jacob is able to embrace his estranged brother in the morning.[37]

Having wrestled with one another, sisters Rachel and Leah are not allowed to embrace and reconcile like Jacob and Esau in Gen 33:1-11 or like Joseph and his brothers in Gen 45:14-15. They do not bury their father in solidarity like Isaac and Ishmael in Gen 25:9, like Jacob and Esau in Gen 35:29, or like Joseph and his brothers in Gen 50:13. In a gesture that simultaneously demonstrates fraternal harmony and sororal strife, Jacob separates the sisters into distinct camps when he reconciles with Esau. Although brothers unite, sisters remain separate even in death. Rachel dies on the road to Ephrat and is buried alone and not in the family tomb. Strikingly, Leah receives that honor, which is recorded in Gen 49:31.

Leah's burial in the cave of Mahpelah appears to settle the sisters' competition that pitted beauty against fertility in favor of fertile Leah. Fertile Leah wins her spot in the family tomb. For Rachel who dies in childbirth,[38] fertility—or rather her selfish desire for it—proves to be lethal. After enduring her sister's seven pregnancies, Rachel finally gives birth and names her son Joseph [יוסף], saying "May God add [יסף] another son for me." Not satisfied with only one son, perhaps when compared with her sister's six, Rachel prays for another. She dies when her prayer is answered. Her death can be seen as harsh judgment for her selfish desire and the agency she exercises to secure it. Rachel's solitary burial between her father's and her husband's homes suggests that she, like Miriam in Numbers 12, is aborted from the family and ends her life in disgrace, marked as dangerous.[39]

As I outline in my introduction, dangerous sisters assert an independent agency that challenges patriarchal authority and threatens the stability of the natal household. In their battle for babies, both Rachel and Leah display independent desire that marks them as dangerous. Leah desires Jacob, and Rachel wants to get pregnant. Yet their desires and their struggles to fulfill them at first seem to serve and not challenge the patriarchal interests of their natal family. As I note above, sororal strife secures the patriline. In the beginning of their story, while they live in Laban's home, it is unclear whose patriline is being supported—Laban's or Jacob's. In Laban's mind, the sisters' rivalry builds his house, and their children are his. Laban informs Jacob of this when he overtakes him in Gen 31:43:

> Laban responded and said to Jacob: "The daughters are my daughters, the sons, my sons, and the flocks are my flocks. All that you see belongs to me. What can I do now about my daughters or the children they have born?"[40]

As long as Rachel and Leah remain in and help build the house of Laban, they seem to function according to my paradigm as ideal sisters whose desire to have children strengthens their natal household. Yet, with the birth of Rachel's first son Joseph, Jacob decides to leave Laban's house, initiating a transformation from the sisters' supportive role within their natal household to a destructive one.

Leaving Laban's house marks a shift in the narrative and draws the sister story to a natural close. Once sisters leave their natal households, like Rebecca in Genesis 24, they primarily function as wives and mothers within their narratives. Yet neither Rachel nor Leah survives narratively as a wife or mother in Jacob's house. As I mentioned above, Rachel dies en route and Leah narratively dies with her. The only subsequent mention of Leah is the incidental mention of her burial. Rachel and Leah's story does not progress outside of the framework of their natal household and therefore remains a sister story. Yet their relationship develops a new dimension.

Before Jacob departs from Laban's home, he summons Rachel and Leah to the field to ask if they are willing to leave their father's house. Together the sisters respond in Gen 31:14-16:

> Rachel and Leah respond and say to him: "Do we still have a share in the inheritance of our father's house? Are we not considered outsiders to him? Indeed, he has sold us and consumed our money.

> Truly, all the wealth that God stripped from our father belongs to us
> and our sons. Now then, all that God says, do."

In solidarity, Rachel and Leah agree to leave Laban's house.[41] Their mutual
consent appears to be financially motivated since they have no claim to their
father's property and, therefore, no place in his house. Feeling like outsiders in
their natal home, they formally renounce their membership in it. Like Rebecca
in Genesis 24, sisters Rachel and Leah agree to leave their father's house. Yet
where ideal sister Rebecca's departure enriches her natal household, Rachel and
Leah's departure depletes their natal household. Their consent to leave is an
overt act of aggression against their father. At this moment, when they align
against their father, Rachel and Leah function like dangerous sisters.

This is not the first time the sisters cooperate, defy patriarchal authority,
and are marked as dangerous. Earlier in the narrative, Rachel and Leah conspire
to subvert patriarchal authority. In Gen 30:14, Leah's eldest Reuben brings his
mother mandrakes, a fruit believed to be an aphrodisiac that promotes fertility.
The mandrakes represent the quality each sister has and the other wants and
brings them together. As an aphrodisiac, the mandrakes represent love—the
quality possessed by Rachel and desired by Leah. As a fruit that promotes
fertility, it represents Leah and the quality desired by Rachel. In this way, the
mandrakes function as a symbol of, and as an impetus for, sororal solidarity.
Seeing the mandrakes, Rachel directly addresses her sister for the first time, and
they strike a deal.[42] Leah purchases Jacob with her mandrakes. In a moment
of sororal solidarity, the sisters compromise and cooperate to get what they
want. They do so at the expense of Jacob's patriarchal authority. As Ilana Pardes
observes, the mandrake episode manifests a "reversal of hierarchies."[43]

Although Rachel and Leah subvert their husband's and not their father's
authority, they do so as *sisters*, using the object, the mandrakes, that symbolizes
their solidarity. This links their action to Dinah's, the paradigmatic dangerous
sister. Like Dinah who independently goes forth [ותצא דינה] from her father's
house, Leah goes forth [ותצא לאה] to greet Jacob and to inform him that
she has acquired him with Reuben's mandrakes.[44] While Dinah's independence
leads to an improper sexual union, Leah's results in a legitimate sexual union
but one that defies the norms of a patriarchal society. At this moment, Leah
behaves like a destabilizing figure. In the biblical world, a woman is not
expected to initiate a sexual encounter with a man. As I mention in my
introduction, a woman's honor depended on being submissive to men and
sexually pure. A man's honor, as Gale Yee notes, depended on controlling a
woman's sexuality.[45] Rarely in the Bible do women initiate sexual encounters

and those that do are either desperate to serve patriarchal interests, like Tamar in Genesis 38 or Ruth, or are dangerous seductresses, like the strange woman in Proverbs 7 or Delilah in Judges 16.[46] With four sons, Leah is not desperate to provide an heir to Jacob. Instead she behaves like her sister Rachel. Leah asserts agency, seeks to satisfy her own desires, and controls her husband's sexuality.

Despite their efforts, sisters cannot determine their fates, and magical substances cannot induce love or fertility. Only God can. Rachel remains desired but infertile (she must suffer through three more of Leah's births),[47] and Leah remains fertile yet unloved.[48] In other words, the competition between the sisters remains unresolved, and their agency did not yield the results they desired. At last, God remembers Rachel and opens her womb in Gen 30:22. It is Joseph's birth that inspires Jacob to leave Laban's home.[49] At this moment, Jacob and Laban formally become rival patriarchs. Over the years, Laban's household has benefited greatly by Jacob's presence. Now it stands to lose a great deal, as Jacob informs Laban in Gen 30:30: "For the little you had before me has grown into much. YHWH has blessed you wherever I turned. And now, when will I provide for my own household?"

Jacob is clearly ready to build his own house apart from, and even at the expense of, Laban's. The two households and their patriarchs stand in obvious tension. Both work to secure their property. In Gen 30:35, Laban surreptitiously protects his property by removing the speckled and spotted goats promised to Jacob: "That day he removed the speckled and spotted he-goats and the speckled and spotted she-goats, all that had white on them and all the black sheep, and gave them into the care of his sons." Interestingly, this is the first time in the narrative that we hear of Laban's sons, the brothers of Rachel and Leah, who actively work to protect their father's house. Unwilling to be outdone by Laban, Jacob practices an effective form of animal husbandry or divination and is able to produce and claim new speckled and spotted flocks. By the end of this chapter, the house of Jacob stands separate from the house of Laban and is both stronger and richer, as Gen 30:42-43 describes: "The feeble flock he did not place. The feeble ones went to Laban and the strong ones to Jacob. The man grew wealthier and wealthier. He had large flocks, female servants, male servants, camels, and asses."

Clearly threatened, Laban's sons inform their father that Jacob is taking and profiting from Laban's property. With tension growing between Laban and Jacob, the time finally has come for Jacob to leave. When Laban is off shearing sheep, Jacob takes his wives, children, and property and leaves Laban's house. Yet Jacob is not the only one to take things from Laban's house. Rachel steals the teraphim, the household gods, from her father's house. The form and function of the teraphim remain unknown. In this narrative, they appear easily transportable, fitting into a camel saddle. Yet, as we see in the next chapter, they appear to be larger. Michal places teraphim in her bed to imitate her sleeping husband and to fool her father. William G. Dever derives several qualities of the teraphim from these narratives; for example, they are transportable and seem to be in the custodianship of women. In terms of my analysis, the most significant quality he derives is their value. Because they represent ancestral deities required to ensure the on-going welfare of the family, Dever considers the teraphim to be "among the most valuable of the family's possessions."[50]

Although the narrative does not explain her action, it implies that Rachel's theft, like her consent to leave, is an act of significant betrayal against Laban. Rachel steals the valuable idols [ותגנב רחל] just as Jacob steals the heart of Laban [ויגנב יעקב את-לב לבן]. Rachel's theft of the teraphim may be an attempt to secure the legal title to her father's estate for Jacob and for her sons,[51] or it may be an attempt to secure the protection and power of his household gods for herself and not for her husband or for her sister.[52] Pardes suggests that Rachel's theft is another manifestation of sororal rivalry. Rachel steals the idols to mark her own son, and not her sister's, as the designated heir.[53]

Whatever her motivation, her theft is a personal act of aggression against her father that seals her fate. Unaware of Rachel's guilt, Jacob condemns the thief to death in Gen 31:32. Rachel's aggression against her father is evident when Laban searches for the teraphim in Gen 31:33-35:

> Laban entered Jacob's tent, Leah's tent, and the tent of the two maidservants, but found nothing. He went out of Leah's tent and entered Rachel's tent. Rachel had taken the teraphim and placed them in a camel saddle and sat upon them. Laban searched the tent but did not find them. She said to her father: "Do not be mad at me for I am unable to rise before you because the way of women is upon me." He searched, but he did not find the teraphim.[53]

Because no one but Rachel knows that she has stolen the teraphim, it seems that Rachel did not intend them for Jacob's benefit. Even in trouble, she does not confess to Jacob and ask for help. Instead, she cunningly hides the teraphim and tells her father that she is menstruating and cannot get up. Rachel's methods of self preservation are clever,[54] but they also have the added benefit of mocking Laban's religious beliefs and his authority. By sitting on the teraphim, symbols of her father's household and his religion, she asserts control over both. Dangerous sister Rachel has Laban and his gods pinned.

Although Rachel may be more dangerous than Leah, both sisters prove themselves to be so. Together, they build the house of Jacob at their father's expense. As the Bible's most developed sister story, their narrative shapes subsequent sister stories like that of Michal and Merav. As we see in the next chapter, the sister story of Michal and Merav shares features with Rachel and Leah's story and includes episodes of wife-swapping and subterfuge that involve household gods. Most importantly, Rachel and Leah's detailed sister story helps illuminate the representation and narrative function of sisters in the Bible. Like other sister stories, their story is concerned with supporting the natal household and reveals the anxieties sisters induce by being marginal figures in those homes, particularly the anxiety of finding appropriate husbands that will enrich and not rival their father's house. At first glance, Jacob seems to be an appropriate suitor, and Rachel and Leah appear to function as ideal sisters who support and strengthen their natal home. Yet as the narrative unfolds, Jacob proves to be a rival patriarch to Laban, and Rachel and Leah function as dangerous sisters, who assert agency and desire and ally against their father. These dangerous sisters damage their father's household.

Their relationship to one another is a pivotal and defining force in their narrative. Although they are rivals, Rachel and Leah display an emotional range in their relationship that transcends their jealousy. Sororal strife and sororal solidarity play significant roles within their story, which demonstrates the benefits to their husband of their rivalry and the dangers to their husband and their father of cooperation. God initiates and sustains the rivalry that builds and fills the house of Jacob, while it weakens and drains the house of Laban. Yet, as the mandrakes episode shows, the sisters are able to capitalize on their jealousy and conspire when necessary to get what they want. When the sisters align, as they do over the mandrakes or when they consent to leave Laban's house, they threaten patriarchal authority. Sororal solidarity induces Jacob to sleep with Leah and Laban to lose his daughters and his property.

Although Rachel and Leah build the house of Jacob, as a sister story their story is essentially about the fall of the house of Laban. By consenting to leave, the sisters formally renounce Laban's house. By stealing his gods, Rachel depletes and denigrates her father's house. In the danger they pose, these sisters clearly serve a crucial purpose. In the greater context of Genesis, Laban is a rival patriarch who must be weakened so that Jacob's household can thrive. Rachel and Leah help weaken Laban's house and strengthen Jacob's. In this way, the sisters are not simply humiliations that Jacob must bear to become the designated patriarch as Levenson suggests. They are not payback for Jacob's deception of Esau as Greenspahn suggests. They are significant figures who advance the biblical narrative and ensure Jacob's success.

Despite their significance, dangerous sisters Rachel and Leah do not experience happy endings. They do not enjoy formal moments of reconciliation, nor do they reap the rewards of being wives and mothers in Jacob's independent house—the house they help build. After they serve their purpose, they are effectively removed from the narrative. In this way, their story remains a sister story because it never advances fully to be a wife or mother story but functions as a cautionary tale that warns against sororal solidarity, agency, and desire. Sororal solidarity overturns patriarchal authority. Sororal agency and desire effectively kill Rachel. Her theft, an act of agency, condemns her to death when Jacob inadvertently promises to kill the thief.[55] Ultimately, it is Rachel's selfish desire for more children that actually kills her.[56] She dies in childbirth on the road to Ephrat, as Gen 35:16-19 recounts:

> They traveled from Beth El. They were at a distance from Ephrat when Rachel went into labor. The labor was difficult. During her difficult labor, the midwife said to her: "Do not fear for this one will also be a son." At the moment of her last breath, for she was dying, she called his name Ben-Oni [lit., son of my affliction], but his father called him Benjamin [lit., son of my strength]. Rachel died and was buried on the road to Ephrat, now Bethlehem.

Dangerous sister Rachel never lives in Jacob's house nor is she gathered to his kin. Buried in the family tomb, Leah appears to fare better. Perhaps she is granted this honor over Rachel because it was desire for Jacob that motivated her and not her own gain as it was for her sister. But once her sister dies, Leah's story essentially stops. Without Rachel, Leah has no place in the text. Her character and her story are defined by her sister.

The house of Jacob is built at the expense of the house of Laban. It is also built at the expense of the sisters Rachel and Leah who, having served their purpose, exit the narrative along with their father. In particular, Rachel suffers in the service of Jacob's house because she dies in childbirth. Before dying, she names her son Ben-Oni, son of my affliction. Yet, Rachel's affliction becomes a symbol of Jacob's strength when Jacob renames the baby. Ben-Oni, son of my (Rachel's) affliction becomes Benjamin, son of my (Jacob's) strength. Rachel and Leah name all their other children. Benjamin is the only baby that Jacob renames. As Fuchs comments, Rachel hopes to inscribe her suffering in her son's name but is overridden by Jacob. Jacob denies Rachel this legacy. Instead, Jacob chooses a name that conveys strength and optimism—a name that communicates his strength.[57] It may be that Rachel's death signals to Jacob the end of his time in Laban's house and his triumph over Laban. He is prepared to enter a new phase in his life and to become the patriarch of his own home. Rachel will not be part of that home. By weakening the house of their father, sisters Rachel and Leah play a crucial role in Jacob's story. Together, the dangerous sisters build the house of Jacob. Their struggles with one another and their suffering ensure that Jacob prevails over Laban.

Notes

1. According to Deut 21:17, the eldest brother receives twice the inheritance of his younger brothers.

2. Greenspahn observes: "Drawing on a father's prerogative to choose whichever child he wishes, it reconciles Israel's doctrine of election with the reality of her political ineffectiveness. The prominence achieved by younger sons throughout the Bible thus asserts Israelite merit while tacitly conceding the weakness of her case." See Frederick E. Greenspahn, *When Brothers Dwell Together: The Preeminence of Younger Siblings in the Hebrew Bible* (Oxford: Oxford University Press, 1994), 109.

3. Deut 7:7 and 9:5 make clear that Israel has no justifiable claim to its status.

4. In Levenson's reading, younger sons acquire the status of firstborn sons through exile and humiliation, and are, like Israel itself, essentially reborn as God's firstborn. See Jon D. Levenson, *The Death and Resurrection of the Beloved Son: The Transformation of Child Sacrifice in Judaism and Christianity* (New Haven: Yale University Press, 1993), 67.

5. Ibid., 66.

6. In Gen 29:18, Jacob asks specifically to marry the younger sister Rachel, knowing that Leah remains unmarried. Block notes: "As a matter of custom parents expected their children to marry in the order of their births (Gen 29:26), but Israel had no laws prescribing this practice." See Daniel I. Block, "Marriage and Family in Ancient Israel," in *Marriage and Family in the Biblical World*, ed. Ken M. Campbell (Downers Grove, IL: InterVarsity, 2003), 57.

7. Gen 29:27.

8. Fighting to preserve their father's property and not to secure their own, the daughters of Zelophehad function as ideal sisters who serve the interests of their natal household.

9. Although paired, I include Lot's daughters in the second part of my study among the incest narratives.

10. Greenspahn, *When Brothers Dwell Together*, 136.

11. Greenspahn writes: "As with rival wives, the Bible's sibling pairs provide the narrator with an opportunity to emphasize certain features of those whom God had chosen by setting them alongside others." See ibid., 137.

12. Athalya Brenner agrees with Greenspahn and considers the pairing of women to be a literary convention that presents the women as rivals and works to induce tension within the narratives. See Athalya Brenner, "Female Social Behaviour: Two Descriptive Patterns Within the 'Birth of the Hero' Paradigm," in *A Feminist Companion to Genesis*, ed. Athalya Brenner (Sheffield: Sheffield Academic, 1993), 207.

13. Brenner identifies motherhood to be the basic motif of their story. See ibid., 209. Leila Leah Bronner includes Rachel and Leah in her study of the Bible's mothers. See Bronner, *Stories of Biblical Mothers: Maternal Power in the Hebrew Bible* (Dallas: University Press of America: 2004), 16–21. In contrast to these scholars, Esther Fuchs views Rachel and Leah primarily in their roles as

wives. For Fuchs, Rachel and Leah's story conforms to the "contest type-scene," which "presents one husband and two co-wives, one of whom is barren. The fertile co-wife humiliates the barren wife intentionally until the latter is redeemed through divine intervention, becoming fertile and giving birth to one or more sons." Fuchs, *Sexual Politics in the Biblical Narrative: Reading the Hebrew Bible as a Woman* (Sheffield: Sheffield Academic, 2003), 150–51.

14. Robert Alter outlines the features of the betrothal type-scene in *The Art of Biblical Narrative* (New York: Basic, 1981), 47–62.

15. Joseph Blenkinsopp comments on the kinship relationship between Jacob and Rachel: "Cross-cousin marriage of this kind, the preferred type in many societies though forbidden in several states in the United States, seems to mark the optimum, the stage of social maturity at which the ancestral lineage could segment, and consequently, Israel as an ethnos came into existence." See Blenkinsopp, "The Family in First Temple Israel," in *Families in Ancient Israel*, ed. Leo G. Perdue, Joseph Blenkinsopp, John J. Collins, and Carol Meyers (Louisville: Westminster John Knox, 1997), 73–74.

16. In my introduction, I argue that Rebecca functions as an ideal sister in Genesis 24.

17. The distinction made between the older and the younger sisters echoes the distinction made in Gen 27:15 between Esau, the older son [הגדל], and Jacob, the younger [הקטן]

18. The meaning of רכות remains unclear. Jacob's description of his children as רכים in Gen 33:13, too weak to travel, suggests that the word indicates a physical condition.

19. Esau is red, hairy, and wild, while Jacob is smooth-skinned and docile. See Gen 25:25-28.

20. Gen 25:28.

21. Gen 37:3.

22. Even when the daughters of Zelophehad fight for property, they do so as a unit. One sister does not claim more than another.

23. Naomi Steinberg differentiates the primary from the secondary wife; she writes: "A primary wife is a woman whose continued status depends on whether there is a marital fund that was established when she was joined with her husband and that would be lost to him if the marriage were to be dissolved. . . . Typically a concubine is a secondary wife, a woman whose involvement with the husband represents a secondary union, both in terms of being an additional wife and of having a lower status than the legal wife." See Steinberg, *Kinship and Marriage in Genesis: A Household Economics Perspective* (Minneapolis: Fortress Press, 1993), 16.

24. See Angelo Tosato, "The Law of Leviticus 18:18: A Reexamination," *CBQ* 46 (1984): 201–2.

25. Ibid., 208–14.

26. Steinberg writes: "In other words, the Rachel-Leah cycle provides us with a social model for resolving heirship in the situation of sororal polygyny. Cross-cultural kinship studies on sororal polygyny lead us to expect multiple heirship among the offspring of Rachel and Leah. Sororal polygyny, then, extends heirship to multiple individuals." See Steinberg, *Kinship and Marriage*, 116.

27. Esther Fuchs observes that the splitting of these qualities justifies polygyny because no one wife can satisfy her husband. See Fuchs, *Sexual Politics*, 161.

28. For a discussion of the various ways beauty functions as a motif in the Bible, see Stuart Macwilliam, "Ideologies of Male Beauty and the Hebrew Bible," *BI* 17 (2009): 265–87.

29. Yee notes the significance of female fertility in ancient Israel. See Gale A. Yee, *Poor Banished Children of Eve: Woman as Evil in the Hebrew Bible* (Minneapolis: Fortress Press, 2003), 46.

30. Brenner outlines Leah's advantages over Rachel: "Leah's seniority is twofold and thus well established (like Sarah's): she is the elder sister who married Jacob first. Rachel is doubly inferior socially: she is younger, a second wife. Unlike Sarah, Leah is not beloved by her husband but is the fertile one." See Brenner, "Female Social Behaviour," 210.

31. See Fuchs, *Sexual Politics*, 154.

32. Fuchs similarly comments on Leah's motivation: "As the names of her first three sons indicate, Leah considers her reproductive capacity not as an end in itself, but as a means by which to win her husband's love (Gen. 29.32-34)." Ibid.

33. In a patrilocal society, a wife's status was particularly dependent on having children, providing her with status and security in her conjugal home. See Yee, *Poor Banished Children of Eve*, 38.

34. Ilana Pardes observes that this passage provides insight into Rachel's emotions and is remarkable in the context of the Bible, which does not usually record its characters' emotional responses. See Pardes, *Countertraditions in the Bible: A Feminist Approach* (Cambridge: Harvard University Press, 1992), 64.

35. Pardes notes the limited role God plays in Rachel's story. See ibid., 65.

36. See Fuchs, *Sexual Politics*, 159.

37. Gen 33:4.

38. Gen 35:19.

39. As Benjamin Cox and Susan Ackerman observe, having died in childbirth, Rachel's corpse is considered dangerous: "(I)f even healthy childbirth is considered to be such a potent source of danger, how exacerbated must the threat become in the case of the mother's death. . . . Not only does a mother's death in childbirth, therefore, introduce another facet of liminality to an already liminal figure, but because that death interrupts the normal progress of delivery before the woman can be reintegrated into her community, it prevents the performance of whatever rites are needed to remove the liminal danger of childbirth. The body of the dead mother is thus left in a perpetual state of liminality." See Benjamin D. Cox and Susan Ackerman, "Rachel's Tomb," *JBL* 128, no. 1 (2009): 145.

40. Nancy Jay suggests that Laban operates within a system of matrilineal descent and assumes his inheritance would be transmitted through his daughters. See Jay, "Sacrifice, Descent and the Patriarchs," *VT* 38, no. 1 (1988): 64.

41. Pardes comments on the sisters' solidarity: "The two have learned to cooperate in times of distress. Enraged by Laban's usurpation of their inheritance and by their status as *nokhriyot* (foreigners) in his household, they do not hesitate to join forces with Jacob against their father." See Pardes, *Countertraditions*, 68.

42. Pardes observes how rarely women dialogue in the Bible. See ibid., 66.

43. Ibid., 67.

44. Gen 30:16.

45. See Yee, *Poor Banished Children*, 46.

46. Claudia V. Camp comments on the strange woman in Proverbs 7: "Far more dangerous is the woman who exists within the boundaries of male-controlled sexuality, but who decides for herself to opt out of them. Such is the wife 'dressed as a prostitute' in Proverbs 7." See Camp, *Wise, Strange and Holy: The Strange Woman and the Making of the Bible* (Sheffield: Sheffield Academic, 2000), 62.

47. Had Leah not met Jacob on his way home and informed him of the hire, presumably he would have gone to Rachel's home, which indicates his desire for Rachel.

48. Leah's choice of names for her sons continues to express her unrequited desire for Jacob.

49. The verse offers no explanation why Jacob decides to leave. It simply says in Gen 30:25: "When Rachel gave birth to Joseph, Jacob said to Laban: "Send me so that I can go to my place, my land."

50. William G. Dever, *Did God Have a Wife? Archaeology and Folk Religion in Ancient Israel* (Grand Rapids, MI: William B. Eerdmans, 2005), 182.

51. Nancy Jay perceives Rachel's theft as an act that secures her inheritance through a system of matrilineal descent. See Jay, "Sacrifice, Descent and the Patriarchs," 65–66.

52. See Karel van der Toorn, *Family Religion in Babylonia, Syria and Israel: Continuity and Change in the Forms of Religious Life* (Leiden: E. J. Brill, 1996), 222–23.

53. Pardes, *Countertraditions*, 71.

54. Rachel may hope to deter Laban with the threat of contamination because according to Lev 15:19-24, impurity can be transmitted to objects touched or sat upon by a menstruating woman.

55. Pardes wonders if Jacob knows the consequence of his promise to Laban that the thief would die. Although she does not doubt Jacob's love for Rachel, Pardes also suggests that Jacob felt threatened by her and may have subconsciously condemned her. See Pardes, *Countertraditions*, 72–73.

56. Rachel's desire to have more children is evident in the name she gives her first son Joseph, meaning "May God provide for me another son." Gen 30:24.

57. See Fuchs, *Sexual Politics*, 56.

2

Michal and Merav

Another sister pair appears in the narratives that relate King Saul's fall from, and King David's rise to, power in the books of Samuel. Although admittedly more fragmentary in its presentation, in significant ways the story of King Saul's daughters Michal and Merav parallels the story of Rachel and Leah.[1] The narratives share common features such as paired sisters, one husband, wife-swapping, and filial subterfuge that involves the household gods. They also share common themes such as romantic love, paternal power and insecurity, and infertility. Despite these similarities, scholars tend to ignore Merav and focus on Michal. They consider Michal's supporting role as daughter, wife, or queen, but not as sister—at least not as Merav's sister—within the Saul-David narratives.[2]

Most often, scholars like J. Cheryl Exum pair Michal with her brother Jonathan to understand her narrative function.[3] Michal and Jonathan share a love for David. Both betray their father to protect David. Although they are siblings, Exum perceives Michal and Jonathan in their roles as Saul's children, who ensure the transfer of kingship from their father to David. Exum observes that though Jonathan and Michal share a narrative function, they do not share a narrative fate. For Exum, gender accounts for the difference in their fates. Whereas Jonathan dies a "hero's death" and is mourned by David, Michal survives to live childless in David's hostile home.[4]

I contend that the Bible intentionally presents Michal in the role of the sister in her narrative. Her sister Merav, who appears at its beginning and is alluded to at its end, provides a narrative framework in which to view Michal as a sister. Given this framework, Michal's story can be read as a sister story concerning the vulnerability of her natal household. As I mentioned in my introduction, I do not argue that Michal functions exclusively in the role of sister or that her story can be read only as a sister story. Just as it is possible to view Rachel and Leah as mothers and wives in the course of their narrative, it is possible to view Michal as David's wife and Saul's daughter—as she is identified throughout her story. But Michal is also a sister, and the Bible presents her as one. Perceiving Michal as a sister provides particular insight into the contours of her narrative while enriching our understanding of the representation of sisters in the Bible.[5]

Furthermore, I contend that the thematic and literary parallels with the Rachel and Leah story that I outline below support identifying Michal's story as a sister story and encourage reading these sister stories in relation to one another. Read together, it is clear that they share a narrative arc and that the sisters serve a similar narrative purpose. In both stories, sisters are destabilizing figures who introduce rival patriarchs that weaken their fathers' households. In other words, Rachel, Leah, Michal, and Merav function within my paradigms as dangerous sisters.

Significant differences are also evident when these two sister stories are read together. Recognizing these differences develops our understanding of how the Bible depicts its sisters. Michal and Merav's interpersonal relationship is *not* a pivotal factor in their story as it was in Rachel and Leah's. Sororal rivalry and solidarity are noticeably absent from their narrative. Although paired, sister is not pitted against sister. They do not compete for husbands or for babies. This reveals that paired sisters do not always function as a "locus of competition" as Greenspahn suggests.[6] Also, Michal and Merav do not align or conspire together. In fact, unlike Rachel and Leah, these sisters do not engage directly with one another. Instead, we see that Michal and Merav appear interchangeable in their narrative. One sister can and does replace the other. By the end of their narrative, their identities merge. The fusion of their characters further supports my premise that without inheritance rights, but able to share a husband, sisters can be interchangeable within the Bible's family narratives. In the Bible, paired sisters are not always rivals. As the story of Michal and Merav reveals, paired sisters, unlike Jonathan and Michal, can share one devastating fate.

First Samuel 14:49 introduces Merav and Michal along with other members of King Saul's family and court: "Saul's sons were: Jonathan, Ishvi,[7] and Malchishua and the names of his daughters were Merav, the firstborn [הבכירה] and Michal, the younger [הקטנה]." Neither sister is described as beautiful, myopic, or fertile. Age alone distinguishes these sisters. The designation of Merav as firstborn and Michal as the younger, recalls the initial description of Rachel and Leah, as well as Laban's justification in Gen 29:26 for switching the sisters by saying that it was not the custom in his land to give the younger daughter in marriage before the elder [הבכירה]. Since this passage evokes Rachel and Leah and marks the sisters and not the brothers as elder and younger, the stage seems set for a battle for a husband and not a battle for the birthright. Yet no battle begins.

The sisters next appear in chapter 18. Saul's rival David has proven himself in battle against the warrior Goliath and has won the love and loyalty of Saul's son Jonathan as well as that of all Israel and Judah.[8] Hoping to ensnare David and to have him killed in battle,[9] Saul schemes to use his daughter Merav as bait:

> Saul said to David: "Here is my eldest daughter Merav. Her I give to you as a wife if you will be for me a warrior and fight the battles of YHWH." But Saul thought: "May my hand not be against him, rather may the hand of the Philistines be against him." David said to Saul: "Who am I, and who is my father's family in Israel that I would be the son-in-law to the king?" When the time came to give Merav, Saul's daughter to David, she was given to Adriel the Mecholatite as a wife. (1 Sam 18:17-19)

Saul appears to observe Laban's custom of marrying the elder sister before the younger and offers Merav to David. David's response to Saul indicates that he is aware of the gravity of Saul's offer. He does not focus on his bride-to-be but questions his personal and his family's status and his right to be the king's son-in-law. David understands fully that his union with Merav would be a union between the house of Saul and the house of David. His rhetorical question "Who am I?" suggests that he feels unworthy to be the king's son-in-law. David's question seems to trigger anxiety for Saul. Understanding that David could prove to be his most dangerous rival as his son-in-law and that his plans to ensnare him could backfire, Saul regrets and retracts his offer. He marries Merav to Adriel.

Like Laban, Saul tricks the groom and takes away his intended bride at the last moment.[10] In both of these stories, the father does the giving and the taking, while the daughter passively accepts her father's maneuverings. Neither Rachel nor Leah reacts when their father substitutes one sister for another. Similarly, Merav expresses no preference for David or for Adriel and registers no reaction upon her marriage.[11] It is her sister Michal who introduces emotion into the narrative:

> Michal, Saul's daughter, loved David. They told Saul, and the matter was pleasing to him. Saul said: "Let me give her to him, and she will be to him a snare so that the hand of the Philistines will be against him." Saul said to David: "Through the second you will become my

son-in-law today (1 Sam 18:20-21)
[בשתים תתחתן בי היום].

As I mentioned in the context of Rachel and Leah's story, the convention of pairing sisters identifies qualities that define each sister while highlighting their differences. Leah is older and fertile, while Rachel is younger and beloved. So far, age alone distinguished Michal from Merav. Now there is another factor. Michal's love for David contrasts with Merav's indifference and defines her character. As Peter D. Miscall comments, in relation to Merav, Michal is the passionate sister. Miscall suggests that Saul capitalized on Michal's love for David, which he recognized in contrast to her sister's indifference. This helps explain why Saul chose to marry Merav to Adriel. Believing Michal's passion will be more useful to him, Saul replaces one sister with the other.[12]

Romantic love and not parental love once again complicates a sister story. For the first time, the Bible states explicitly that a woman romantically loves a man.[13] Rebecca expresses maternal love for Jacob.[14] Clearly, Leah desires Jacob's love, but the text never explicitly states that she loves him. First Samuel 18:20 relates that Michal loves David. It also implies that she actively pursues him by informing Saul, or having someone inform him, of her desire. Notably, Michal's love for David does not instigate sororal competition. Merav remains indifferent to David. Unlike Rachel and Leah, these sisters do not wrestle with one another and engage in a battle for a husband or for babies. Instead, Michal's love, a manifestation of sororal desire because Michal is presented as a sister, feeds the rivalry between the houses of Saul and David.

Initially, Saul enthusiastically embraces Michal's love of David. He thinks he can use Michal to his advantage just as he had planned to use Merav. In exchange for Michal, Saul asks David for one hundred Philistine foreskins in the hopes that David will die paying the bride-price. In Saul's eyes, the sisters are functionally interchangeable and command the same price. Even the similar meaning in their names reflects their interchangeability. They are Merav, "from plenty," and Michal, "from all." Saul is just as happy to use one sister as the other. Either Merav or Michal could ensnare David and put him at the mercy of the Philistines, as the repeated expression "may the hand of the Philistines be against him" makes clear in 1 Sam 18:17 and 21. Either daughter can deliver David to the Philistines; either one is worth 100 Philistine foreskins. While negotiating with David, Saul clearly names the position David will acquire but not which daughter, saying "through the second [בשתים], you will become my son-in-law today." The phrase "through the second" implies Michal, but it can also mean "through both," suggesting that either sister will do.

Recognizing that the sisters are functionally interchangeable, that either sister can trap David through marriage, some commentators consider Merav's story, which does not appear in the Codex Vaticanus, iterative. These scholars suggest that Merav's story reflects an alternative, and less original, version of David's marriage to one of Saul's daughters. For them, David's marriage to Michal is more likely to reflect historical reality than Merav's, which, they argue, is a later literary invention.[15] Although Merav's story may be a later addition to the narrative, I do not consider it redundant or irrelevant. Instead, I contend that it serves a critical narrative purpose because Merav's presence transforms Michal into a sister. The Bible intentionally introduces Michal as a sister. Without Merav, Michal would function in her narrative first as a daughter and then as a wife.[16] As the on-going parallels with the Rachel and Leah story support, the narrative frames their story as a sister story.

Unmarried sisters Michal and Merav induce anxieties as marginal figures within their natal household. If following the paradigm of ideal sisters, they will serve the needs and desire of their patriarch and marry well. Like Rebecca's marriage to Isaac, their marriages should enrich and support their father's house. If following the paradigm of dangerous sisters, they, like Rachel and Leah, would assert agency and desire to support a rival patriarch that threatens their father's house. From the very beginning of their story, David is clearly Saul's rival. Yet Saul eagerly offers his daughters to David in order to protect his house. It was Saul's idea to marry Merav to David. He approves of the union between Michal and David.[17] Although he welcomes his rival into his home, he expects Michal and Merav to remain loyal to him and to help him destroy David. In other words, he expects them to behave like ideal sisters that protect their natal household against rival patriarchs—even if it means they will have to marry them to betray them.

Yet Saul makes a foolish and tragic mistake. He underestimates David's ability. David does not die in battle but delivers two-fold on the bride-price, bringing Saul two hundred Philistine foreskins.[18] He also underestimates Michal's desire. He believes he can use Michal's love to his advantage. As the ensuing events show, Michal's love for David proves stronger than her loyalty to her father. It is a dangerous force that makes her a dangerous figure in relation to her father's house. In 1 Sam 18:28-29, Saul recognizes the danger and implications of Michal's desire for David:

> Saul saw and knew that YHWH was with David and that Michal, Saul's daughter, loved him. Saul grew more afraid of David and became an enemy of David ever after.

At this moment, Saul realizes that Michal's love for David is no longer an asset but a threat to his household. He understands that God and Michal love David and that their love of David comes at his expense. Like God, Michal chooses David over Saul.

Michal's choice is evident in the next chapter when she saves David's life. Realizing the extent of the threat David poses, crazed Saul sends emissaries to David's house to kill him. Michal warns David in 1 Sam 19:11:

> Saul sent messengers to David's house to keep watch over him and to kill him in the morning. Michal, his wife, said to David: "If you do not escape tonight, tomorrow you will be killed.

Noticeably, this passage refers to Michal as David's wife and not as Saul's daughter, as she was in the previous chapter. Also, she now resides in David's house [בית דוד], which is separate from Saul's house. Given this designation and the setting of the conjugal house, Michal's story, unlike Rachel and Leah's story, appears to have progressed from a sister to a wife story. Yet it is clear from this passage, as well from what happens next, that she remains tied to her father's house and that her story remains focused on her natal household. Thus, the locus of the sister story, the natal household, remains intact.

Michal is privy to information from her father's house and is aware of Saul's plot to kill David. The text does not reveal how Michal knows of her father's plans. Perhaps servants inform her—or maybe even her sister. Saul himself may be informing Michal because he believes that ultimately she will be loyal to him. What happens next suggests that Michal, indeed, feels a measure of loyalty to her father. Yet Michal's loyalty to her husband comes first, and at her father's expense. This is clear when she helps David escape in 1 Sam 19:12-13:

> Michal lowers David through the window. He flees and escapes. Michal took the teraphim and placed them in the bed. She put a quilt made of goat's hair over its head and covered it in a blanket.

Once again, a father's teraphim figure prominently in a sister story. The inclusion of this episode is a direct link to Rachel and Leah's story and reveals that Michal and Merav's story conforms to the Bible's overarching sister narrative in which sisters weaken their fathers' homes to support the Bible's designated patriarchs.

Just as the stealing of her father's teraphim was a pivotal moment for Rachel, Michal's manipulation of her father's teraphim proves to be a pivotal moment for Michal. It determines her fate and manifests her narrative function.

Like dangerous sister Rachel, Michal asserts agency, as Exum notes, and dupes her father with his household gods.[19] And once again, the symbolism could not be clearer. As household gods or as ancestor figures, the teraphim represent and protect Saul's household, just as they represented and protected Laban's. Rachel's theft of her father's teraphim was an aggressive act against her father. When fleeing from her father's house, Rachel steals her father's property—the symbols of his ancestors and his gods. Feigning impurity, she then sits upon them, mocking her father's authority and the potency of his gods. Similarly, Michal's use of the teraphim to save David's life is an aggressive act against her father, mocking Saul's authority and religion. She places her father's gods, the symbol of his household, in her husband's bed. By covering the teraphim with a wig and a blanket, Michal mocks idols that can be dressed up like dolls. She shows that her father's gods have no real power and warrant no respect. By placing her father's idols, the symbol of his vitality, in her conjugal bed, she makes it clear that her husband has now replaced her father as her primary patriarch and that David controls the fate of Saul's house.

Michal helps David escape through the window, and remains in his house to confront her father:

> Saul sent messengers to take David, but she said: "He is sick." Saul sent the messengers to see David, saying: "Carry him from the bed and bring him to me to kill him." The messengers entered, and there were the teraphim in the bed with the quilt of goat's hair on its head. Saul said to Michal: "Why have you deceived me in this way and sent forth my enemy so that he escaped?" Michal said to Saul: "He told me, 'Send me forth! Why should I kill you?'" (1 Sam 19:14-17)

The confrontation between Michal and Saul leaves no doubt that in Saul's mind, Michal chose her husband over her father. Saul understands what it means to find his household gods in his rival's bed. He also knows who must have put them there. He immediately accuses Michal of treason for assisting David whom Saul refers to as "my enemy." Saul's question to Michal "Why have you deceived me? [למה ככה רמיתני]" reveals his hurt and anger. It also serves as another link to Rachel and Leah's story by recalling Jacob's outrage when he discovers that Laban deceived him with Leah.[20] Just as Jacob felt betrayed by Laban, Saul feels betrayed by Michal. He holds Michal entirely responsible for David's escape. In response, Michal lies to her father to protect herself from her father's wrath, just as Rachel lied to Laban to protect herself after stealing his teraphim.

Michal informs Saul that David threatened to kill her and therefore coerced her into betraying her father. The interesting fact that she remains in David's house and does not escape with him lends credence to her lie. Michal does not escape with David because she would not accompany someone who threatened her life. In truth, the text does not reveal the real reason why Michal does not leave with David. Both David J. A. Clines and Exum suggest that it was not Michal's choice to remain behind. Michal remains because David chooses not to take her with him.[21] Unlike Clines and Exum, I suggest that Michal continues to exert agency and chooses not to escape with David. Although not explicitly stated, her choice to remain behind, I suggest, reveals a core loyalty to her father and a desire not to break ties with him completely. Unlike Rachel and Leah, Michal does not abandon her father for her husband. Although she defies him and helps his rival, Michal remains tied to her natal household. Her lie to her father enables Michal to maintain this linkage since Saul cannot blame a threatened woman for helping his rival escape. Unsurprisingly, it is Michal's relationship to David that appears strained, if not severed, after this episode. Once Michal helps David escape, she does not speak with her husband again until he returns as king.

Like Rachel's, Michal's deception proves effective, but her actions have enormous consequences. David escapes, lives as an outlaw, and marries other women. Michal reenters the narrative when the text lists David's new wives:

> Abigail quickly rose and mounted an ass with five maidservants attending her. She followed David's messengers and became his wife. David took Ahinoam of Jezreel and both of them became his wives. Saul gave Michal, his daughter, David's wife, to Palti son of Laish from Gallim. (1 Sam 25:42-44)

Clearly, Michal has returned to her father's house and is under his direct control once again. For a second time, Saul overturns his daughter's marriage; this time, giving Michal to Palti. Having almost shared a husband, the sisters now share the common experience of having a marriage overturned. Sisters Michal and Merav both fall victim to the whims of their father's matrimonial machinations. At least for Merav, the marriage to David had not yet taken place. But Michal was married to David and belonged to him. The passage does not relate Saul's motivation for marrying Michal to Palti. He may act aggressively against David *and* Michal for betraying him. He also may be acting compassionately toward Michal, who must now share the role and status of David's wife with two more women.[22] Either way, Saul reasserts his paternal authority over Michal by marrying her to Palti. Yet despite Saul's despotic behavior, verse 44 refers to Michal as Saul's daughter and David's wife, capturing Michal's on-going marginal position in both houses. Although her father determines her fate and effectively annuls her marriage with David, Michal still remains caught between her first husband and her father, between the house of David and the house of Saul.

Tensions between these houses continue even after Saul's death, recorded in 1 Samuel 31. As David's house grows stronger, Saul's house grows weaker. At last, preparing to assume kingship over Israel and Judah, David makes pacts with Abner, Saul's cousin and general, as well as Saul's son Ish-Boshet, Michal's brother. In 2 Sam 3:13-16, David sets the terms. He has one condition, the return of Michal:

> He said: "Good, I will make a pact with you, but I demand one thing from you. You will not appear before me unless you bring Michal, Saul's daughter, when you come to see me." David sent messengers to Ish-Boshet, Saul's son, saying: "Give me my wife Michal whom I betrothed for one hundred Philistine foreskins." Ish-Boshet sent and took her from the man, from Paltiel son of Laish. Her husband followed after her crying until Bahurim. Abner said to him: "Return home!" And he returned.

David wants Michal back despite the fact that biblical law, as reflected in Deut 24:1-4, prohibits a man from remarrying his former wife if she had married another man in the interim. By the standards set by Deuteronomy, Michal should be undesirable, if forbidden to David.[23] Yet David seems as intent as Saul was in 1 Sam 25:44 to assert his authority over Michal. Saul asserts his paternal authority when he marries Michal to Palti. David asserts his conjugal authority when he tells Ish-Boshet that he had paid the bride-price of one hundred Philistine foreskins. Michal, he makes clear, belongs to him.

In a gesture that marks the final demise of Saul's house and the transmission of power and authority to David, Ish-Boshet returns Michal to David. After reclaiming Michal, David can now become king. It is interesting to note that this is the only moment in Michal's narrative where siblings directly interact. Ish-Boshet takes Michal from Paltiel's house. The exchange of Michal resonates with the events of another sister story—Genesis 34. Just as Dinah's brothers take their sexualized sister from Shechem's house (Gen 34:26), ויקחו את-דינה מבית שכם Ish-Boshet takes his sexualized sister from Paltiel's home, ויקחה מעם איש. He gives her to David.

Although Dinah's fate is not described, one imagines that she remains within her natal home for the rest of her life and is a constant reminder of her own violation and of the violation of her father's house. Sexually violated and unmarried, Dinah cannot progress happily in her life to become a wife or a mother. She must remain in the role of a violated sister-daughter for the rest of her life. Similarly, Michal's presence in David's house represents her father's defeat and is a constant reminder of the destruction of his household. Yet unlike Dinah, Michal does not return to her natal house. Instead, she is restored to her first husband's house. As a married woman, Michal could live a happy life in David's house as a wife and as a mother—that is, if she happily returns to him.

Just as Merav's feelings were not described when Saul marries her to Adriel, Michal's feelings are not mentioned when she is taken from Paltiel. Instead, Paltiel weeps as he watches his wife leave. His sorrow conveys the emotional costs of switching brides and revoking marriages. It also may communicate indirectly that Michal may be emotionally devastated at the thought of leaving Paltiel and returning to David. Paltiel's sorrow may reflect Michal's. It has been some time since the text mentioned Michal's love for David, and a lot has happened to test that love. As I noted earlier, David does not take Michal with him, nor does he send for her later, even though Michal helped David escape. Having acquired other brides, David seems to have had no need or desire for Michal except as a trophy symbolizing her father's defeat.

Given what happens next, it appears that Michal no longer loves David, certainly not in the way that she had at the beginning of her story. In 2 Samuel 6, King David solidifies his power and brings the ark of God into the city of David. In 2 Sam 6:16, Michal watches from her window as David parades with the ark and celebrates:

> When the ark of YHWH entered into the City of David, Michal, Saul's daughter, watched through the window. She saw King David leaping and whirling before YHWH, and she despised him in her heart.

This is the second mention of a window in which Michal and David stand on opposite sides—the first being when Michal helps David escape. Once again, Michal is inside, while David is outside. In both cases, their physical separation indicates an emotional distance. David has no desire to take Michal, or she has no desire to go with him when he escapes through the window in 1 Samuel 19, and Michal has no desire to celebrate with her husband as he escorts the ark in 2 Samuel 6. Also, the placement of Michal at a window, as Exum observes, reflects her status as a marginal person in David's house.[24]

The image of the woman at the window is a common one throughout ancient art and literature according to Nehama Aschkenasy.[25] As openings to the home, windows and doors mark the places where the home is most vulnerable and are associated in the Bible with individuals who exist on the margins of their families and are themselves vulnerable.[26] This is made brutally clear in Judges 19 in the story of the raped concubine who collapses across the threshold of her host's home, desperate for, yet denied its protection. Similarly, Queen Jezebel is tossed from a window to her death when she is deposed in 2 Kgs 9:33. As temporary members of their natal households, sisters inherently are threshold figures. Seth Daniel Kunin argues that biblical sisters, like daughters, are structurally dangerous figures who threaten the cohesion of a family by creating openings to the outside.[27] In their narratives, sisters and daughters function as the windows or doors of their natal homes, who may allow dangerous outsiders to come within.

As discussed in other chapters of this book, the doorway is a feature that marks marginality in the sister stories of Lot's daughters (chapter 4) in Genesis 19 (a story that resonates with Judges 19) and of Tamar (chapter 6) in 2 Samuel 13, as well as in the sisterhood story of Jephthah's daughter in Judges 11.[28] In Michal's story, it is a window that marks her marginality. As Saul's daughter, who is also David's wife, and as a sister, Michal is a threshold figure. Looking out the window, Michal recognizes her marginal status and reacts viscerally to David's celebratory behavior. As Saul's daughter trapped within David's house, Michal watches the ark enter the City of David, cognizant of what this means for her father's household. Now that both God and Michal reside within David's house, the house of David is firmly established. Saul recognized the destructive power of this combination back in 1 Sam 18:28. Now Michal understands it.

Although she expresses no regret for the role she played in Saul's demise, Michal, with chagrin, seems to recognize David as Saul's triumphant rival. As verse 16 relates, she sees him as the king [ותרא את-המלך דוד] and comes to despise him [ותבז לו בלבה]. Her reasons for despising him remain obscure. Perhaps, as she says, she is genuinely disgusted by his dancing before the ark and by his exposing himself before the maidservants. Perhaps she continues to feel loyal to her father. Perhaps she realizes that all along she was a pawn in David's plot to usurp Saul and that he never loved her.[29] Whatever the reason or reasons, her love clearly has soured.

As they did at the beginning of her narrative, Michal's emotions once again dictate her actions. Initially, Michal's love drove her to David and made her betray her father. Now, her hatred of David causes her to confront him:

> When David returned to bless his household, Michal, Saul's daughter, went out [ותצא מיכל] to greet David and said: "How honored is the King of Israel today who reveals himself today before the maidservants as one of the worthless ones reveals himself!" (2 Sam 6:20)

David returns home after offering sacrifices, blesses every man and woman in Israel, and provides them with celebratory food. In this passage, Michal's isolation and alienation from David is apparent—she was not there with everyone else to receive his blessing. Yet she does not wait for him to return home. Instead, as sister Leah does in Gen 30:16 and sister Dinah in Gen 34:1, Michal exercises agency and crosses the threshold of her house. Remarkably, she "goes out" as "Saul's daughter" and accuses David of demeaning himself and not behaving like a proper king of Israel. Once again, her allegiance has shifted, this time in favor of her father over her husband. Michal implies that Saul would never have behaved in this way. David's response to Michal indicates that he has understood her in this way:

> David said to Michal: "It is before YHWH who chose me over your father and over all his household to appoint me as ruler over YHWH's people, over Israel! I will celebrate before YHWH and dishonor myself more than this. I will be disgraced in my own eyes but among the maidservants whom you mentioned, I will be honored." Michal, Saul's daughter, had no children until the day of her death. (2 Sam 6:21-23)

In his rebuke, David makes one thing absolutely clear to Michal: God chose him and his household over Saul and his household. By referring to Saul as "your father," David associates Michal with Saul and his house and condemns them both, as the final verse in this passage implies. Following David's rebuke, the text states that Michal, Saul's daughter, dies childless. Although the text does not explicitly indicate a causal relationship between David's rebuke and Michal's barrenness, it is easy to assume one. Either David curses Michal with infertility or with a sexless marriage.[30] It is also equally possible that, from this moment on, Michal abstains from sex with David as Exum suggests.[31]

Whether she is cursed or scorned by David, or abstains from sex herself, childless Michal, again referred to as Saul's daughter, represents the destruction of her father's house, at least through her own line. Michal is doomed to live a marginal existence—a kind of living death—within David's house.[32] Without children, she cannot participate fully in the construction of David's house, as Rachel and Leah participated in the construction of Jacob's house. Childless, perhaps in a sexless marriage, and with her father dead, Michal cannot continue as a mother, wife, or even as a daughter in her story. The only role she can continue to fill is that of sister.

The final episode in Michal's story reintegrates Merav into the narrative and confirms Michal's status as a sister. In 2 Samuel 21, God informs David that the famine Israel is experiencing is caused by a bloodguilt borne by the house of Saul because of their deception of the Gibeonites. To remove the bloodguilt and end the famine, the Gibeonites demand that seven of Saul's sons be killed. David agrees, though he spares Jonathan's son. Second Samuel 21:8-9 describes the murder of Saul's other sons:

> The king took Armoni and Mephiboshet, the two sons Rizpah, daughter of Aiah, bore for Saul and the five sons of Michal, Saul's daughter, which she bore for Adriel son of Barzillai the Mecholatite. He handed them over to the Gibeonites who impaled them upon the mountain before YHWH. All seven fell together. They were killed in the first days of the harvest, the beginning of the barley harvest.

The confusion this passage causes by referring to Michal and Adriel's five sons is easily remedied. The simplest solution is to follow the Septuagint, the Syriac, and the Vulgate to emend the text and to substitute Merav, Adriel's true wife, according to 1 Sam 18:19, for Michal. The emended text would record that the king kills Merav's children and not Michal's.

Yet my reading of this passage embraces its ambiguity,[33] and suggests that 2 Sam 21:8 intentionally blurs the identities of Michal and Merav, ending their story as it began with two sisters and one husband. It brings their story full circle. In my reading, both sisters are present in this passage as shadow figures to one another, just as they were at the start of their narrative. One sister should not be substituted for the other through emendation but should coexist within the confused text that means to evoke both Michal and Merav. In the beginning of their story, Saul considers them functionally interchangeable and equally valued. Either one was worth one hundred Philistine foreskins and could ensnare David. At the end of their narrative, the textual confusion proves that the sisters are indeed interchangeable. Unlike Rachel and Leah, these paired sisters are not oppositional figures within their narrative. Instead, they blend together. Their characters and their fates are fused to reflect the fate of their father. At this moment in the narrative, whether from murder or from barrenness (it does not matter which), *both* sisters die childless. As the fate of these sisters convey, David, indeed, destroys the house of Saul.

Michal and Merav's fate and story, like Rachel and Leah's, reflect and contribute to the vulnerability of their natal households. As dangerous sisters, Michal and Merav introduce a rival patriarch who threatens to usurp their father's authority and weaken his house. Like Rachel and Leah, Michal and Merav secure the position of the Bible's designated patriarch at their father's expense. Their stories reveal that dangerous sisters, like brothers, play a significant and positive role in the biblical narrative. It is also interesting to observe that younger sisters, like younger brothers, are particularly destabilizing figures and appear to be the focus of their narrative. We see this pattern continue in the stories of Rebel Israel and Faithless Judah, discussed in the next chapter.

Yet, unlike younger brothers, sisters—whether younger or older—are not rewarded with blessings and property even though they help remove unwanted patriarchs from the biblical narrative. The Bible wants David to succeed at Saul's expense, just as the Bible wants Jacob to succeed at Laban's expense. Yet dangerous sisters do not experience happy endings to their stories, perhaps because they challenge patriarchal authority—Rachel and Michal directly, Leah and Merav by association. Rachel, Leah, Michal, and Merav do not become happy wives or happy mothers in their narratives.

Arguably, Michal and Merav's fate is much worse than Rachel and Leah's. Whereas Rachel and Leah built the house of Jacob at the expense of the house of Laban, Michal and Merav destroy the house of Saul but do not build the house of David. In particular, Michal serves as a chilling reflection of Saul's fate. At the beginning of her story, Saul hopes Michal will entrap David within his house in order to destroy him. In the end, Michal is trapped within David's house. Immediately after declaring Michal childless until her death, the Bible records God's promise to establish an eternal house and dynasty for David.[34] As 2 Sam 7:16 makes clear, God, not Michal, builds David's בית נאמן, his secure and steadfast home. Sister Michal remains childless in David's home, a symbol of God's rejection of the house of Saul and his election of the house of David.

Notes

1. David J. A. Clines notes the specific difficulty in identifying Michal's independent story within the Saul-David narratives. See Clines, "The Story of Michal, Wife of David, in its Sequential Unfolding" in *Telling Queen Michal's Story: An Experiment in Comparative Interpretation,* ed. David J. A. Clines and Tamara C. Eskenazi (Sheffield: Sheffield Academic, 1991), 129–30.

2. In her analysis, J. Cheryl Exum does not fully consider the role Merav plays in these narratives. She focuses only on Michal in the role of Saul's daughter or David's wife—roles, Exum argues, Michal cannot inhabit simultaneously. See Exum, *Tragedy and Biblical Narrative* (Cambridge: Cambridge University Press, 1992), 83–84.

3. See J. Cheryl Exum, *Fragmented Women: Feminist (Sub)versions of Biblical Narratives* (Valley Forge, PA: Trinity, 1993), 42.

4. See Exum, *Tragedy and Biblical Narrative*, 92.

5. Similarly, Ellen White encourages reading Michal's story as a wife story—Paltiel's wife. See White, "Michal the Misinterpreted," *JSOT* 31, no. 4 (2007): 457.

6. Frederick E. Greenspahn, *When Brothers Dwell Together: The Preeminence of Younger Siblings in the Hebrew Bible* (Oxford: Oxford University Press, 1994), 136.

7. Scholars suggest that Ishvi's name is a variation of "man of God" and consider it to be either an official or theologically corrected variation of the name of Saul's son Ish-Boshet mentioned in 2 Sam 2:8. See P. Kyle McCarter Jr., *1 Samuel* (New York: Doubleday, 1980), 254.

8. See 1 Sam 18:1, 16.

9. Peter D. Miscall raises the possibility that Saul wants to keep David in battle and away from him so that Saul does not kill him. See Miscall, "Michal and Her Sisters," in *Telling Queen Michal's Story*, 248.

10. The phrase "when the time came" indicates that David expected to marry Merav.

11. Miscall comments on Merav's silence: "What is note-worthy is that Merab, the king's oldest daughter, is merely an object, whether reward or not, to be handed back and forth. We know nothing of her feelings and reactions to the plans and to the change in plans. David doesn't even mention her by name." See Miscall, "Michal and her Sisters," 248.

12. Ibid.

13. Similarly, Robert Alter observes: "Michal leaps out of the void as a name, a significant relation (Saul's daughter), and an emotion (her love for David). This love, twice stated here, is bound to have special salience because it is the only instance in all biblical narrative in which we are explicitly told that a woman loves a man." See Alter, *The Art of Biblical Narrative* (New York: Basic Books, 1981), 118.

14. Gen 25:28.

15. See Hans Wilhelm Hertzberg, *I & II Samuel*, trans. J. S. Bowden (Philadelphia: Westminster, 1964), 160; McCarter Jr., *I Samuel*, 306. Zafrira Ben-Barak summarizes the scholarly debate and concludes: "In the view of most scholars the Michal narrative is authentic and reflects historical reality, while the Merab narrative is dismissed as colourless imitation." See Ben-Barak, "The Legal Background to the Restoration of Michal to David," in *Telling Queen Michal's Story*, 79.

16. Of course even without Merav, Michal would still be a sister—Jonathan's sister—but she never engages directly with him in her narratives.

17. The text notes in verse 20 that Michal's love for David was a "good thing to his eyes [וישר הדבר בעיניו]."

18. First Sam 18:27.

19. See Exum, *Tragedy and Biblical Narrative*, 83.

20. In Gen 29:25, Jacob asks Laban: "Why have you deceived me? [למה רמיתני]"

21. See Clines, "The Story of Michal," 131 and Exum, *Tragedy and Biblical Narrative*, 83.

22. Exum suggests that Saul married Michal to Palti to prevent the outlaw David from claiming the throne. See Exum, *Tragedy and Biblical Narrative*," 83.

23. Shulamite Valler discusses how the rabbis justified David's remarriage to Michal in "King David and 'His' Women: Biblical Stories and Talmudic Discussions" in *A Feminist Companion to Samuel and Kings*, ed. Athalya Brenner (Sheffield: Sheffield Academic, 1994), 133–34.

24. See Exum, *Fragmented Women*, 50.

25. See Nehama Aschkenasy, *Woman at the Window: Biblical Tales of Oppression and Escape* (Detroit: Wayne University Press, 1998), 13.

26. See Aschkenasy, 17–18.

27. See Seth Daniel Kunin, *The Logic of Incest: A Structural Analysis of Hebrew Mythology* (Sheffield: Sheffield Academic, 1995), 138.

28. A window figures in the Rebecca wife-sister story in Genesis 26.

29. Alter attributes Michal's scorn to a variety of factors: "The scorn for David welling up in Michal's heart is thus plausibly attributable in some degree to all of the following: the undignified public spectacle which David just now is making of himself; Michal's jealousy over the moment of glory David is enjoying while she sits alone, a neglected co-wife, back at the provisional palace; Michal's resentment over David's indifference to her all these years, over the other wives he has taken, over being torn away from the devoted Palti; David's dynastic ambitions—now clearly revealed in his establishing the Ark in the "City of David"—which will irrevocably displace the house of Saul." See Alter, *Art of Biblical Narrative*, 123.

30. Perhaps David refuses to have sex with Michal because of the prohibition against remarrying a former wife who has been married in the interim.

31. Although unlikely, Exum believes that it would not be out of character for Michal to abstain from sex with David. See Exum, *Tragedy and Biblical Narrative*, 88.

32. According to Exum, Michal suffers a symbolic and narrative death. See ibid., 90.

33. Edward Greenstein argues for a similar intentional ambiguity in Genesis 37, which records that either the Ishmaelites (Gen 37:27; 39:1) or the Midianites (Gen 37:28, 36) sold Joseph to Potiphar in Egypt. According to Greenstein, ancient audiences could tolerate textual inconsistencies that appear to contemporary audiences as discrepancies. For Greenstein, the Genesis text intentionally confuses the Ishmaelites with the Midianites to highlight God's role in the narrative. See Edward L. Greenstein, "An Equivocal Reading of the Sale of Joseph," in *Literary Interpretations of Biblical Narratives, Volume II*, ed. Kenneth R. R. Gros Louis and James S. Ackerman (Nashville: Abingdon, 1982), 117.

34. Second Samuel 7.

3

Israel and Judah

Paired sisters married to a single husband appear in the books of Jeremiah and Ezekiel as part of the prophet's depiction of Israel as God's promiscuous wife. Scholars credit the eighth-century prophet Hosea for introducing the marriage metaphor into prophetic literature when he compares his relationship with his own unfaithful wife Gomer to God's relationship with Israel.[1] Subsequent prophets develop the metaphor. Piecing together the prophetic texts that evoke the marriage metaphor, scholars like Gerlinde Baumann construct a narrative for Israel as God's wife that extends from youth through adulthood and that reflects the stages of her marriage to God.[2] At first, God loves Israel.[3] Lustful Israel challenges that love when she pursues other lovers.[4] Enraged, God brutally punishes Israel and divorces her.[5] Having administered justice, God then reconciles with Israel and renews his covenant with her.[6]

Although Hosea is the first to evoke the metaphor, most scholars do not locate its origin in Hosea's troubled marriage. Scholars like Gale Yee attribute the development of the metaphor to social and political changes in ancient Israel's society. Yee suggests that Hosea responds to Israel's increased engagement with foreign powers during the eighth century when it shifted from a native-tributary mode of production to a foreign-tributary mode. Hosea, Yee posits, constructed an effective rhetoric that castigates any political, social, and religious engagement with foreign powers.[7] Others, like Alice A. Keefe and Christl M. Maier, situate the metaphor within a long history that associates land with women and women's bodies with the body politic.[8] For Keefe, women's bodies in the Bible represent the social body. A violated woman like Dinah or a promiscuous woman like Gomer represent social chaos and signify Israel's vulnerable, if not breached, society.[9]

Given the sexual nature of the marriage metaphor, recent scholarship has focused on its rhetorical impact—ancient and contemporary.[10] Explicit images of a female Israel spreading her legs for everyone who passes by and of masturbating with gold phallic images[11] raises the question of whether these passages should be considered pornographic.[12] This identification may seem anachronistic and unnecessarily provocative, but it focuses attention on the craft of these passages and on their intended audience. In this reading, the marriage metaphor is carefully constructed to elicit a strong response from the prophets' audience. As Yee observes, the prophets address an audience of elite males and use the marriage metaphor as a provocative way to shame their audience into reform by calling them loose women. Yee thinks the marriage metaphor in Hosea "feminizes" the ruling male elite and symbolically castrates them, thereby deterring them from engaging with foreigners.[13]

Prophets Jeremiah and Ezekiel introduce and develop a unique element within the metaphor of Israel as God's wife. Jeremiah 3:6-11, Ezek 16:44-63, and Ezekiel 23 portray Israel and Judah (and in the case of Ezekiel 16, Sodom as well) as sexually promiscuous sisters, married to God. Although married to God, these paired sisters pursue other lovers and are violently punished by God. Given that Israel and Judah are two distinct kingdoms that share, to some degree, a national and religious identity, the introduction of sisters into the marriage metaphor may seem logical and not particularly innovative.[14] It makes sense in the context of the marriage metaphor that two kingdoms would mean two wives for God. This certainly would have been a natural image during Hosea's lifetime when the Northern Kingdom still stood. Yet by the time of Jeremiah and Ezekiel, Israel had long ago fallen to Assyria, and Judah alone faced the threat of Babylon.[15] Therefore, I contend, these prophets chose to evoke the memory of Israel and chose to portray Israel and Judah as sisters—as opposed to two unrelated wives.

Jeremiah and Ezekiel's choice to portray Israel and Judah as sisters confirms that sisters are dangerous yet powerful figures. In the paired sister stories already studied, we have seen the narrative power of sisters, who destabilize their natal households and work to remove rival patriarchs from the narrative to strengthen the position of the Bible's designated patriarchs. In Jeremiah and Ezekiel, we see the rhetorical power of sisters, who can be evoked to persuade Israel to change its sinful behavior. These sisters are a core part of what Mary E. Shields calls the prophets' "subversive discourse," designed to enable people "to identify themselves in a new way" so that they behave differently.[16] In other words, these sisters are rhetorically destabilizing figures. The prophets want their targeted male audience to identify as sisters married to God. We also see how Jeremiah and Ezekiel's particular incorporation of sisters works to expand the marriage metaphor. It makes room for not only one more wife, but it stretches the metaphor to include Israel and Judah's mother, other sisters, and their daughters. In the rhetoric of these prophets, the sisters become a sisterhood not unlike those I will discuss in part 3.[17] This, I argue, enables the prophets to reach a broader audience—one that extends beyond the male elite to include women.

The prophets' portrayal of Israel and Judah as sisters shares significant elements of the sister stories already discussed along with distinct features. Most notably, as part of the prophetic literature, Israel and Judah do not exist as characters within constructed narratives in the same way that Rachel, Leah, Michal, and Merav do. The figures of Judah and Israel conform to the contours of the Bible's paradigmatic sister story. Yet, as masters of rhetoric, the prophets are more interested in the impact these sisters make as disturbing figures than they are in telling a coherent story. Thus, it is appropriate to consider sisters Israel and Judah as potent rhetorical devices intentionally employed by the prophets rather than as developed characters within defined sister narratives. Because the prophets did not write such narratives but used sisters as part of their rhetoric, I analyze this material differently. Instead of examining each prophet independently, I bring together the sister texts from Jeremiah and Ezekiel to examine common themes, concerns, and rhetorical strategies. Although Ezekiel prophesied after Jeremiah and offers a fuller portrait of the sisters than Jeremiah,[18] the prophets' portrayal of Israel and Judah as sisters reflects shared anxieties raised by sisters as destabilizing figures.[19] Fears of sororal desire, agency, and solidarity are evident in Jeremiah and Ezekiel's portrayal of Israel and Judah as sisters, as they were in the sister narratives.

As part of a rhetoric that condemns Israel, there can be no doubt that Jeremiah's Rebel Israel and Faithless Judah and Ezekiel's Oholah (Israel) and Oholibah (Judah)[20] fit the paradigm of dangerous sisters who, like the sisters already discussed, pose a formidable threat to their patriarchal household. Their interpersonal relationship creates a sister bond that fosters confidence in themselves and defiance of their patriarchs. Their insatiable passions introduce rival patriarchs into their households.

In Israel and Judah's case, these sisters threaten the patriarchal household that belongs to their husband God. Their story uniquely focuses on the conjugal and not the natal household. With the focus on the conjugal home, one could argue that Israel and Judah function primarily as wives and not as sisters in the prophetic texts. Yet, as I demonstrate, the sisters' relationship to each other is a central concern of the prophets, just as it was a central concern of the Rachel and Leah narratives. Also, though God functions primarily as husband in the metaphor, both prophets present God in the role of adoptive father as well. God tells Israel:

> I said I would place you among my children and would give you
> desirable land—the most glorious among the nations. I had said that
> you would call me "my father," and from me you would not stray.
> (Jer 3:19-20)

Remarkably, God not only adopts Israel in this passage, God seems prepared to
allow his adopted daughter to inherit property along with his sons.[21] Similarly,
Ezek 16:1-6 offers a detailed description of God's adoption of Israel whom
he discovered as a bloody infant abandoned in a field. Embedded within the
marriage metaphor, and in close proximity to the sister passages, these passages
suggest that God functions as both father and husband to Israel and to Judah. In
other words, the natal and the conjugal homes are intertwined.

I contend that Jeremiah and Ezekiel intentionally portray Israel and Judah
as sisters, thereby injecting particular anxieties into the metaphor of the
wayward wife that become an essential part of their rhetoric. The metaphoric
depiction of Israel as sisters heightens tensions and expresses terrors related
to Israel's demise, while it also conveys what is necessary to secure Israel's
redemption.[22] Dangerous sisters Israel and Judah destroy their patriarchal
household and come to represent its destruction. Naked, shamed, and maimed,
these paired sisters embody the fall of the house of Israel, God's house, just
as barren and trapped Michal embodied the fall of Saul's house. Yet unlike
Saul's house or Laban's house, God's house must be protected. The prophets
employ the rhetoric of the dangerous sisters to protect God's house. Once again,
dangerous sisters serve the Bible's goals and values but are not rewarded for the
essential role they play.

The sisters' grim fate, which Ezekiel recounts in graphic detail, warns
Israel against political and religious apostasy.[23] It also implicitly warns Israel's
women against sororal solidarity and desire by telling them what they must do
to overturn their fate. If the sisters break their bond and relinquish their role
as sisters and if they redirect their desire appropriately, they can reconcile with
God. Metaphorical sisters Israel and Judah must drink the cup of poison so that
live Israel can restore its relationship with God and return to God's house.

Sororal Solidarity

Jeremiah and Ezekiel recognize that sisters Israel and Judah are alike and that
there is a fundamental and threatening bond between them. Like Merav and
Michal, sisters Israel and Judah are essentially interchangeable. In the prophets'
depiction, the sisters behave alike and bear the same fate. As the prophet Ezekiel
says, each is her sister's sister [אֲחוֹת אֲחוֹתֵךְ] (Ezek 16:45), and there is one

path for them both [דרך אחד לשתיהם] (Ezek 23:13). Having walked the same path, the sisters must drink from the same deadly cup and suffer the same fate [בדרך אחותך הלכת ונתתי כוסה בידך] (Ezek 23:31). Similarly, Jeremiah makes clear that Faithless Judah behaves just like Rebel Israel and, therefore, deserves a similar fate. According to Jer 3:7-8, younger sister Judah learns to behave promiscuously by watching her older sister:

> I said, after doing all this, she will come back to me, but she did not return. Her sister Faithless Judah watched. She saw that on account of Rebel Israel's adultery,[24] I sent her off and gave her a bill of divorce, yet her sister Faithless Judah was not afraid and also behaved promiscuously.

Following Israel's example, Judah should expect God to divorce her, just as God divorced her sister.

Despite their fundamental similarity, the convention of pairing sisters, as we have seen, highlights their differences. Although the sisters behave similarly, each prophet identifies one sister as behaving worse than the other. Younger sister Judah is portrayed as more wretched than elder sister Israel. As I note in the previous chapter, a pattern emerges among the Bible's paired sisters in which younger sisters are portrayed as more assertive and, therefore, more problematic than elder sisters. Motivated by jealousy of her sister, Rachel challenges Jacob and demands that he give her sons. She initiates the exchange for Leah's mandrakes and steals her father's teraphim. Michal's love for David triggers the downfall of her father's house. Like Rachel, Michal betrays her father with his teraphim.

As I observed, the pattern of the problematic younger sister resembles the pattern manifest in the Bible's paired brother stories in which younger brothers destabilize their natal families and are the focus of their narratives. Yet, whereas the Bible supports younger brothers Isaac, Jacob, and Joseph even when they betray and deceive as Jacob does, the Bible holds younger sisters Rachel, Michal, and Judah accountable for their destructive behavior.

Because Faithless Judah refused to learn from her sister's example, Jeremiah considers her more wretched than her sister. In fact Faithless Judah makes Rebel Israel look good, as Jer 3:11 states: "YHWH said to me: Rebel Israel is more righteous than Faithless Judah." Likewise, Ezekiel's Oholibah learns to misbehave by watching her older sister Oholah. A voyeur, as Yee notes, Oholibah "becomes even more degenerate than her sister in her own tireless nymphomania."[25] When it becomes clear that the younger has surpassed the elder in sin, she is condemned by the prophet:

> But Shomron did not sin half your sins. Your abominations were more than theirs. You made your sister more righteous with all the abominations you did. Indeed you must bear the shame of interceding on behalf of your sister. Since you have sinned more abominably than they, they appear more righteous than you. Be disgraced, bear shame because you have made your sisters look righteous. (Ezek 16:51-52)

Recognizing that the bond between the sisters inspires bad behavior, Jeremiah and Ezekiel attempt to dissolve it. Both prophets use Israel's fate as a deterrent and warn Judah not to behave like her elder sister. The above passage from Ezekiel suggests that the sisters do more than imitate each other. Not only do the sisters behave alike, they are loyal to one another. No matter how egregious Israel's sin, Judah is willing to fight on her sister's behalf. The prophet directly admonishes Judah for acting on her sister's behalf, and tells Judah she must "bear the shame of interceding on behalf of your sister." Thus, the bond between the sisters does more than teach and perpetuate bad behavior, it challenges patriarchal authority. Loyal to each other, sisters become a united front, even before God. Sororal solidarity emboldens sisters to assert agency apart from, and even over, their patriarchs. Ezekiel 16:45-46 makes clear that Israel and Judah's relationship poses a general threat to patriarchal authority:

> You are your mother's daughter, who despises her husband and sons. You are your sisters' sister, who despise their husbands and children. Your mother is Hittite, your father Amorite. Your elder sister Shomron, she and her daughters sit upon your left; and your younger sister Sodom and her daughters sit upon your right.

In this passage, sisterhood appears contagious as the prophet expands the dangerous sisterhood to include a broader community of women who come together to defy their husbands and sons. Now there are three sisters, as well as daughters, who sit together in solidarity. The community continues to grow in Ezek 23:10 as Oholah's reputation spreads among the women [ותהי־שם לנשים]. As I mention above, scholars often assume that the prophets address an elite male audience and, therefore, select images that will be the most rhetorically effective for their audience. Attempting to shame their male audience into reform, the prophets force them to identify with a promiscuous wife, the "most shameful individual of Israelite society," according to Yee.[26]

Although I believe men to be the primary target of the prophets' rhetoric, I contend that the expansion of the metaphor from dangerous sisters to a dangerous sisterhood suggests an expansion in the perception of the prophets' intended audience, if not of their live audience, to include women and an expansion in the metaphor's rhetorical impact.[27] Not only do the prophets want to shame their male audience, they seek to control their female audience—whether directly or indirectly through their husbands—by making an example of these promiscuous sisters.

As Ezekiel says, Oholah's reputation is growing among women. Earlier in Ezek 16:27, the prophet observes how the Philistine women are horrified by Israel's behavior. Both of these passages present women as Israel's audience who witness her behavior. Having witnessed her crime, women also must witness her punishment, as Ezek 16:41 reveals:

> They will burn your houses in fire and execute judgment upon you
> in the sight of many women. I will put a stop to your promiscuity,
> and you will pay no more fees.

In Ezek 23:46-48, the prophet comes closest to recognizing women among his intended audience and revealing his rhetorical strategy:

> For thus says Lord YHWH:

> Summon a crowd against them and make them an object of horror
> and spoil. Let the community pelt them with stones and cut them
> with their swords. They will kill their sons and their daughters and
> burn their houses. I will stop wantonness in the land, and all women
> will be warned not to act according to your depravity.

In this passage, Ezekiel's explicit description of the sisters' punishment serves to warn women not to behave promiscuously. Ezekiel may in actuality only be addressing men and calling them women, but the implications of his message reaches a broader audience.[28] His depiction of dangerous sisters Israel and Judah encourages women to remain sexually, emotionally, and socially submissive to their patriarchs. As Renita J. Weems observes, it supports a patriarchal ideology in which a husband has absolute control and authority over his wife physically and emotionally.[29]

As I show below, loyalty is manifest mostly as sexual fidelity in the marriage metaphor. Yet, as the fate of these sisters reveals, loyalty also means emotional fidelity. Sororal solidarity is dangerous. Not only do sisters learn bad behavior from one another, they align with one another at the expense of their patriarch. Unlike Rachel and Leah who align effectively, but only occasionally, Israel and Judah are partners in crime. Their constant allegiance to one another overturns the patriarchal norms of society. If unstopped and if the sisters continue to align with one another and defy patriarchal authority, they will come to embody the Bible's ultimate patriarchal nightmare. They will be, at once, dangerous sisters, adulterous wives, and murderous mothers who defile and destroy God's house, as Ezek 23:36-39 describes:

YHWH said to me:

Human, will you judge Oholah and Oholibah and tell them their abominations? For they committed adultery; blood is on their hands. They committed adultery with their idols and their sons, which they bore for me, they offered as food. Even more they did to me; they defiled my sanctuary on that day and profaned my Sabbaths. They slaughtered their children to idols and brought them into the sanctuary on that day to profane it. Indeed they did so within my house!

Sororal Desire

The Ezekiel passage quoted above continues and describes how the sisters brazenly invite foreign men into God's home where the adorned Oholibah lies coquettishly before a set table. This image of Oholibah lying before a table welcoming her lovers captures the sisters' most dangerous shared quality—their insatiable sexual appetite. Both Jeremiah and Ezekiel portray Israel and Judah as sexually active and, even more shocking in the context of the Bible, as sexually proactive women. As I have already noted, the Bible's patriarchal ideology is not comfortable with a sexually aggressive female. A promiscuous female, as Rashkow and Shields observe, is considered to be out of control and dangerous.[30]

Anxieties induced by the sexually proactive woman are evident in Rachel and Leah's and Michal and Merav's story. In chapter 4, I reveal similar anxieties manifest in the story of Lot's daughters. The marriage metaphor provides the Bible's most articulate manifestation of this anxiety, playing directly on male fears and, perhaps as Weems suggests, male fantasies of the sexually aggressive female.[31] Jeremiah accuses Rebel Israel in Jer 3:6 of pursuing her lovers and enjoying them everywhere:

YHWH said to me in the days of King Josiah:

Have you seen what Rebel Israel did, going to every high mountain and under every lush tree and behaving promiscuously there?

In Jer 3:8, Faithless Judah behaves like her sister and goes off to meet her lovers [ותלך ותזן גם-היא]. Clearly, these dangerous sisters actively seek to satisfy their sexual desires. When compared to Jeremiah, Ezekiel presents a more graphic and disturbing account of the sisters' lust, which I suggest reveals this prophet's particularly deep-seated fears of female sexuality and desire. Although Jeremiah condemns the sisters for their promiscuity, at least he envisions an initial period of love and romance between God and young Israel.[32] For Jeremiah, Israel and Judah were once innocent and pure but became corrupt over time.[33] For Ezekiel, sisters Israel and Judah were never innocent and pure. Ezekiel 16 describes Israel as an abandoned and despised infant that only God could love.[34] Ezek 23:2-3 describes sisters Oholah and Oholibah's sullied youth:

Mortal, there were two women, daughters of one mother. They were promiscuous with Egypt in their youth. There, their breasts were squeezed, and there the breasts of their maidenhood were pressed.

Shockingly, in Ezekiel's depiction of the marriage metaphor, God marries damaged goods. Sisters Israel and Judah were not virgins when they married God, but had spent their youth as Egypt's lovers.

As I suggest above, this detail in the marriage metaphor may reflect Ezekiel's deeply engrained fear of, or perhaps repulsion by, female sexuality. Yet it also provides rhetorical punch and narrative coherence to the marriage metaphor. As Yee observes, Ezekiel titillates his audience with an account of "child porn."[35] One assumes this would be as shocking and, therefore, as effective with an ancient audience as it is with a modern one.[36] Given their youthful indiscretions, there can be no surprise when the sisters behave true to form and resume their promiscuities.[37] In this way, Ezekiel explains Israel and Judah's demise and attributes it to sororal desire almost entirely. Both Ezek 23:8 and 23:19 describe the sisters' engrained lust:

> She did not abandon her whoring in Egypt for they laid with her in her youth, they pressed the breasts of her maidenhood, they poured their lust upon her.

> She increased her lust to remember the days of her youth when she whored in the land of Egypt.

It is clear from these passages that Oholah and Oholibah are easily stimulated and sexually hungry. Unable to satisfy their desire, they brazenly pursue their lovers:

> She lusted after the Assyrians: governors and prefects, guardsmen—wearers of finery, horsemen, riders—all desirable men. I saw how she defiled herself. One path for both of them; she increased her whoring, she saw men incised upon the wall, Chaldean figures engraved in red, girded waistbands upon their loins, trailing turbans upon their heads, all of them looking like officers, all the image of Chaldeans, the land of their birth. At the sight of them, she lusted after them and sent messengers to them, to Chaldea. The Babylonians came to her for lovemaking and defiled her with their lust, and she defiled herself with them until she turned away. (Ezek 23:12-17)

Once again, the sisters follow one treacherous path. Just as Oholah lusted after the Assyrians, Oholibah lusts after the Chaldeans. Mere pictures of Chaldean soldiers arouse Oholibah, who then invites her lovers to satisfy her lust [ותשלח מלאכים אליהם]. With this image, Ezekiel suggests that brazen Judah actively pursues Babylon. As Yee describes, she flirts with elite foreigners.[38] Like Rachel and Michal, Judah proves to be a threshold figure that allows a dangerous outsider into her home.[39] In other words, Judah is responsible for her own ruin. For God, this is the last straw. In Ezek 23:18, God rejects Judah just as he rejected her sister: "She revealed her promiscuities and her nakedness. I turned from her in disgust, as I turned from her sister in disgust." Sororal desire and solidarity seal the sisters' fate.

PUNISHMENT AND REDEMPTION

Just as Ezekiel goes into great detail to describe Israel and Judah's crimes, he goes into great detail to describe their punishment. God plans a multipronged assault on the sisters, as Ezek 23:25-26 outlines:

> I will be zealous toward you, and they will deal with you in fury. They will remove your nose and ears, and what remains will fall by the sword. They will take away your sons and daughters, and what remains will be consumed by fire. They will strip you of your clothes and take the objects of your glory.

Stripped and then stoned, Oholah and Oholibah bear the punishment of murderers and adulterers.[40] What is most striking about the sisters' punishment is not its brutality but its precision. In their youth, lovers fondled the sisters' breasts.[41] Now the sisters are made to feel pain where they once felt pleasure, as Ezek 23:32-34 describes:

> Thus says Lord YHWH:
>
> You will drink your sister's cup,
> Deep and wide.
> It will be for mockery and scorn,
> It holds so much.
> You will be full of drunkenness and sorrow,
> The cup of desolation and horror,
> The cup of your sister Shomron.
> You will drink it and suck (upon it),
> And devour its shards.
> You will remove your breasts,
> For I have spoken—declares Lord YHWH.

Ezekiel evokes the cup of wrath from which Oholah has already drunk, and from which now Oholibah must drink.[42] Like Michal and Merav, the paired sisters share one fate. But Oholibah does more than drink from her sister's cup—she must suck it dry. The use of the verb מצי, to slurp, is related to the roots מצץ (m-ṣ-ṣ) or מוץ (m-w-ṣ) meaning to suck or to nurse. Fondled by their Egyptian lovers, the sisters' breasts had been the initial site of their lust. Now in shame, God forces Oholibah to suck from a different kind of breast—a lethal one—while she cuts off her own breasts.[43]

With this brutal act of self-mutilation, Ezekiel eliminates the threat of sororal desire by removing the site of the sister's lust. Oholibah's double mastectomy effectively neuters her. Without breasts and without her sister (Oholah has already drunk from the poisonous cup), sororal desire and solidarity do not pose a threat. Oholibah is no longer dangerous. She can return to her husband God, as Ezek 16:60-61 relates:

> I will remember my covenant with you from the days of your youth, and I will establish with you an eternal covenant. You will remember your ways and be ashamed and when you receive your older sisters and your younger sisters, I will give them to you as daughters though they are not from your covenant.

God transforms her sisters into daughters and renews his covenant only with Judah. In this family reconfiguration, redeemed Judah is no longer a sister though she must remember that she was one once.[44]

As I have noted and will indicate in Chapter 6, a sexualized sister cannot be redeemed in the Bible. She can be avenged like Dinah, punished like Israel and Judah, or imprisoned like Tamar (Chapter 6), but she cannot be redeemed. Once sexualized, she does not resume her position as a sister in her natal family and progress forward in her life and narrative. By transforming Judah's sisters into daughters, Ezekiel removes the image of sexualized sisters from his rhetoric to enable Judah's story to progress. Judah's story continues but only as a shamed and silent wife and mother.[45] With her sisters now her daughters, God reclaims his bride—no longer presented as a sexualized sister.

Unlike Ezekiel, Jeremiah does not describe the sisters' punishment though he also expresses hope for reconciliation. Having divorced Israel, God waits for Judah to return to him. Remarkably, God is willing to forgive Judah her promiscuity and to take her back. God's openness to reconciliation challenges the laws of Deut 24:1-4 that prohibit a man from remarrying a former wife who has been married in the interim.[46] We already have seen these laws challenged in another sister story. Like David with Michal, God is willing to reconcile with a wife even though she has been with another man. Yet unlike Michal, Judah is not forced to return. Instead, God wants her to return on her own, and with a full heart, as Jer 3:10 describes:

> Indeed, through all this, her sister Faithless Judah did not return to me with all of her heart but rather in deceit, declares YHWH.

Like Ezekiel, Jeremiah is concerned with sororal desire. Yet, whereas Ezekiel amputates sororal desire, Jeremiah seeks to redirect it. God wants Judah to *want* to come back to him. In Jeremiah, God hopes that Judah will behave like an ideal sister who channels her desire for the good of her patriarch and comes home to him.

The stories of Rachel and Leah and Michal and Merav reveal the narrative power of sisters. These dangerous sisters introduce rival patriarchs that threaten their fathers' households to bolster the houses of Jacob and David. The incorporation of sisters into Jeremiah and Ezekiel's prophecy reveals the rhetorical power of sisters to move and to disturb an audience. Like the dangerous sisters of the narratives, the prophets' sisters threaten their patriarchal home. Yet this home belongs to God, and the Bible is invested in its security. To protect God's house, Jeremiah and Ezekiel use sisters as a potent part of a rhetoric that encourages proper behavior among the community of Israel at large and, more specifically, among its women. Jeremiah and Ezekiel warn Israel (and its women) not to behave like dangerous sisters whose uncontrolled desires and misplaced loyalties threaten their patriarchal home. Instead, Israel must control her desire and remain exclusively devoted to her patriarch God. If she does, then God will welcome her back into his family. Once again, dangerous sisters serve the Bible's ideology and interests; yet, as Ezekiel's prophecy makes clear, they are not rewarded. Israel reconciles with God, but she returns scarred, silent, and most importantly, no longer a sister. All that remains for her is a painful and shameful memory of having once been a sister.

Notes

1. In Hos 1:2, God commands Hosea to marry a promiscuous woman because Israel has strayed from God.

2. Gerlinde Baumann locates the metaphor in the following texts: Isa 1:21; 50:1; 54:1-6; 57:6-13; 62:4-5; Jer 2:1-3, 13; 4:1-31; 13:20-27; Lam 1:1-22; Ezekiel 16 and 23; Hos 2:4-25; 9:1; Mic 1:6-7; Nah 3:4-7; Mal 2:10-16. See Gerlinde Baumann, *Love and Violence: Marriage as Metaphor for the Relationship between YHWH and Israel in the Prophetic Books* (Collegeville, MN: Liturgical, 2003), 41–42.

3. See Hos 2:17 and Jer 2:1.

4. See Hos 2:7-9 and Ezek 16:25.

5. See Jer 3:8 and Ezek 16:37-42.

6. See Hos 2:16-24; Ezek 16:60; Isa 54:1-6.

7. See Gale A. Yee, *Poor Banished Children of Eve: Woman as Evil in the Hebrew Bible* (Minneapolis: Fortress Press, 2003), 97–98.

8. See Christl M. Maier, *Daughter Zion, Mother Zion: Gender, Space, and the Sacred in Ancient Israel* (Minneapolis: Fortress Press, 2008), 60–93 and Alice A. Keefe, *Woman's Body and the Social Body in Hosea* (Sheffield: Sheffield Academic, 2001), 162–89.

9. Ibid., 174–77.

10. Renita J. Weems addresses the rhetorical impact of the metaphor for both an ancient and a contemporary audience in *Battered Love: Marriage, Sex, and Violence in the Hebrew Prophets* (Minneapolis: Fortress Press, 1995).

11. Ezek 16:17, 25.

12. On the question of pornography, see T. Drorah Setel, "Prophets and Pornography: Female Sexual Imagery in Hosea," in *Feminist Interpretation of the Bible*, ed. Letty M. Russell (Philadelphia: Westminster, 1985), 86–95; Fokkelien van Dijk-Hemmes, "The Metaphorization of Woman in Prophetic Speech: An Analysis of Ezekiel XXIII," *VT* 43:2 (1993): 162–70; and Robert P. Carroll, "Whorusalamin: A Tale of Three Cities as Three Sisters," in *On Reading Prophetic Texts: Gender-Specific and Related Studies in Memory of Fokkelien van Dijk-Hemmes* (Leiden: E. J. Brill, 1996), 67–82.

13. See Yee, *Poor Banished Children of Eve*, 98–99.

14. Although the Bible presents Israel and Judah as sharing a national and religious identity, scholars challenge the degree to which they were similar. According to Israel Finkelstein and Neil Asher Silberman, there were always two distinct kingdoms, and the Northern Kingdom was the stronger, more ideologically defined kingdom than the Southern one; they write: "Put simply, Israel and Judah experienced quite different histories and developed distinctive cultures. In a sense, Judah was little more than Israel's rural hinterland." See Israel Finkelstein and Neil Asher Silberman, *The Bible Unearthed: Archaeology's New Vision of Ancient Israel and the Origin of Its Sacred Texts* (New York: Free Press, 2001), 159.

15. Mary E. Shields notes the "temporal displacement" assumed by the metaphor. See Mary E. Shields, *Circumscribing the Prostitute: The Rhetorics of Intertextuality, Metaphor, and Gender in Jeremiah 3.1–4.4* (London: T&T Clark, 2004), 86–87.

16. See Mary E. Shields, "Circumcision of the Prostitute: Gender, Sexuality, and the Call to Repentance in Jeremiah 3.1–4.4" in *Prophets and Daniel: A Feminist Companion to the Bible (Second Series)*, ed. Athalya Brenner (Sheffield: Sheffield Academic, 2001), 123.

17. Baumann also notes how the marriage metaphor expands with the inclusion of sisters. See Baumann, *Love and Violence*, 144.

18. Jeremiah begins his prophecy in the 13th year of King Josiah's reign, which is dated 627 BCE. Ezekiel is among the first exiles in Babylon and receives his inaugural vision some time after 597 BCE.

19. Scholars consider the sister texts of Jeremiah and Ezekiel to be related, though they debate which prophet was the first to portray Israel and Judah as sisters. For a discussion of the various opinions, see William L. Holladay, *Jeremiah I* (Philadelphia: Fortress Press, 1986), 116.

20. Yee notes the sexual connotations of the sisters' names which mean "her tent"—Oholah—and "my tent is in her"—Oholibah in Ezekiel: "In addition, tents are typically female spaces of erotic expression or allusion." See Yee, *Poor Banished Children of Eve*, 124.

21. Janet L. R. Melnyk suggests that this passage reflects the formal procedure of adoption. See Janet L. R. Melnyk, "When Israel Was A Child: Ancient Near Eastern Adoption Formulas and the Relationship between God and Israel" in *History and Interpretation: Essays in Honour of John H. Hayes* (Sheffield: JSOT, 1993), 253.

22. Because Judah is the only kingdom existing during Jeremiah and Ezekiel's lifetime, I use Israel to refer to the national entity and its identity and not to the geographic kingdom.

23. Maier comments on the political and religious implications of the marriage metaphor: "Asking again for possible historical references of the narrated metaphor, the elder sister's "whoring" in Ezekiel 23 mirrors Samaria's political jockeying between Assyria and Egypt. During the reign of King Jehu (843–816 BCE), Samaria became a vassal of Assyria. . . . According to the scholarly discussion of vassal treaties, the vassal status includes at least a minimal participation in the Assyrian state cult." See Maier, *Daughter Zion, Mother Zion*, 128.

24. My translation, *she saw*, follows the LXX and the Syriac and does not read with the more difficult MT text, *I saw*.

25. Yee, *Poor Banished Children of Eve*, 126.

26. Ibid., 99.

27. Although women may be included in the prophets' intended audience, they may be indirectly addressed through their husbands and fathers. Dijk-Hemmes similarly comments: "Coming back now to the question whether the text speaks differently to men and to women, we can state the following. YHWH's speech to Ezekiel transforms the people of Israel and thus the intended audience, males and at least indirectly also females, into his metaphorical wives. Both sexes are thus required to identify with these women, and especially with the second one Oholibah, since Oholah figures chiefly as a warning signal for her sister." See Dijk-Hemmes, "The Metaphorization of Woman," 169.

28. Jacqueline E. Lapsley also notes a shift in the audience addressed by the text. See Lapsley, "Shame and Self-Knowledge: The Positive Role of Shame in Ezekiel's View of the Moral Self" in *The Book of Ezekiel: Theological and Anthropological Perspectives,* ed. Margaret S. Odell and John T. Strong (Atlanta: Society of Biblical Literature, 2000), 162.

29. See Weems, *Battered Love*, 61.

30. See Ilona N. Rashkow, *Taboo or not Taboo: Sexuality and Family in the Hebrew Bible* (Minneapolis: Fortress Press, 2000), 32–38 and Mary E. Shields, "Multiple Exposures: Body Rhetoric and Gender in Ezekiel 16" in *The Prophets and Daniel: Feminist Companion to the Bible (Second Series),* ed. Athalya Brenner (Sheffield: Sheffield Academic, 2001), 144.

31. See Weems, *Battered Love*, 41.

32. In Jer 2:2, God states: "I remember for your benefit the devotion of your youth, the love of your bridal days."

33. Jer 2:21 conveys God's surprise at Israel's transformation: "I planted you as choice grapes, all true seed. How did you become a putrid and alien vine?"

34. Ezek 16:5 states: "No eye had mercy upon you to do one of these things for you compassionately. On the day you were born, you were cast out into the field, despised."

35. Yee, *Poor Banished Children of Eve*, 122.

36. Yee writes: "Ezekiel's descriptions of pedophilia are geared rhetorically to arouse his male elite audience sexually and to indict them at the same time." See ibid., 122–23.

37. Gerlinde Baumann comments on Ezekiel's portrayal of the sisters' parentage and sullied past; she writes: "Reference is made to history, to the imaginary biographical background of the 'woman,' to establish a foundation for her determination to 'play the whore.'. . . 'Her' parental origins (ch. 16) and the experiences of 'her' youth (ch. 23) have already laid the foundations for what will later be manifested in 'her' falling away from YHWH." See Baumann, *Love and Violence,* 142.

38. Yee, *Poor Banished Children of Eve*, 126.

39. As I will argue in the context of Tamar's story, the use of the verb "to send" conveys intentional agency.

40. See Ezek 16:38.

41. Ezek 23:3, 8, 21.

42. See also Jer 25:15-16 and Ps 75:9. For more on this image, see Else K. Holt, "King Nebuchadrezzar of Babylon, My Servant, and the Cup of Wrath: Jeremiah's Fantasies and the Hope of Violence," in *Jeremiah (Dis)placed: New Directions in Writing/Reading Jeremiah,* ed. A. R. Pete Diamond and Louis Stulman (London: T&T Clark Continuum, 2011), 209–18.

43. Yee similarly writes: "Oholibah's crazed behavior is dreadfully manifested in oral and mammary self-mutilation: she will gnaw the cup's broken shards and use them to tear out her breast (Ezek 23:34). The mouth that imbibes the cup is gashed; the breasts foreign men once enjoyed are lacerated." See Yee, *Poor Banished Children of Eve*, 133.

44. God insists that Judah remember her paths [דרכיך]—the paths she once walked with her sister (Ezek 23:13, 31).

45. Although God takes Judah back, it is clear in Ezek 16:63 that God does not expect her to live a happy life: "Thus you will remember and feel shame, and you will no longer open your

mouth because of your shame upon my forgiving you for all that you have done, says Lord YHWH."

46. Jer 3:1 and 3:8 refer to the laws of divorce and remarriage found in Deut 24:1-4.

PART II

Incestuous Sisters

4

Lot's Daughters

In the first part of this study, I looked at the Bible's paired sisters—Rachel and Leah, Michal and Merav, and Israel and Judah. My reading of their stories suggests that the Bible tells a distinct sister story about the vulnerable patriarchal household. As temporary members of a natal household who typically cannot inherit their father's property, sisters induce particular anxieties that are evident in the Bible's sister stories. The Bible, I argue, presents two distinct paradigms of sisters that reflect its implicit gender ideology. An ideal sister, like Rebecca as she functions in Genesis 24, supports her natal household by behaving appropriately and marrying well, whereas a dangerous sister, like Rachel, weakens her natal household by asserting agency and introducing rival patriarchs.

I further argue that dangerous sisters play a significant role in the Bible. They destabilize their natal households in order to secure the Bible's designated patriarchs. As we saw in part 1, paired sisters Rachel and Leah, Michal and Merav, and Rebel Israel and Faithless Judah function as dangerous sisters. All three paired-sister stories establish the sisters' conjugal home at the expense of their natal homes. Rachel and Leah weaken Laban's house but strengthen Jacob's. Michal and Merav decimate Saul's house to establish David's. Rebel Israel and Faithless Judah weaken God's house, which, as I mention in chapter 3, conflates the sisters' natal and conjugal homes but ultimately serve as warnings that protect it. As we saw in chapter 3, Israel reconciles with God solely in her role as wife. Thus, even in the prophet's metaphorical rendering of the sister story, the conjugal home triumphs over the natal.

Although dangerous-sister stories advance the Bible's narrative in important ways, they also serve as cautionary tales that bolster the Bible's patriarchal ideology by demonstrating the consequences of inappropriate behavior. In particular, the paired sister stories illustrate how sororal solidarity poses a threat to patriarchal norms and authority. When sisters ally, like Israel and Judah, or conspire, like Rachel and Leah, they assert an agency that is independent from, if not in defiance of, their patriarchs. Loyal to each other, Israel and Judah defy God. Rachel and Leah conspire to control their husband's sexuality and ally against their father. Along with sororal solidarity, sororal desire is a devastating factor in the paired-sister narratives. In each, sisters desire men from outside the natal household—Jacob, David, and, in the case of Israel and Judah, the Babylonians—and integrate them into their homes. Ultimately these men prove to be rival patriarchs who threaten the sisters' natal home.

The next selection of sister stories shows that unsuitable relationships can also be formed within a natal household and not just between allied sisters or between sisters and threatening outsiders. Incest anxieties are evident throughout the Bible and are particularly focused on the sister. The Bible includes a number of narratives in which incest occurs or is a motif, and sisters play a prominent role within these narratives. In Genesis, Lot's daughters, another sister pair, seduce their father; Abraham and Isaac introduce their wives as their sisters; Jacob, by marrying his wife's sister, might be committing incest or at least evoking the motif.[1] If marriage, as Gen 2:24 asserts, creates "one flesh," then one's spouse's family becomes one's family, and one's wife's sister is considered a consanguine and not an affine. Later, in chapter 9, I explore this further in the context of levirate marriage. No doubt Amnon, who rapes his half-sister Tamar in 2 Samuel 13, commits incest. Even King David may have married his sister Abigail.[2]

In this section, I examine three incest narratives featuring sisters: Genesis 19 and 20 and 2 Samuel 13. Given the biblical prohibitions against brother-sister incest found in Lev 18:9 and 11; 20:17; and Deut 27:22, one expects sisters in the incest narratives to be dangerous because their behavior defies the norms set by the biblical laws. Yet in each of the narratives I consider, marriage to a sister benefits, or at least potentially benefits, the patriarchs involved. Since the households of Lot, Abraham, and David could be enriched and secured by incestuous sisters, it seems that incestuous sisters can function as ideal sisters who support their natal homes.

Recent scholarship has shed light on the Bible's conflicted attitude toward incest. Recognizing a more tolerant attitude toward incest in the biblical narratives than in the law codes, scholars work to align the legal material that condones incest with the narratives. Specifically addressing the brother-sister incest found in 2 Samuel 13, William H. Propp suggests that the narrative's tolerance of incest reflects an earlier period in Israel's development than is reflected in the laws and conforms to the norms practiced by Israel's neighbors Egypt and Phoenicia.[3] In contrast to Propp, Sabine Huebner challenges the ubiquity of brother-sister marriage in ancient Egypt, noting that the majority of evidence of such unions comes from official census returns from Roman Egypt dating to the first to third centuries CE—long after the setting of the biblical narratives.[4] Offering another explanation for the dissonance between the Bible's incest laws and narratives, Calum Carmichael argues that the Bible's legal prohibitions respond directly to the incest narratives and serve as a polemical legal commentary on the more permissive stories.[5]

Also addressing the discrepancy between the Bible's narratives and its laws, Seth Daniel Kunin offers a provocative perspective, suggesting that the narratives do not express a tolerance for actual incest. Rather, they indulge in the fantasy of incest. For Kunin, the tension between the incest narratives and the prohibitions reflects Israelite society's acceptance of a qualified exogamy, marriage to an Israelite outside one's immediate family, despite its clear preference for endogamy.[6] Endogamous marriages have economic and social benefits as Karel Van der Toorn observes. They prevent threatening outsiders from infiltrating a family and claiming its property—precisely the anxiety manifest in the Bible's paired sister-stories.[7]

According to Kunin, Israel perceived itself as the one nation directly descended from God. Therefore, its kinship relations are designed to maintain the purity of the Israelite line and to protect its property.[8] The ideal wife, like Rebecca, is the woman closest in kin yet still distantly enough related that she does not violate the incest laws.[9] In Kunin's reading, the family narratives work to literarily transform a wife into a sister so that she becomes the purest partner for the patriarch, as the wife-sister narratives illustrate.[10] Following Kunin, an incestuous sister is the ultimate ideal sister who supports her natal household by protecting the property and purity of the Israelite line.

My reading of the incestuous sister stories challenges Propp's, Carmichael's, and Kunin's basic argument that the narratives present a positive attitude toward incest. I particularly challenge Kunin's assertion that incestuous sisters reflect biblical fantasies and are ideal. Close examination of their narratives proves incestuous sisters to be dangerous. Like paired sisters, incestuous sisters threaten their patriarchal natal homes and can even come to represent their demise. Their stories are nightmares not fantasies. They serve as cautionary tales that warn against sororal agency and desire although with a distinctly inward focus. When a sister directs sexual desire or attention toward members of her natal family as Lot's daughters do, or she is an object of desire of someone within her family as Tamar is, she threatens the stability of her natal home.

Although they are destabilizing figures, incestuous sisters, like paired sisters, serve the Bible's patriarchal ideology. By illustrating the dangers of incest, their stories are cautionary tales that preserve the boundaries and roles of the patriarchal family. Seen in this way, the Bible's incest narratives are aligned ideologically with its prohibitions. As Carol Meyers contends, the incest laws function as "coping mechanisms" that counter sexual feelings that develop between family members living in extended-family compounds. They help to preserve order within these homes and work to ensure marriages that will most benefit the family.[11] As cautionary tales, I argue that the incest narratives have a similar function; they preserve order within the home.

The incestuous-sister stories demonstrate that family is strongest when the roles within it are not violated, and when sexual desire and relations are appropriately contained. Sisters should not sleep with their father. A brother should not marry his sister. Although incestuous sisters serve the Bible's ideology and, as we see later in this chapter, help advance its narrative, they are not rewarded. Like paired sisters, incestuous sisters do not have happy endings to their stories—at least not as sisters. Lot's daughters give birth to Israel's enemies. Like their father, they are effectively written out of Israel's story until Ruth can redeem them (at least the Moabites), as I discuss in chapter 9. Sarah must relinquish her role as Abraham's sister to restore order to her family. Tamar remains desolate within her brother's house.

Genesis 19 tells the Bible's most explicit tale of incest. Having survived the destruction of Sodom and now safe in a mountain cave, Lot's two daughters have sex with their father and conceive sons. Certainly Genesis 19 is a story about a father and his daughters, but it is also intentionally constructed as a sister story, just as Michal and Merav's story is constructed as a sister story. To perpetuate Lot's line, one daughter would have sufficed. Yet the narrative chose to include two daughters—a sororal pair—marking Genesis 19 as a sister story that strikingly conforms to the sister stories discussed in the first part of this study.[12]

Like the Bible's other paired and dangerous sisters, Lot's daughters remove a rival patriarch to strengthen the position of its designated patriarch. At this point in the Genesis narrative, Lot is a liability. Although God promised Sarah that she would have the child that would receive God's blessing (Genesis 17), in Genesis 19 she remains childless. Ishmael, Abraham's son through Hagar, and his nephew Lot are Abraham's nearest kin and therefore potential heirs.[13] In Genesis 21, Sarah ousts Ishmael and removes him as a contender for Abraham's blessing. In Genesis 19, I argue that Lot's daughters, a pair of incestuous sisters, remove Lot as yet another contender for Abraham's blessing. Although his birth is not recorded until Genesis 21, Isaac is the designated patriarch. With the help of dangerous sisters, the Bible clears a path and ensures that there are no rival heirs to Isaac.

From the start of the story, Lot appears as a compromised patriarch in a distressed household. At a crisis moment, he uses his daughters as a means to secure his household. As Saul foolishly did, Lot hopes that his two daughters will function as ideal sisters who will secure their natal household. By the end of the story, it is clear that Lot's daughters are in fact dangerous sisters. Sororal solidarity and sexual agency—this time internally focused—decimate Lot's household and taint his line. This pair of incestuous sisters removes Lot and his descendants from Israel's story for generations to come.

The story begins with two divine messengers who intend to inform the righteous of Sodom about its impending destruction. The messengers arrive at the city's gate in the evening, as Gen 19:1-3 relates:

> Two messengers arrived at Sodom in the evening while Lot was sitting at Sodom's gate. Lot saw and rose up to greet them, bowed to the ground, and said: "Please, my lords, turn toward the house of your servant, spend the night, wash your feet, then you can get up early and go on your way." They responded: "No. We will spend the night in the square." But he beseeched them, and they turned toward him and entered his house. He prepared a feast for them and baked unleavened bread, and they ate.

From its beginning, location matters in this story though it is difficult to determine throughout the narrative which place is safest and more desired—the public, the private, or the space in between. We first meet Lot at a space in between—at the city gate. Since city gates served as civic centers in the ancient world, Lot's position at the gate could indicate his privileged status in the town and his involvement in the town's affairs.[14] Yet, as points of entry into the city, gates, like the windows and doors of a house, are also vulnerable places and can be associated with marginal people, such as the lepers who sit outside the city's gates in 2 Kgs 7:3.

Just as Michal's position at the window in 2 Samuel 6 marked her marginality in David's house, I contend that Lot's position at the gate reflects his marginal status in Sodom and his vulnerability. This border-dweller is found at the spot where local identity can be violated, and where the distinction between inside and outside—and insiders and outsiders—is blurred. Lot's position at the city gate reflects his outsider position within Sodom and suggests that he is not, in fact, fully integrated into the city. His conversation with the Sodomites later, who identify Lot as a sojourner and not as a native, affirms this.[15] Since the gate provides a social area for people to gather and talk, I suggest that Lot seeks to engage with the Sodomites in order to elevate his status. Perhaps if Lot sits with them, the Sodomites will welcome him into their society.

While at the gate, Lot sees the messengers and offers to bring them from the public square into his home. This distinction between public and private space remains important throughout the narrative. Lot's invitation to the messengers reflects genuine hospitality. After their long journey, Lot wishes to give them food and respite in his home. He also seems to want to protect them, either because he feels that private space is always safer than public, or because he senses the Sodomite public space is particularly dangerous.[16] Lot's hospitable behavior resembles Abraham's. A chapter earlier, Abraham invites these same divine messengers into his home for food and respite. Yet, as Brian Doyle observes, there are significant differences in how Abraham and Lot engage with their guests that suggest a difference in their characters. Whereas Abraham addresses his visitors as "my Lord," indicating that he recognizes them as God's representatives, Lot addresses the messengers as "my lords" as if he does not recognize them to be God's emissaries.[17] Noticeably, the messengers respond differently to Lot's offer than they did to Abraham's. Whereas the messengers accept Abraham's offer, they initially refuse to follow Lot home. They state explicitly that they prefer to sleep in the public square.

The messengers' refusal suggests that they see no benefit or reason to enter Lot's home. From this it appears that the messengers have no intention of saving Lot in particular but had come to Sodom to make a general proclamation in the public square and enable any righteous folks to respond. Support for this reading is found in Genesis 18. When Abraham negotiates with God on behalf of the righteous of Sodom, he does not argue specifically for Lot. Also, the messengers do not inform Lot of Sodom's looming destruction until later in the chapter. Perhaps they did not assume that Lot was among the righteous of Sodom. If so, then Lot's household appears to be in danger from the beginning of this narrative.

The messengers' reluctance to accept Lot's invitation only makes Lot insist harder.[18] At last, he convinces them to come home with him. After the messengers are safe inside Lot's house, the townspeople surround it and threaten its inhabitants:

> Before they lay down, the men of the city, the men of Sodom, surrounded the house—from young to old, every last one. They called to Lot and said to him: "Where are the men that came to you

tonight? Bring them out to us so that we may know them." Lot came out the door to them, shut the door behind him, and said: "Don't, my brothers, behave badly. I have two daughters that have not known a man. Let me bring them out to you, and you can do to them what is good in your eyes. Only to these men, don't do a thing for they have entered within the shelter of my walls." (Gen 19:4-8)

Every male Sodomite surrounds Lot's house and demands to know, נדעה, Lot's guests. The verb used implies carnal knowledge. The Sodomites want to rape the messengers and assert dominion over them. As Tikva Frymer-Kensky asserts, rape is an act of "hostility and aggression, not sexual interest." She compares the Sodomites proposed rape to jailhouse rape, which Frymer-Kensky describes as "the assertion of dominance and the dishonoring of the man forced to submit."[19]

Their specific request for Lot's guests registers the Sodomites hatred of outsiders. It also must be seen as a direct attack on Lot's household and his honor since the Sodomites threaten to violate the people within Lot's home. As we have mentioned, a patriarch is supposed to protect the members of his house, particularly their sexual purity. As guests within his home, the messengers are members of Lot's house who require protection. Once again, Lot proves to be a man on the margins. To protect his household, Lot crosses his threshold and closes the door behind him.[20] The precise narrative detail is notable. This time Lot stands with his neighbors at the gate of his home and not the city. By shutting the door behind him, Lot seals the inside from the outside and protects those within. He also places himself outside among the Sodomites.

As if he were one of them, Lot addresses the Sodomites as "brothers" and implores them not to do this terrible thing. Hoping to protect his house guests, Lot then offers his two daughters to the mad crowd. He wants to bring his daughters outside [אוציאה-נא אתהן] so that the Sodomites could rape them instead of his guests. Appropriately, paired sisters enter the narrative when their patriarchal household is most vulnerable. Lot's particular use of the verb יצא resonates with other sister narratives, yet highlights the passivity of these sisters. Unlike dangerous sisters Dinah, Leah, and Michal, Lot's daughters do not assert agency and go forth from their homes. Instead, these sisters will be brought out of the house by their father who, just a few verses before, himself goes forth [ויצא אלהם לוט] to talk to the Sodomites.

Lot's willingness to sacrifice his daughters' sexual purity to protect his guests suggests that Lot values hospitality over family and that he considers his guests precious and his daughters expendable. From a contemporary perspective, it is easy to condemn Lot for valuing strangers, even divine strangers, over family.[21] Yet within the context of the biblical family narratives, Lot's actions appear to be a reasonable strategy. Guests belong inside the home, whereas daughters and sisters ultimately belong outside their natal homes. As we have already seen, daughters and sisters are essentially threshold figures because one day they will leave their natal homes to join their husbands' households. To protect his household, Lot initiates an inevitable reality by pushing his daughters across his threshold and outside his home.

Lot's willingness to barter their sexuality does not have to be seen as a callous father's willingness to sacrifice his daughters' lives and happiness. Like Jacob in Genesis 34, Lot may feel that his daughters legitimately could marry these outsiders. As I mention in my introduction and explore further in chapter 7, this openness to exogamous marriage may reflect a father's particular perspective, which contrasts with a brother's. As the head of the house, a father may be more concerned than his sons with forming alliances with his neighbors. Lot may genuinely want his daughters to marry Sodomites so that he can fully integrate into their community. This helps explain why Lot was at the city gate with the Sodomites in the first place, and why he now addresses them, perhaps wishfully, as brothers. But the Sodomites, like the messengers, refuse Lot's offer:

> They said: "Stand back! The one who sojourns among us judges us! Now we will do worse to you than to them!" The men pressed hard against Lot, and they approached to break down the door. But the men extended their hands and brought Lot to them inside of the house and closed the door and struck the men at the threshold with blindness, from smallest to largest so that they could not find the door. (Gen 19:9-11)

The Sodomites react to Lot's moralistic tone and reject his offer in principle. They refuse to be told how to behave by someone they clearly consider to be an outsider. Furious, they now personally attack Lot and his household. At this point, it is clear that Lot belongs inside his home. Yet, he is overpowered by the Sodomites. It takes a miracle to get him back across the threshold that he had crossed a moment before and over which he was willing to expel his daughters. The divine messengers must reach out, retrieve Lot, and bring him inside. With a blinding flash, they are able to do what Lot cannot. They seal his doorway and protect Lot's household.

No longer able to protect his home, Lot is clearly a compromised patriarch. It is time for Lot and his family to leave. The messengers command Lot to flee with his family before Sodom's destruction. Oddly, the messengers do not mention Lot's wife but focus on their children and list his sons-in-law first.[22] Mentioned for the first time, it is unclear who these sons-in-law are. Rabbinic tradition and the Septuagint assume that they refer to the husbands of Lot's married daughters who live outside his home. It is also possible that they refer to Lot's *future* sons-in-law who are betrothed to the daughters Lot offers to the Sodomites. If so, these men are justifiably angry with Lot for seeing greater benefit in offering his daughters to all of the Sodomites than in honoring their betrothals. Perhaps to placate them, Lot addresses them directly. The interaction between Lot and his sons-in-law conveys tension between them in Gen 19:14:

> Lot went out and spoke to his sons-in-law, takers of his daughters, and said: "Get up and leave this place because YHWH is destroying the city!" But he was like one who jests in the eyes of his sons-in-law.

Once again, Lot goes forth [ויצא] from his house. As in verse 6, the use of this verb could imply that Lot leaves home to negotiate with people he considers to be foreign or hostile to him.

Just as he hoped to reason with the attacking Sodomites, he hopes to reason with his sons-in-law who also seem to be Sodomites. Although his intentions appear to be good, the text pointedly refers to his sons-in-law as "takers of his daughters." Although לקח is a standard verb meaning "to marry,"[23] its unique form as a participle referring to Lot's sons-in-law may convey a distance, or even mistrust, between Lot and his sons-in-law. Like Laban who accuses Jacob in Gen 31:26 of stealing his daughters, Lot may accuse his sons-in-law of a similar crime. Also, since the text explicitly says that all the Sodomites surround Lot's house, it is plausible that his sons-in-law were among them and that Lot bears a grudge. Clearly, the hostility is mutual. The response of the sons-in-laws conveys that they do not respect Lot's authority or take him seriously. Either they laugh at what he says, or they laugh at him.[24]

Lot is unable to convince his family to leave Sodom. Once again, the messengers must intervene:

> When dawn came, the messengers urged Lot saying: "Get up, take your wife and your two remaining daughters, lest you are swept away because of the iniquity of the city." He delayed, so the men grabbed his hand, his wife's hand, and the hands of his two daughters

for YHWH's compassion was upon him. They brought him out [ויצאהו] and placed him outside [מחוץ] of the city. (Gen 19:15-16)

Lot's hesitation forces the messengers to take action. They must physically grab hold of Lot, ויחזקו, and remove him [ויצאהו], his wife, and his daughters from the city.[25] The man who offered to bring his daughters outside—one assumes against their will—is now brought outside against his will. The verb חזק appears in other contexts in which force is applied against the will of an individual, most notably in the laws of rape found in Deut 22:25, in the rape of Tamar in 2 Sam 13:14, and in the rape of the concubine in Judg 19:25. Judges 19:25 closely echoes our text: "The man grabbed [ויחזק] his concubine and brought (her) [ויצא] to them outside [החוץ]." Like the concubine who is cast outside by her husband, Lot is overpowered for the second time and is forced to act against his will. Unable to protect his home, persuade his family, and, now, even save himself, Lot is an impotent patriarch.

Lot recognizes his weakness and the debt he owes the messengers. Afraid he cannot reach the mountains, he begs the messengers to allow him to flee to the closer town of Zoar:

Lot said to them: "No, my Lord.[26] I have found favor in your eyes and the kindness [חסדך] that you have done me is great to save my life [להחיות את-נפשי], but I am unable to flee to the mountains, lest the calamity clings to me and I die. There is a closer town to flee to, and it is very small. Let me escape there; is it not small? Let me survive." (Gen 19:18-20)

As we see below, Lot's words echo Abraham's in the wife-sister narratives in Genesis 12 and 20. Like Lot, Abraham acts to save his own life [וחיתה נפשי] when he asks Sarah to pose as his sister.[27] Abraham, also like Lot, considers Sarah's compliance to be an act of kindness[28] [זה חסדך]. Both Abraham and Lot are concerned with their own life and safety and not the lives and safety of their families. Abraham's wife-sister scheme ensures his safety at Sarah's expense. When Lot begs to go to Zoar, he makes no mention of his wife or his daughters. He only wants to save himself [אמלטה] by fleeing to tiny Zoar. Clearly he no longer behaves like a patriarch who supports, protects, and rules his home. Even the name of the town, Zoar, indicates Lot's reduced status and household. It's a "little place" for a little man.

The messengers agree to let Lot escape to Zoar. Although he makes no mention of them, his wife and daughters remain with him. En route, Lot's wife turns to look at the devastation and, famously, becomes a pillar of salt. Her transformation is significant since her fate demonstrates that Lot's fears were justified.[29] In verse 19, he worries that the calamity would cling to him and that he would die. This is precisely what happens to his wife. The calamity clings to her, and her body becomes like the sulfurous fire that rains down upon the city. It is also evident from verse 26 that Lot was unable to protect his wife. Lot's wife looks מאחריו, from behind *him,* and becomes a pillar of salt. In other words, Lot stands between his wife and the destruction, but he cannot shield her. Once again, Lot appears powerless. Perhaps most significant of all, her transformation into a pillar of salt removes Lot's wife from the narrative. Had she stayed, the story could have gone in a very different direction. By removing first Lot's sons-in-law and then his wife, the narrative reduces Lot's family and curtails its ability to reproduce.[30] There are no husbands for his daughters, and he has no wife. There is only one logical opportunity to ensure the continuity of Lot's patriarchal line.

After the destruction of the cities of the plain, Lot and his two daughters leave Zoar and settle in a mountain cave. Once settled, the two sisters plot in Gen 19:31-32:

> The elder said to the younger: "Our father is old, and there is no man in the land to come to us in the way of all the world. Come, let us make our father drink wine so that we can lie with him and sustain our father's seed."

Ironically, the expendable sisters who Lot was willing to cast outside his home conspire to save their father's line through incest. Initiating the action and speaking in the first person, the eldest sister's motivation is clear. She offers two justifications for the action that she proposes: Lot is an aged father, and there are no men left in the world to become sexual partners for the sisters. Although Lot is able to impregnate women as the narrative will reveal, the sisters are concerned that their father's potency is waning. Perhaps they recognize that Lot no longer behaves like a potent patriarch because he was unable to save his home and family. They assume he will soon be sexually impotent as well.

After the cataclysm, the sisters also assume that they are alone in the world. The logic of this assumption is suspect because it remains unclear what happened to the inhabitants of Zoar during the cataclysm.[31] Still, at this moment in the narrative, Lot and his daughters live isolated in a mountain cave.[32] Their circumstances have dramatically changed since the start of their story, when they lived within the walls of their home and their city. Now, both home and city are destroyed. With their father's house in ruins, the sisters desperately, and with seemingly good intentions, work to secure his line.

Assuming they are alone in the world with an aging father, the sisters resort to incest to sustain their father's seed [ונחיה מאבינו זרע]. There is no doubt that Lot's daughters believe that incest is necessary for the welfare of their father's house. Their desire to preserve their father's seed echoes God's command to Noah in Gen 7:3 to bring his family and representatives of all the animal species onto the ark to preserve their seed [לחיות זרע על-פני כל-הארץ]. By preserving their father's seed, Lot's daughters, like Noah, act like saviors—though on a smaller scale. They appear to behave like ideal sisters who support, protect, and sustain their natal household. Although their intention may be good, their means of salvation, we will see, is suspect within the biblical context and proves them to be dangerous.

The sisters' plan to secure Lot's patriline includes three actions as verse 32 outlines: Let us make our father drunk [נשקה]; let us lie with him [נשכבה]; let us sustain his seed [נחיה]. Pairing the sisters enables conspiracy and demonstrates the dangers of sororal solidarity. Although the elder sister devises the plot, she speaks in the first person plural and indicates that the sisters will ally together to exert power over their father.

Once again, sororal solidarity overturns patriarchal power and authority. In Rachel and Leah's story, sisters defy patriarchal conventions when they barter for their husband's sexuality but stay within the appropriate constructs of the patriarchal family. In the story of Lot's daughters, sisters defy patriarchal convention and the constructs of the patriarchal family by seducing their father.

The sisters enact their plot in Gen 19:33–35:

> They cause their father to drink wine that night. The eldest comes and lies with her father, but he did not know when she lay down or when she arose. The next night the eldest said to the youngest: "Last night I lay with my father. Let us give him wine tonight. Go and lie with him so that we can sustain our father's seed." They made their father drink wine that night. The youngest got up and lay with him, but he did not know when she lay down or when she arose.

The wine renders Lot completely helpless and unaware of his daughters' presence, let alone that he is having sex with them. He does not know [ולא-ידע] when they lie down or when they get up.

The use of the root ידע, to know, recalls the demand of the Sodomites that Lot release his guests so that they could know them [ונדעה אתם]. As

I mention above, the Sodomites want *to know* Lot's guests, which means to assert power over them by raping them. For the sexual aggressor, carnal knowledge communicates power. At this moment, Lot's daughters are the sexual aggressors. As such, they defy the patriarchal norms of behavior in which men control women's sexuality, evident throughout the Bible, but particularly earlier in this narrative when Lot offered these sisters to the Sodomites.

Lot's lack of knowledge indicates his weakness and his submission to the sisters. The eldest sister's instruction to the younger reflects this power dynamic. Her command, "Go and lie with him [שכבי עמו]," evokes the command of Potiphar's wife to Joseph in Gen 39:12 [שכבה עמי] and, as we see, Amnon's to Tamar in 2 Sam 13:11 [שכבי עמי]. In all three narratives, a more powerful character demands sex from a less powerful character. In Genesis 19, sisters assert power and rape their father—not once, but twice. Two sisters enable two rapes. Had it happened only once, Lot would have proven himself to be the weak patriarch that he has been throughout his story. The fact that it happens twice proves that Lot is not just weak; he is completely broken.

The sisters successfully sustain their father's seed, as Gen 19:36-38 records:

> Lot's two daughters conceive from their father. The elder bears a son and names him Moab. He is the ancestor of Moab until this day. The younger also bears a son and names him Ben-Ammi. He is the ancestor of the Ammonites until this day.

The sisters' success suggests that the ends justified the means. As Esther Fuchs observes, the birth of male heirs in the Bible is usually a sign of divine approval.[33] Since incest successfully perpetuates Lot's line, the birth of Lot's sons-grandsons also supports Kunin's assertion that an incest fantasy underlies the Bible's family narratives. Yet, as Fuchs notes, though the Bible rewards Lot's daughters with sons and does not overtly condemn their actions, the text implicitly does.[34] For Fuchs, the repetition of the rape and the specific mention of the fact that the sisters lay with their father, condemns the sisters as the villains of the narrative but exonerates Lot.[35] In Fuchs's reading, drunken Lot cannot be held responsible for his actions since he did not know what was happening to him. He may be weak, but he is not guilty.

I agree with Fuchs that the text neither hails nor rewards Lot's daughters as heroes, though I disagree that it exonerates Lot. Even though Lot's daughters successfully birth male babies, as I mention above, their actions invert and defy the norms of the patriarchal household and of Israel. As we have already noted, the Bible generally condemns sexually aggressive women. In the more specific context of its sister stories, we have seen how sororal solidarity and desire are destabilizing factors. As two sisters who conspire and are sexually aggressive toward their father, Lot's daughters must be condemned in the context of the Bible's gender ideology. But the text also condemns Lot, holding him accountable for his weakness and proving him to be a failed and undesignated patriarch.

The daughters' so-called reward turns out to be their punishment, as well as a punishment for their father, because they give birth to the ancestors of the Moabites and the Ammonites—Israel's national enemies.[36] By naming these children, Lot's daughters continue to exert power over their father while publicly proclaiming the nature of his legacy. With names Moab, "from father," and Ben-Ammi, "from my kinsman," there is no doubt that Lot fathers his own grandchildren. His line may be perpetuated, but it is forever tainted by incest. In time, it is even made taboo because Deut 23:4 unequivocally states: "No Ammonite or Moabite will enter into YHWH's community, even unto the tenth generation none will enter into YHWH's community forever."

Although Lot's house and line is physically sustained by the sisters, it is cut off from the line of Abraham and Israel. With his descendents marked as outsiders, Lot cannot be counted among the patriarchs of Israel. Effectively, this is the end of Lot's story, and the Bible can now focus on Abraham and his descendants—its designated patriarchs.[37] Thus, Lot is not exonerated by the text. The text condemns him *and* his daughters. Whereas Lot is condemned for weakness, his daughters are condemned for sororal solidarity and, above all, for asserting a sexual agency—one that is internally focused.

By initiating incest with their father, paired sisters again remove a rival patriarch from the biblical narrative. They violate their father, defile his lineage, and destroy his legacy among Israel. In other words, Lot's daughters behave like typical dangerous sisters who weaken their natal households. Like other dangerous sisters, Lot's daughters are victims of their own success and are not rewarded for their actions. As the mothers of the Ammonites and the Moabites, these sisters, like their father, have no place in Israel's story. After they serve their purpose, they disappear from the narrative. One imagines that if their narrative were to continue, they would remain stuck in their natal households, like Dinah and, as we will see, like Tamar, unable to become legitimate wives and mothers in their husbands' homes. Although their story conforms to the contours of the Bible's previously identified dangerous-sister story, it includes a new element. In an interesting twist, Lot's daughters do not introduce outsiders into their natal home. They produce them. Lot's daughters seduce their father and give birth to Israel's enemies. In this incest narrative, the outsider comes from within, and the natal home implodes.

Notes

1. In his book that explores incest in the Bible, Seth Daniel Kunin asserts that Rachel functions "mythologically" as Jacob's sister even if she is not considered to be his biological sister. See Kunin, *The Logic of Incest: A Structuralist Analysis of Hebrew Mythology* (Sheffield: Sheffield Academic, 1995), 121–22.

2. In 1 Samuel 25, David meets and marries a woman named Abigail. According to 2 Chr 2:15-17, David's sister's name was Abigail. Jon D. Levenson and Baruch Halpern suggest that they are the same woman. See "The Political Import of David's Marriages," *JBL* 99, no. 4 (1980): 507–18.

3. See William H. Propp, "Kinship in 2 Samuel 13," *CBQ* 55 (1993): 44.

4. See Sabine R. Huebner, "Brother-Sister Marriage in Roman Egypt: A Curiosity of Humankind or a Widespread Family Strategy?" *The Journal of Roman Studies* 97 (2007): 23.

5. Carmichael writes: "My assumption is that the biblical lawgivers set out to tackle the ethical and legal problems they encountered in their reading of these tales. Biblical laws consequently constitute commentary on matters arising in the national folklore." See Calum M. Carmichael, *Law, Legend, and Incest in the Bible: Leviticus 18–20* (Ithaca: Cornell University Press, 1997), 6.

6. Kunin describes a tension between exogamy and endogamy in Israelite society that is reflected in the Bible's narratives. See Kunin, *Logic of Incest*, 161.

7. See Karel Van der Toorn, *Family Religion in Babylonia, Syria and Israel: Continuity and Change in the Forms of Religious Life* (Leiden: Brill, 1996), 200–201.

8. Kunin, *Logic of Incest*, 91–92.

9. Ibid., 56–57.

10. Kunin writes: "Sarai's relationship as wife, representative of the outside, is problematic, so the text creates the possibility that she is sister, working on an essential building block of the system." See Kunin, *Logic of Incest*, 67.

11. See Meyers, "The Family in Early Israel," in *Families in Ancient Israel*, ed. Leo G. Perdue, Joseph Blenkinsopp, John J. Collins, and Carol Meyers (Louisville: Westminster John Knox, 1997), 18.

12. Ilona N. Rashkow offers an interesting explanation for the inclusion of two daughters; she writes: "And although the daughters in this instance appear to be the active initiators of the incestuous behavior, the fact that more than one daughter is involved brings the story closer into line with clinical incest in which the incestuous father commonly moves from older to younger daughters." See Rashkow, *Taboo or not Taboo: Sexuality and Family in the Hebrew Bible* (Minneapolis: Fortress Press, 2000), 109.

13. In the event that the deceased has no children, Num 27:11 enables the nearest kin to inherit property.

14. In ancient Near Eastern cities, the gate area served as a civic center where affairs could be handled publicly. For example, Hamor and Shechem consider Dinah's brothers' conditions with their clansmen at the city gates in Gen 34:20.

15. Gen 19:9.

16. Lot's impulse to protect his guests is explicit in Gen 19:8.

17. See Brian Doyle, "'Knock, Knock, Knockin' on Sodom's Door': The Function of פתח/ דלת in Genesis 18–19," *JSOT* (2004): 434.

18. Doyle observes how Lot "urges" the messengers in 19:3, just as the Sodomites will urge Lot in 19:9. See ibid., 437.

19. See Tikva Frymer-Kensky, *Reading the Women of the Bible: A New Interpretation of Their Stories* (New York: Schocken, 2002), 124. For a fuller discussion of rape in the Bible, see Susanne Scholz, *Sacred Witness: Rape in the Hebrew Bible* (Minneapolis: Fortress Press, 2010).

20. Doyle observes how the use of the words פתח/דלת in this passage captures Lot's marginality. See Doyle, " 'Knock, Knock, Knockin' on Sodom's Door," 441.

21. Katherine B. Low offers a contemporary interpretation that condemns Lot's actions from her perspective as a daughter of a sexually abused mother. See Low, "The Sexual Abuse of Lot's Daughters: Reconceptualizing Kinship for the Sake of Our Daughters," *JFSR* 26, no. 2 (2010): 40.

22. By not including her among those who should escape with Lot, Low argues that the text dismisses Lot's wife. See Low, "Sexual Abuse of Lot's Daughters," 41.

23. Nowhere else in the Bible is the participle used to describe individuals who are engaged or married.

24. Low suggests that the sons-in-law challenge Lot's masculinity; she writes: "Lot's relationship with his sons-in-law further demonstrates Lot's demasculinization among his fellow men." See ibid., 45–46.

25. Notably, Lot is the only male saved.

26. It is interesting to note that Lot now addresses the messengers as "my Lord," echoing Abraham in chapter 18, and not as "my lords," as he did at the beginning of the narrative. Perhaps being miraculously saved by the messengers, Lot recognizes they are God's emissaries.

27. Gen 12:13.

28. Gen 20:13.

29. Rabbinic tradition suggests that her punishment fits her crime. Having refused to give salt to her guests, she becomes salt. See *Bereshit Rabba* 50:4. Scholars offer an etiological explanation and link the story to one of the strange rock formations that inhabit the area.

30. Rashkow notes how the association between salt and fertility makes Lot's wife's transformation particularly apt. See Rashkow, *Taboo or not Taboo*, 109.

31. Esther Fuchs considers the first justification correct and the second erroneous; she writes: "The daughter's misperception, on the other hand, refers to her concern about the survival of the entire human species. She is wrong to interpret the destruction of Sodom and Gomorrah as the destruction of the entire earth." Fuchs, *Sexual Politics in the Biblical Narrative: Reading the Hebrew Bible as a Woman* (Sheffield: Sheffield Academic, 2003), 66.

32. Rashkow remarks on the cave: "The image of the cave is quite potent: generally speaking, it signifies movements of descent to a lower world." See Rashkow, *Taboo or not Taboo*, 107.

33. See Fuchs, *Sexual Politics*, 69.

34. See ibid., 67–68.

35. Fuchs writes: "The repetition of the 'fact' that the daughters colluded in the inebriation of Lot, and especially the repeated phrases 'and she lay with her father' and 'I lay last night with my father' . . . seems to serve as an implicit condemnation of the daughters' deceptive and incestuous initiative. In addition, the repeated emphasis on the 'fact' that the women both planned and executed their plan exonerates Lot of any responsibility for the action." See ibid., 68.

36. Fuchs similarly notes: "For Moab and Ammon, the Transjordanian neighbors of the Israelites, are also their national enemies. Giving birth to Israel's national rivals is, to say the least, a highly ambivalent compliment." See ibid., 69.

37. Low agrees with my reading: "When Lot becomes father of independent nations, the narrative has no need to continue with Lot. He disappears from the family in Genesis (only two other references exist, in Deut 2:9, 19). With Lot out of the picture, as father of a separate nation, the narrative fully legitimates Abraham's patrilineal line for Israel." See Low, "Sexual Abuse of Lot's Daughters," 46.

5

Sarah

In the last chapter, I argued that the story of Lot's daughters can be read as a dangerous-sister story in which the sisters' successful conspiracy to seduce their father subsequently results in the destruction of their natal household. My reading counters Seth Daniel Kunin who considers Genesis 19 to be a fantasy of incest in which Lot effectively marries his daughters to ensure the purity and continuity of his line.[1] Contrary to Kunin, I consider incest to be a destructive force within the narrative. Incest is the means through which Lot is deposed as a rival patriarch to Abraham.

Surprisingly, incest appears in the Bible's next narrative but involves a brother-sister relationship. In Genesis 20, at first glance, incest does not appear as a destructive force. In this narrative, the motif of incest, as manifest in the presumed brother-sister relationship between Abraham and Sarah, seems a productive force that enriches Abraham. Genesis 20, along with its companion narratives found in Gen 12:10-20 and Gen 26:6-11, offer the Bible's most positive narrative representation of incest. Abraham (twice) and Isaac (once) present their wives as their sisters in an effort to protect themselves from foreigners.[2] Despite the repetitive subject matter, the differences in narrative detail, as well as the placement of these stories within the broader framework of Genesis, argue for their careful inclusion and intentional design.

Placed immediately before or after moments of covenantal promise or fulfillment, these narratives provide tension by prolonging and complicating the fulfillment of God's promise to the patriarchs while at the same time describing how the patriarchs were enriched and had their status elevated among the nations. Each time the ruse is discovered, the patriarchs do not suffer for acting deceitfully. On the contrary, they prosper when the duped foreign kings offer gifts of appeasement that also serve as an incentive to leave. In this way, the wife-sisters function as ideal sisters who bring benefit to their patriarchal homes, which in this context, as they were in Jeremiah and Ezekiel, are a conflation of the conjugal and natal households. As I note in chapter 3, God is both Israel's father and husband in the marriage metaphor developed by these prophets. Therefore God's house is Israel's conjugal and natal home. Similarly, Abraham and Isaac are presented as Sarah's and Rebecca's brother and husband, respectively. Their houses also conflate the conjugal and natal homes and, therefore, provide the appropriate focus of a sister-story.

Given the outcome of the three wife-sister stories, it is easy to see why scholars like Kunin identify them as fantasies. For Kunin, Genesis 19 and 20 function as a narrative unit that reflects a common ideological preference for endogamy.[3] Through the shared motif of incest, they work to transform problematic (in a literary sense) outsider wives into privileged insider wives to enable the patriarchs to procreate appropriately. In Genesis 19, Lot's daughters replace his outsider wife to preserve his line after the cataclysmic destruction of Sodom. In Genesis 20, Sarah transforms into Abraham's sister to ensure the fertility and purity of Abraham's line. After she is re-designated as a wife-sister, Sarah can give birth to Abraham's designated heir Isaac in Genesis 21.[4]

Like Kunin, J. Cheryl Exum also argues that the three wife-sister stories encode fantasies. Although she acknowledges the possibility of an underlying incest fantasy,[5] Exum argues that the primary shared fantasy of the three wife-sister stories is that the patriarch's wife will have sex with another man. Within Exum's psychoanalytic-literary reading, the fantasy reflects the patriarchs' fears and desires and offers a means to work through them.[6]

Although the text is not explicit, Exum offers several insights into the nature of these fears and desires. As the text states clearly, the patriarchs fear for their lives. While traveling in foreign territory, Abraham and Isaac fear that foreigners will kill them in order to take their beautiful wives. As neither patriarch tests the waters to see if this is true before passing off his wife as his sister, Exum notes that his action all but guarantees that his wife will be taken.[7] For Exum, this suggests that latent desires other than self-preservation might be at work. Perhaps the patriarch wants to know that his wife is attractive to foreigners, which, by implication, would affirm the patriarch's ability to have attracted a beautiful wife. Perhaps the patriarch wants to rid himself of a problematic wife like Sarah who has been unable to conceive a child. Perhaps Abraham unburdens himself of the responsibilities a wife brings.[8]

For both Kunin and Exum, the wife-sister stories reflect male fantasies. The consequences related in the stories show each patriarch in a stronger position than when he first encountered the foreigners. Although Isaac does not receive money or livestock directly from the foreign king as Abraham does, he enjoys great agricultural fertility in the wake of the wife-sister episode and grows quite prosperous.[9] The fertility and fortune gained by the patriarchs at the conclusion of the narratives appear to justify their actions. For Kunin, a wife must become a sister before the heir apparent can be born. For Exum, a wife must become a sister to work through the patriarchs' latent fears and desires. Thus, the wife as sister is essentially a positive figure. Either she is an ideal figure, or she is a necessary means through which the patriarch can achieve emotional and financial stability.

In this chapter, I offer a different reading of the wife-sister narratives, particularly those of wife-sister Sarah. In my reading, the wife-sisters are threatening figures whose stories manifest the anxiety of incest as opposed to the fantasy of incest. Perhaps more than any other figure I have discussed, the wife-sister evokes the image of the sexualized sister. She is a destabilizing object of internally and externally focused desire. Like the story of Lot's daughters, the wife-sister narratives warn against crossing boundaries within one's family. Wives should remain wives; sisters should remain sisters.

Sarah assumes her role as Abraham's sister when Abraham and his household are most vulnerable. I contend that Sarah functions as a dangerous sister who reflects, and contributes to, the vulnerability of Abraham's household. To restore order to Abraham's household, as well as to the households that she enters as a sister, Sarah must relinquish her role as sister and resume her sole status in the narrative as Abraham's wife. In this way, her story resembles Israel's story as told by the prophet Ezekiel, which I discuss in chapter 3. Like Israel, Sarah must relinquish her role as sister and assume her role as wife. In each story, the conjugal house triumphs over the natal house.

In significant ways, my reading of the wife-sister narratives aligns with the reading offered by Esther Fuchs, who includes the wife-sister stories within the adultery type-scene in which a powerful king "threatens to or actually succeeds in appropriating to himself another man's wife."[10] For Fuchs, the wife-sister narratives serve to present polyandry—the practice where a wife has multiple husbands—as a sin.[11] Like my reading, Fuchs's reading highlights the vulnerability of the patriarch traveling in foreign territory. For Fuchs, it is Abraham's vulnerability that causes him to subvert the "ideal order" and present his wife as his sister, thereby enabling her to have more than one husband.[12] As Fuchs observes, Abraham is forced to do this, like Lot in Genesis 19 and, therefore, cannot be held morally accountable for what happens.[13] Divine intervention restores Sarah and order to Abraham's house. The role God plays in the narratives, as well as the riches rewarded to the patriarchs, makes clear that uxorial monogamy is the ideal.[14]

Our readings differ in that Fuchs perceives the patriarchs to be righteous victims within the narratives. She observes how God clearly sides with the patriarchs,[15] and how the disparity in status between the patriarchs and the foreign kings justifies the patriarchs' actions.[16] She also suggests that within each retelling of the wife-sister story, the patriarchs look more and more innocent.[17] In contrast to Fuchs, I perceive the narratives to condemn the patriarchs, particularly Abraham in Genesis 20. I argue that Genesis 20 presents Abraham as an ineffective patriarch and prophet, similar to the way the text presents Lot in Genesis 19, and accuses him of violating the incest prohibition whether in thought or in deed.[18] In this narrative, incest threatens Abraham's home just as it threatened Lot's home in Chapter 19; however, because Abraham is the designated patriarch, ultimately order is restored to his household. Removing the dangerous sister from the narrative and, with her, the threat of incest preserves Abraham's house and line.

Although Genesis 20 is the most developed of the wife-sister narratives, events unfold quickly and cryptically in verses 1-2:

> Abraham journeyed from there to the area of the Negev and settled between Kadesh and Shur. Abraham said of Sarah, his wife, she is my sister. Abimelech, King of Gerar, sent and took Sarah.

All three wife-sister narratives begin with a patriarch on the move and take place outside of the biblical heartland. The first wife-sister story occurs in Egypt, whereas the second and third stories take place in the Canaanite city of Gerar.

In the first wife-sister story, the mention of famine, Egypt, Pharaoh, and plagues suggests that its setting is significant. In this story, Abraham and Sarah personally experience Israel's mythic history—first famine, then enslavement, and ultimately prosperity in the exodus from Egypt. Kunin observes that Egypt provides an apt setting for a wife-sister story because brother-sister marriage was practiced there.[19] The setting of the other two narratives seems less laden with meaning because the Bible attributes no particular significance to Gerar, a prosperous city in the western Negev. Yet its name enables a significant word play. Abraham sojourns in Gerar [ויגר בגרר]. Like Lot in Sodom, Abraham is a temporary resident, a גר, of Gerar. As we saw in Gen 19:9, temporary residents are treated suspiciously. The play with the root גור, emphasizes Abraham's tenuous status among the residents of Gerar. He is a sojourner among sojourners, a stranger, גר, in a land of strangers. From the beginning of this narrative, Abraham and his household are marked as vulnerable in a dangerous place.[20]

While in Gerar, Abraham presents his wife Sarah as his sister without explanation. In the first wife-sister story (Genesis 12), Abraham justifies himself to Sarah. This initial explanation helps explain his actions in Genesis 20. On the road to Egypt, Abraham says to Sarah:

> I know that you are a beautiful woman. When the Egyptians see you, they will say, "This is his wife," and they will kill me and keep you alive. Say you are my sister so that things will go well with me because of you, and I will live because of you. (Gen 12:11-13)

Below, I address the question of whether or not Sarah is really Abraham's sister. Here, I note that Abraham asks Sarah to behave like an ideal sister while in Egypt. She must submit to her brother's will to protect and to benefit him, as Abraham explicitly says, "so that things will go well for me because of you."

To contemporary readers, Abraham's demand that Sarah presents as his sister seems callous if not repugnant, just as Lot's offering of his daughters to the Sodomites did in Chapter 19. Yet ancient norms and customs help explain the actions of each patriarch. Patrilocal marriage customs and, perhaps, an openness to intermarriage help explain Lot's actions. He is willing to sacrifice his nubile daughters, who are temporary members of his household, to protect his guests and the integrity of his home. The practice of sexual hospitality in which men exchanged women for security while in foreign territory might explain Abraham's action.[21] In Egypt and Gerar, Abraham is willing to sacrifice his wife for his own security.

Whatever his reasoning, each patriarch appears self-centered in his willingness to sacrifice a woman in his household for personal security. Although a reader assumes the whole household is in jeopardy while traveling in foreign territory, Abraham is noticeably concerned with his own safety. Like Lot who begged the messengers to allow him to escape to Zoar to save his life,[22] להחיות את-נפשי, and only his own life, Abraham schemes to save *his* life in Egypt, וחיתה נפשי. Sarah's safety—or even her life—is not his concern.[23] In fact, Abraham appears content after Pharaoh takes Sarah into his home in Gen 12:16. He enjoys Pharaoh's gifts until God intervenes and plagues Pharaoh's house.

Immediately after Abraham proclaims Sarah to be his sister in Gen 20:2, Abimelech, King of Gerar, takes her. Just as quickly, God intervenes. Like Lot in Sodom, Abraham in Gerar is a compromised patriarch at the mercy of foreigners. Like Lot, Abraham requires divine intervention to protect his household.[24] God comes to Sarah's rescue in Gen 20:3-7:

> God came to Abimelech in a night dream and said to him: "Indeed you will die because of this woman that you took, for she is married!" But Abimelech had not approached her, and he said: "My Lord, would you indeed destroy a righteous nation? Did he not say to me she is my sister and she said he is my brother? With pure heart and hands, I did this." God said to him in the dream: "Indeed I know that you did this with a pure heart. I prevented you from sinning against me. Therefore, I did not allow you to touch her. Now return this man's wife, for he is a prophet. He will pray on your behalf so you may live. But if you don't restore (her), know that you will die and all that is yours!"

In the biblical context, God's interaction with Abimelech is remarkable. Not only does God provide a Canaanite king with prophecy, but God also allows Abimelech to justify himself and then affirms Abimelech's innocence. In this way, God's intervention not only protects Sarah, it protects Abimelech as well by allowing him to prove his innocence.

Abimelech claims innocence in both intention and deed. Remarkably, he uses language that echoes Abraham when he negotiates with God on behalf of the righteous Sodomites in Genesis 18. Abimelech's question to God, "Would you indeed destroy a righteous nation?" echoes Abraham's challenge to God before the destruction of Sodom in Gen 18:23: "Will you destroy the righteous with the wicked?" Abimelech is as concerned with the innocent as Abraham and does not want to see anyone unjustly punished. Not only does Abimelech sound like pious Abraham, but his declaration that he is a righteous man with a pure heart and clean hands echoes the words of Ps 24:3-4. The Psalm asks: "Who can stand in His holy place?" The response is "One clean of hands and pure of heart." Abimelech suggests that he is able and willing to stand in God's company, just as Abraham stood before God in Gen 18:22.[25] At this moment Abimelech, and not Abraham, stands before God. At this moment, I suggest, Abimelech appears more righteous than Abraham.

Most importantly in the context of the narrative, Abimelech declares that he did not touch Sarah and that their relationship was never consummated. Because Isaac is born in Genesis 21, this information from Genesis 20 is crucial for clarifying his parentage. There is no possibility that Abimelech is Isaac's father. Also, Abimelech asserts that he bears no responsibility for what *could* have happened because he was deceived when he brought Sarah into his home. Abraham said that Sarah was his sister, and Sarah confirmed this. Genesis 20 is the only wife-sister story in which the woman speaks, although indirectly. Sarah appears to have affirmed her status to Abimelech.[26]

It is also the only wife-sister story in which the foreign king directly addresses the woman, as he does in verse 16. In the other wife-sister stories, the matriarch's silence suggests her passivity but not her complicity. In these stories, the matriarch does not act but is acted upon.[27] In contrast, Sarah appears as a more significant actor in Genesis 20, one who is able to dialogue directly with King Abimelech. Abimelech implies that he might not have believed Abraham if Sarah had not affirmed directly that she was his sister. Her confirmation convinces Abimelech that Sarah is available. By affirming her status, Sarah actively participates in the ruse and willingly assumes the role of Abraham's sister.

In the context of these narratives, the roles of wife and sister are mutually exclusive. In each of the wife-sister stories, when in foreign territory the matriarch must relinquish her status as wife and assume the sole status of sister for the scheme to work. Isaac explicitly states that Rebecca is his sister and *not* his wife in Gen 26:6-7:

> Isaac dwelt in Gerar. The people of the place asked after his wife. He said: "She is my sister," for he was afraid to say "my wife," thinking, "the people of the place will kill me because of Rebecca for she is beautiful."

By agreeing to present as Abraham's sister, Sarah relinquishes her position as Abraham's wife. Her consent raises the possibility that Sarah was as eager to be rid of Abraham, as Exum suggests, as Abraham was to be rid of Sarah.

In Genesis 20, Sarah enters Abimelech's house in the role of a sister—Abraham's sister. Because their relationship is not consummated, Sarah never becomes Abimelech's wife but remains functionally a sister throughout the narrative. A sister removed from her natal house and placed within a conjugal household is essentially a sexualized sister, whether in actuality or in potential and, therefore, functions within the narrative as a destabilizing figure. Sister Sarah threatens Abimelech's house, just as she threatened Pharaoh's house a few chapters earlier. In Genesis 12, God attacks Pharaoh's household, בית פרעה, with plagues because of Sarah,[28] ואת-ביתו על-דבר שרי. In Genesis 20, Abimelech's household similarly suffers because of Sarah's presence, as the final line in the story narrates: "God had closed every womb in

Abimelech's house [בית אבימלך] because of Sarah, Abraham's [29] wife [על דבר שרה אשת אברהם]. " Only in Genesis 26 does God spare the foreign king's house. But in this narrative, Rebecca does not actually enter his house. Abimelech observes Isaac sporting with Rebecca through a window and figures out what is going on. Because he does not bring the dangerous sister inside, his household is spared.

In Genesis 20, God commands Abimelech to return Sarah, אשת-האיש, to Abraham. Notably, Sarah returns to Abraham marked as his wife and not as his sister. Yet simply returning Sarah to Abraham is not enough. God insists that Abraham, the prophet, pray on Abimelech's behalf to avert impending disaster. God's insistence that Abraham function as intercessor on behalf of Abimelech restores Abraham's power, which was compromised a moment ago by the need for divine intervention. As he did in Genesis 18, Abraham must once again pray on behalf of the innocent—this time Abimelech and his household. God's demand that Abraham intercede on Abimelech's behalf also bolsters Abraham's reputation as God's true prophet, lest Abimelech, the dreamer-prophet, consider himself to be God's chosen. One expects Abimelech to heed God and to quickly ask Abraham to pray on his behalf. The narrative seems to be heading in this direction by having Abimelech "get up early," a gesture of obedience as Abraham does in Gen 22:3 when he rushes to fulfill God's command to sacrifice Isaac.

Instead of immediately asking Abraham to pray on his behalf, Abimelech gathers his own servants and informs them of what has happened. In response to his prophecy, the people are filled with awe [וייראו האנשים מאד]. Abimelech then confronts Abraham:

> Abimelech calls Abraham and says to him: "What have you done to us? What sin have I committed against you that you bring upon me and my kingdom this great sin? Things which should not be done, you do to me." Abimelech said to Abraham: "What have you seen that you do this thing?" (Gen 20:9-10)

Not only does Abimelech not rush to obey God, he also does not ask Abraham to pray on his behalf.[30] Instead, he demands to know what wrong he has committed against Abraham such that he betrayed him in this way and jeopardized his household and kingdom. Abimelech views Abraham's deception to be an aggressive act against him and his people. His tone is one of righteous indignation—"How have I sinned against you?"—and is accusatory—"You do things which should not be done!"

Abimelech may be held accountable for what has happened, but he is innocent. It is Abraham who is guilty. Certainly in Abimelech's eyes, and I contend within the greater perspective of the narrative, Abraham is not portrayed as the innocent victim, as Fuchs believes.[31] With the persistence of one who knows he is right, Abimelech insists that Abraham justify his actions.

Put on the defensive, Abraham responds:

> Abraham said: "Indeed I thought there was no fear of God in this place and that they will kill me on account of my wife. Also, it is true she is my sister, she is the daughter of my father but not the daughter of my mother, and she became my wife. When God made me wander from my father's house, I said to her, this will be your kindness that you will do for me in every place we enter. Say about me, he is my brother." (Gen 20:11-13)

From the beginning of his defense, Abraham does not sound like a powerful patriarch or an effective prophet. He reveals his weakness to Abimelech. He confesses that he feared for his life because he assumed that there was no fear of God, אין-יראת אלהים, in Gerar—an assumption that the narrative proved wrong in verse 8 when the people of Gerar respond to Abimelech's account of his prophecy with great awe [וייראו האנשים מאד]. Ironically, Abraham the prophet failed to assess the situation properly when he arrived in Gerar. Abimelech hints at Abraham's inadequacy as a prophet when he asks in verse 9, "What have you seen that you do this thing?" Abraham, the seer, has seen nothing.[32]

As Abraham continues his defense, he further reveals his weakness as a patriarch and unknowingly condemns his own actions. He justifies himself by claiming that he was not lying. Sarah is his sister, albeit his half-sister. They share a father, but not a mother. Although possible, there is no biblical evidence that Abraham and Sarah are half-siblings; Sarah's lineage is not given when she is first introduced in Gen 11:29.[33] In Genesis 26 we know that Isaac is lying to Abimelech when he introduces Rebecca as his sister, which shows that patriarchs are willing to deceive to protect themselves.

Although Abraham hopes to justify his actions, he in fact incriminates himself. His claim אחתי בת-אבי היא אך לא בת-אמי, "she is my sister, the daughter of my father but not the daughter of my mother," echoes the incest prohibition of Lev 20:17:

> A man who marries his sister, daughter of his father or daughter of his mother [בת-אביו או בת-אמו], and he sees her nakedness and she

sees his nakedness, it is a disgrace [חסד]. They will be cut off in the sight of their people. He has revealed the nakedness of his sister; he shall bear his iniquity.

Whether or not based on reality, the verbal associations with the incest prohibition make the incest motif blatant in the narrative and condemn Abraham by indicating that he has violated the biblical prohibition. He claims to have married *the daughter of his father, not the daughter of his mother*, precisely the relationship restricted by Lev 20:17. Surely, if inventing a relationship, Abraham easily could have presented Sarah as his full sister. This would prevent Abraham from directly violating the incest prohibitions *as written* in Leviticus since, as many commentators have noted, the full sister may be implied but is not explicitly mentioned in the prohibitions.[34] At least he would appear less culpable.

Both the narrative and the prohibition use the word חסד, though in seemingly opposite ways. In Gen 20:13, Abraham employs the more common and positive meaning of the word, gracious act. As a favor to him, Sarah should say that she is Abraham's sister. Her willingness demonstrates her loyalty to him and enables her to behave like an ideal sister who actively supports her brother.[35] Yet in Lev 20:17, חסד has the euphemistic meaning of "shame."[36] The use of חסד links Genesis 20 to the incest prohibition. It alludes to a shared meaning and implies that Abraham violates the incest prohibition whether in deed, by actually marrying his half-sister, or in kind, by presenting his wife as his half-sister. In this reading of חסד, Sarah's act of grace is, in truth, an act of disgrace that reflects poorly upon Abraham and works to his detriment and not to his benefit.[37] Abraham should not have married his sister or even presented Sarah as his sister. Such behavior compromises and shames the patriarch.

Abraham's final explanation to Abimelech may be his most revealing. Yet again, Abraham denies culpability as he did earlier when he blamed the non-God-fearing Gerarites for his deception. This time he says that God made him do it. Yet Abraham does more than blame God. He confesses feeling vulnerable ever since "God made me wander from my father's house."[38] With this statement, Abraham may wish to deflect blame or to evoke sympathy. Yet he also reveals his perception of his existential reality. While wandering in foreign territory, Abraham finds it hard to feel and act like a patriarch. Forced to leave his father's house, Abraham may in fact identify more with a sister who, also upon marriage, must leave the patriarchal household.

While traveling, Abraham is a marginal and vulnerable figure like a sister within her natal household. As a *ger* in Gerar, Abraham may project his feelings of insecurity and marginality onto Sarah. His projection transforms Sarah into a sister. Exum suggests this when she describes Abraham's fantasy that Sarah is his sister as a "narcissistic striving . . . whose realization can only be imagined in his mirror-image from the opposite sex (she is what he would be if he were a woman)."[39] As a mirror-image of Abraham, Sarah as sister not only contributes to the vulnerability of the patriarchal household, she represents it. Like Michal in David's house, Sarah in Abimelech's house reflects the distress and vulnerability of Abraham's own house.

The vulnerability of Abraham's house is not just existential. Clearly, he must defend himself against a justly enraged foreigner. To restore order within both affected households, the sister is removed from the house and from the narrative. Restitution is made, and Sarah is reintegrated within Abraham's house as his wife.

> Abimelech took sheep, cattle, male and female servants and gave them to Abraham. He returned to him Sarah, his wife. Abimlech said: "Indeed, my land is before you. Dwell where it pleases you." To Sarah he said: "I gave a thousand pieces of silver to your brother; it will be for you as vindication before all who are with you and before all, you are vindicated." Abraham prayed to God, and God healed Abimelech, his wife, and his female servants so that they could give birth for God had closed every womb in Abimelech's household because of Sarah, Abraham's wife. (Gen 20:14-18)

Abimelech returns Sarah to Abraham as his wife and not as his sister [וישב לו את שרה אשתו]. The final words of the story confirm Sarah's status. She is "Sarah, wife of Abraham." Similarly, the wife-sister story in Genesis 12 concludes: "Pharaoh commanded men and sent forth him and his wife [אשתו] and all that was his."[40] Likewise the ending of the third wife-sister story refers to Rebecca only as Isaac's wife[41] [אשתו]. Reunited with his wife, Abraham reclaims his patriarchal and prophetic power and prays on behalf of Abimelech. With the dangerous sister removed, households are healed or enriched, and order is restored. Abraham can resume his position as the most powerful patriarch in the Bible's central story.

After proper roles are resumed in Abraham's family, the narrative can proceed in Genesis 21 with the much anticipated birth of Isaac, Abraham's designated heir. Within its broader biblical narrative, Genesis 20 could be viewed as functioning like a typical sister story. It uses a dangerous sister to weaken the rival patriarch Abimelech in order to strengthen the designated family of Abraham. Wealthy Abraham can now sire his heir. Yet in significant ways, Genesis 20 continues the particular sister story begun in Genesis 19.

Incest is an unsettling motif in both narratives, in which sisters play a central role. Given these fundamental similarities, like Kunin, I perceive Genesis 19 and 20 to be a narrative unit. Yet unlike Kunin, I do not believe that these stories reflect incest fantasies. Rather, I contend that they reflect incest anxieties, particularly focused on the sister. Lot's daughters, a pair of sisters, taint Lot's line through incest. As his wife-sister, Sarah cannot protect Abraham despite his hopes that she will. She is a dangerous and destabilizing figure who threatens the households of Pharaoh, Abimelech, *and* Abraham. Wife-sister Sarah puts Abraham on the defensive and brings plagues and barrenness into the homes of Pharaoh and Abimelech. Not only does she make households vulnerable, but she signifies the vulnerability of these households. Sarah's marginal status as a sister reflects Abraham's marginal status as a sojourner. Abraham transforms Sarah into his sister when he feels most vulnerable and most like a sister himself.

Genesis 19 and 20 both warn against trespassing defined roles within the family. Genesis 19 shows that incest does not secure the patrilineage. With its allusion to Lev 20:17, Genesis 20 condemns Abraham for violating in thought or in action the incest prohibition. In both stories, incest does not empower the patriarch, nor does it protect his household. Like the incest prohibitions, these incest narratives make clear that individuals should fulfill one role within the family. Wives should only be wives; daughters should only be daughters; and sisters should only be sisters. Genesis 19 and 20 reveal the devastating consequences of sisters who are not confined to their proper role within the family. Unleashed, incestuous sisters can seduce their fathers, give birth to enemies, enrage foreigners, bring plagues, and cause barrenness. In Genesis 19, incestuous sisters destroy the house of Lot. In Genesis 20, an incestuous sister threatens Abraham. Being one of the Bible's designated patriarchs, Abraham, unlike Lot, is not destroyed. Instead, he survives and thrives. Yet, as this narrative reveals, even Abraham and his household cannot escape the dangerous sister.

Notes

1. In Kunin's reading, Lot's daughters function as insiders who replace Lot's outsider wife in order to induce his fertility. Kunin recognizes that Lot is Abraham's rival and suggests that the Bible uses daughters as opposed to sisters in this incest fantasy to diminish Lot's status. See Seth Daniel Kunin, *The Logic of Incest: A Structural Analysis of Hebrew Mythology* (Sheffield: Sheffield Academic, 1995), 83.

2. Noting the similarities between these three narratives, scholars often argue that they are different versions of the same story rather than three independent narratives. As Elizabeth Boase notes, "Gen. xii 10-20 provides the basic structure from which the other two units gain their form." See Elizabeth Boase, "Life in the Shadows: The Role and Function of Isaac in Genesis: Synchronic and Diachronic Readings," *VT* 51, no. 3 (2001): 323.

3. Kunin writes: "The placement of this text immediately after the previous text is significant. Both texts serve identical purposes, to make the wife (outside) inside." Kunin, *Logic of Incest*, 84.

4. Kunin observes: "*Wife/Sister 2* is the final preparation for the birth of Isaac. Like *Wife/Sister 1*, this text resolves the ambiguous position of Sarah. She is completely transformed from wife (outside) to sister (inside)." See ibid., 83.

5. Like Kunin, Exum attributes the incest fantasy to the Bible's desire to have the patriarch's partner be as close in kinship as possible. See J. Cheryl Exum, *Fragmented Women: Feminist (Sub)versions of Biblical Narratives* (Valley Forge, PA: Trinity, 1993), 167.

6. Exum attributes the fear and desire to the "narrator" and suggests that the text is working through the narrator's "intra-psychic conflict." See ibid., 154.

7. See ibid., 158.

8. Exum writes: "This is the male fantasy of sex without commitment; he will be free to have other women, unhampered by the domesticity that the wife represents." See ibid., 159.

9. Gen 26:12-14 describes Isaac's wealth and fertility: "Isaac sowed in that land and reaped a hundredfold that year. YHWH blessed him, and the man grew increasingly richer until he was quite rich." Kunin acknowledges that the Isaac-Rebecca wife-sister narrative does not result in the birth of the designated heir since Jacob and Esau are already born. He suggests that the incident results in Isaac's increased agricultural fertility symbolized by his re-digging of the wells in Gen 26:18. See Kunin, *Logic of Incest*, 108–9.

10. Fuchs, *Sexual Politics in the Biblical Narrative: Reading the Hebrew Bible as a Woman* (Sheffield: Sheffield Academic, 2003), 118.

11. See ibid., 122.

12. Fuchs observes: "It is the husband's vulnerability that leads to the destabilization of the ideal order, namely, one in which the husband's control over his wife is uncompromised by outside intervention." See ibid.

13. See ibid., 123.

14. See ibid., 122–23.

15. Ibid., 120.

16. Fuchs writes: "The 'real' victim in the adultery type-scene is the husband. His political weakness and vulnerability is highlighted by the immense power of his rival, the monarch." See ibid., 124.

17. Ibid.

18. Fuchs and I offer consistent readings of the representation of the patriarchs in both Genesis 19 and 20. Whereas Fuchs believes the text exonerates Lot and Abraham, I argue that both are presented as ineffective patriarchs.

19. See Kunin, *Logic of Incest*, 68. As I mention in chapter 4, Sabine R. Huebner challenges the ubiquity of brother-sister marriage in ancient Egypt.

20. Robert L. Cohn observes: "The wife-sister stories demonstrate the dangers that threaten the integrity of this outsider family as it wanders in lands occupied by others." See Cohn, "Negotiating (with) the Natives: Ancestors and Identity in Genesis," *HTR* 96, no. 2 (2003): 154.

21. Cohn suggests that the practice of sexual hospitality is behind the wife-sister narratives; he writes: "What lies behind this literary topos, says anthropologist Julian Pitt-Rivers, is the ancient Mediterranean custom of "sexual hospitality," the use of women to establish patron-client bonds between host and guest. On this reading, the patriarch gives over his woman in order to dwell in the land unmolested . . . protected by the 'king' and permitted to graze his flocks and

herds." Ibid., 153. Cohn suggests that the stories work as a polemic against the custom. See ibid., 155.

22. Gen 19:19-20.

23. Fokkelien van Dijk-Hemmes notes that Abraham, Lot, and the Levite in Judges 19 are all men who sacrifice women for their own safety. See van Dijk-Hemmes, "Sarai's Exile: A Gender-Motivated Reading of Genesis 12.10–13.2" in *A Feminist Companion to Genesis,* ed. Athalya Brenner (Sheffield: Sheffield Academic, 1997), 229–30.

24. Of course, it remains unclear whether Abraham wants God's help. In both stories, he complies with the wishes of the foreign king and does not appeal to God to intervene after Sarah is taken.

25. Gen 18:22 reads: "Abraham remained standing [עמד] before God."

26. In contrast to my reading, Exum dismisses the significance of Sarah's indirect affirmation that she is Abraham's sister; she writes: "If her only speech is one reported by another character in the narrative, the matriarch can hardly be said to become a narrative presence in any real sense. She is merely the object in a story about male relations (and we shall inquire below how the two men respond in relation to the object)." See Exum, *Fragmented Women,* 151-52.

27. Exum observes: "The woman has no voice in determining her sexual status and no control over how her sexuality is perceived or used." See ibid., 165. Similarly, Fuchs notes that the women's voice is "consistently suppressed." See Fuchs, *Sexual Politics,* 130.

28. Gen 12:17.

29. Van Dijk-Hemmes considers the various meanings of the phrase על-דבר שרה, and suggests that *dvr* may refer to Abraham's "word-deed" or "speech act" through which Abraham names Sarah his sister and thereby terminates their marriage. See van Dijk-Hemmes, "Sarai's Exile," 231.

30. Although Abraham prays in Gen 20:17, Abimelech never asks him directly to pray on his behalf.

31. Fuchs, *Sexual Politics,* 124.

32. As 1 Sam 9:9 records, prophets were initially called seers in Israel.

33. Without a biblical account of her lineage, we cannot speculate whether Sarah was indeed Abraham's half-sister.

34. See Jacob Milgrom, *Leviticus 17–22* (New York: Doubleday, 2000), 1753.

35. This is how the *JPS Hebrew-English Tanakh* translates Gen 20:13: "Let this be the kindness that you shall do me."

36. For a similar use of the word, see Prov 14:34; 25:10.

37. Gershon Hepner suggests the verse implies both meanings of the word חסד; he writes: "The word חסד is a Janus word that implies 'disgrace' as well as lovingkindness. When Abraham uses it to describe his relationship with Sarah he refers not only to her חסד, *lovingkindness,* but also the חסד, *disgrace,* caused by violation of the Holiness Code's prohibition of incest." See Hepner, "Abraham's Incestuous Marriage with Sarah: A Violation of the Holiness Code," *VT* 53, no. 2 (2003): 148.

38. The first wife-sister story occurs immediately after God commands Abraham to leave his father's house.

39. Exum, *Fragmented Women,* 167.

40. Gen 12:20.

41. Gen 26:11.

6

Tamar

Whereas brother-sister incest may only be a motif in Genesis 20, actual incest occurs in 2 Samuel 13. In this story, Amnon rapes his sister Tamar. In the first two incest narratives that I examined in Genesis 19 and 20, incest could be seen as an act intended to benefit the natal household. Through incest, Lot's daughters hope to preserve their father's seed, and wife-sister Sarah attempts to protect husband-brother Abraham. My reading of these narratives challenges that perception and argues that incest is a destructive force associated with a vulnerable natal household. This conclusion is also evident regarding the incest that occurs in 2 Samuel 13. Amnon's rape of Tamar brings about fratricide and civil war within the house of David. In this chapter, I argue that 2 Samuel 13 is a sister story that is unambiguously about the vulnerability of the natal household.

Ironically, the vulnerable household belongs to David, the very household dangerous sisters Michal and Merav helped establish and that God promised would remain steadfast in 2 Sam 7:16. David jeopardizes the security of his own home when he commits adultery by sleeping with Uriah's wife Bathsheba and then plotting to have Uriah killed.[1] Furious at David, God sends the prophet Nathan to condemn David's behavior and to deliver the prophecy that David's house will never again experience peace. Immediately after this, the rape of Tamar by Amnon fulfills Nathan's prophecy of doom to David in 2 Sam 12:11: "Thus says YHWH: 'I will make calamity rise against you from within your house.'" Indeed, calamity rises from within David's house in the figure of a dangerous sister whose sexual violation tears her father's house apart.

Although a sympathetic figure, Tamar jeopardizes the security of her father's house. As an object of her brother's desire, we see that Tamar is both symptomatic and emblematic of a household in distress. In her reading of this narrative, Esther Fuchs also considers Tamar's story to be about the destabilized patriarchal household. Yet, in Fuchs's analysis, it is Amnon's rape of Tamar more than the act of incest itself that upends the norms of the patriarchal household. Fuchs connects Tamar's story with Dinah's and reads both as rape stories in which the custodial patriarch is the true victim.[2] The family's honor is violated more than the sister's safety.[3] Like Shechem's crime, Amnon's crime was to circumvent the proper betrothal channels—whether before or after having sex—that help sustain patriarchal order.

Amnon defies the laws of Exod 22:15 and Deut 22:28-29 that compel a rapist to marry his victim and to compensate her father.[4] In both narratives, brothers intervene to avenge their sisters and to restore order to their households. For Fuchs, the avenging brothers are the intended heroes of these narratives at the expense of their sisters. Dinah's story ends when her brothers remove her from Shechem's house. Similarly, Tamar disappears from the narrative after she enters Absalom's house. For Fuchs, the disappearance of the sister enables the brothers to avenge their own honor, which has been compromised by the violation of their sisters and is the central concern of the narratives.[5]

Although Fuchs makes many astute observations about the patriarchal ideology that underpins the narrative, her reading effectively turns a sister story into a brother story. My reading restores the sister as the focus of 2 Samuel 13 and contends that the incestuous sister is the central concern of the narrative. It is Amnon's passion for his sister that upends the household. As the dangerous object of desire, Tamar embodies incest anxieties. Her fate reveals what happens to a household in which boundaries are crossed, and incestuous desires are fulfilled. Like Dinah in her brothers' house and Michal in David's house, Tamar in Absalom's house becomes a living fossil. This dangerous sister becomes a שממה, a desolation, who lives as a symbol of her own violation and of David's vulnerable and fractious home.

The story begins by introducing its characters who are clearly marked by their position within David's family, as well as their relationship to one another:

> Time passed. Absalom, son of David, had a beautiful sister whose name was Tamar. Amnon, son of David, loved her. Amnon grew sick over Tamar, his sister because she was a maiden and it seemed impossible to Amnon that he could do anything to her. Amnon had a friend whose name was Jonadab, son of Shimah, David's brother, and Jonadab was very wise. He said to him: "Why are you sick like this, o son of the king, every day? Can you not tell me?" Amnon said to him: "Because Tamar, Absalom's sister, my brother, I love." (2 Sam 13:1-4)

This passage marks each of the characters by their familial roles. Interestingly, the males occupy two roles within the family and are identified in relation to David. Absalom and Amnon are brothers and David's sons, whereas Jonadab is a son and David's nephew. In contrast, Tamar is described with only one attribution—that of sister. Although she is David's daughter, she is not identified as such. Instead, she is seen only in relation to her brothers and will remain functionally a sister throughout her narrative. Repeatedly, the text refers to Tamar as sister. As Phyllis Trible observes, the structure of the first line of the narrative conveys that Tamar is caught between her two brothers. She is a sister to Absalom and an object of desire to Amnon.[6]

Because of the role he plays in the narrative, commentators assume that Absalom is Tamar's full brother and Amnon is her half-brother. Like Dinah's full brothers Simeon and Levi, Absalom avenges his violated sister. Another reason for considering Amnon to be a half-brother is Tamar's later suggestion that David would not oppose their marriage. Although unstated, it is reasonable to assume that David would be more open to marriage among half-siblings as opposed to full, even though, as I mention in chapter 5, the Bible specifically only prohibits marriage to one's half-sister. For these reasons, I identify Amnon as Tamar's half-brother throughout my analysis though I recognize that the text never makes this distinction. In contrast, the Bible clearly states Amnon's relation to Absalom. Second Samuel 3:1-3 records that Amnon was David's son by Ahinoam and that Absalom was David's son by Maacha. Yet it remains unclear who shares a mother with Tamar. First Chronicles 3:1-9 lists David's sons by birth mother and by location of their birth. Tamar is included at the end of the passage without indicating her birth mother. She is simply identified as "their sister."

From its beginning, the narrative manifests incest anxieties. Incest overtly enters the story when Amnon admits he loves his sister, but it is also covertly alluded to in the characters' names. The name Amnon resonates with Ben-Ammi, progenitor of the Ammonites, born to Lot and his second daughter in Genesis 19.[7] Tamar shares her name with Judah's daughter-in-law who sleeps with her father-in-law in Genesis 38.[8] For readers today, a sexual relationship between a father-in-law and daughter-in-law would not be considered technically incestuous since there is no blood relation. Yet, Lev 18:15 includes this union among other prohibited sexual relationships between immediate family members, suggesting that the Bible may consider it to be an incestuous relationship. As I mentioned in chapter 4 when discussing sororal polygyny and will discuss further in the context of Ruth, in the ancient world, marriage may have constructed a blood relationship among members of the co-joined patriarchal household. If, as Gen 2:24 states, husbands and wives become one flesh—indicating a blood relationship between them—then a husband's father is his wife's father as well, just as a husband's sister is considered to be his sister. By having sex, Tamar and Judah engage in incest. Bearing these names, Tamar and Amnon seem fated for an incestuous union.

Initially, Amnon does not act upon his incestuous desire, but his hesitation is not because he considers his desire to be inappropriate. Later, Amnon proves that he has no problem indulging his desire. Rather, Amnon hesitates because he does not know how to attain her. Being with Tamar seems impossible to him, though Amnon does not specify why. When asked by Jonadab why he appears despondent, Amnon admits that he is upset because he loves Tamar, "*Absalom's* sister, my *brother.*" His response to Jonadab suggests that Absalom is the impediment to their union. Perhaps Tamar's full brother Absalom will negotiate her marriage as Laban does for Rebecca in Genesis 24. If so, Amnon may fear that Absalom will not violate the prohibitions against marrying a half-sister and will deny him access to Tamar.[9]

Fraternal rivalry offers another explanation why Amnon perceives Absalom as the impediment to their union. If Absalom perceives Amnon to be a political rival, he may not relinquish his sister to him. In this reading, violating the incest prohibitions is not Absalom's concern. Rather, Absalom fears that an incestuous marriage between Tamar and Amnon would preserve the purity of David's line and secure Amnon's position as David's successor.[10] Whatever prevents Amnon from acting on his desires and taking Tamar, it is clear from the beginning of the story that Tamar belongs to Absalom. She is marked more directly as Absalom's sister and, as such, she is out of Amnon's reach. In the events that follow, Amnon claims her for himself.

Jonadab devises a plan for Amnon to acquire Tamar that is enacted in 2 Sam 13:5-6:

> Jonadab said to him: "Lie upon your bed and feign illness. When your father comes to see you, say to him: 'Let Tamar, my sister, come. Let her feed me bread, let her make food [הבריה] before me so that I can see and eat from her hand.'" Amnon lay down and feigned illness. The king came to see him. Amnon said to the king: "Let Tamar, my sister, come and prepare before me two cakes so that I can eat from her hand."

Capitalizing on Amnon's love-sickness, Jonadab plots rape, not marriage. He does not suggest that Amnon negotiate with David for Tamar's hand in marriage. Instead, he figures a way for Amnon to use David to circumvent Absalom and have sex with Tamar. In this way, Jonadab makes David a crucial actor in the events that unfold.

David's role in this narrative resembles the roles assumed by other fathers in dangerous-sister stories. Like Laban, Saul, and particularly Lot, David is a compromised father who is unable to protect Tamar and prevent a sexual relationship from occurring that threatens his home. Although sisters are the primary destabilizing figures in their narratives, we have seen that all four fathers are also accountable to some extent for the demise of their households. Laban and Saul welcome rival patriarchs into their homes. Drunken Lot sleeps with his daughters. Easily manipulated by his son, David enables Amnon to rape his half-sister.

Granting Amnon's request, David sends Tamar to prepare a meal for Amnon:

> David sent [וישלח] for Tamar at home saying: "Go to the house of Amnon, your brother, and prepare food for him." Tamar went to the house of Amnon, her brother. He was lying down. She took the dough, kneaded it, and made the cakes before him and cooked the cakes. She took the pan and served him, but he refused to eat. Amnon said: "Everyone, get out!" Everyone left him. Amnon said to Tamar: "Bring the food into the room so that I can eat from your hand." Tamar took the cakes that she made and brought them to Amnon, her brother, into the room. (2 Sam 13:7-10)

Although David sends Tamar to Amnon, it remains unclear whether David was aware of what lurked behind Amnon's request that Tamar bake cakes and feed him. Either David was duped by his son when he sends Tamar to nurse Amnon, or he was overpowered by his son when he sends Tamar to satisfy Amnon's desires.

To understand David's motivation, we must ascertain if Amnon's request that Tamar bake cakes for him was unusual. According to Tikva Frymer-Kensky, young women in the ancient world were involved in healing practices. Thus, Amnon's request that Tamar prepare healing food is not unusual.[11] When devising the plot, Jonadab tells Amnon to ask that Tamar prepare בריה for him, a word whose root may come from ברא, meaning healthy or fat. This specific request would indicate to David that Amnon only seeks medical attention.[12] Yet, when Amnon speaks to David, he asks that Tamar specifically prepare לבבות for him—heart cakes. These cakes may have been heart shaped as some have suggested and were perhaps intended to *enhearten* and heal the sick. They also could have been "cakes of desire" that refer to any type of cake that Amnon would have an appetite for.[13] In other words, Amnon's specific request for לבבות, as opposed to the more medicinal בריה communicates Amnon's desire to David and his hopes that his desire will be fulfilled.

I contend that Amnon indeed conveys his desire to David and that David knowingly grants his son's request. By sending [וישלח] for Tamar and commanding her to go to Amnon's house, David initiates the events that follow, just as he did in the preceding narrative about Bathsheba. At the start of 2 Samuel 11, David sends [וישלח] Joab and his soldiers to battle.[14] He then sees Bathsheba bathing on her rooftop and *sends* messengers first to confirm her identity and then to bring her to him.[15] After Bathsheba informs David that she is pregnant, he *sends* for Uriah, her husband.[16] Ultimately, he *sends* Uriah to his death.[17] The repeated use of the root שלח in the David and Bathsheba story communicates that David acts with intentionality and therefore is culpable for his actions. Certainly God and Nathan hold David accountable for his actions in 2 Sam 12:7-12. The striking reappearance of the root שלח in Tamar's story conveys that David acts with intentionality in this story as well. Like Joab, Bathsheba, and Uriah, Tamar is subject to David, who knowingly relinquishes her to Amnon.

In light of Nathan's post-Bathsheba prophecy that calamity will arise from within David's house, David must be well aware of the tensions within his household. Given Amnon's appetite for heart cakes, he is also well aware of Amnon's desires. David's acquiescence to Amnon may be a misguided attempt of a compromised patriarch to assert control over and to protect his household. David believes it is in his best interest to satisfy Amnon's desire. Like Amnon, he may consider Absalom to be an impediment. David's willingness to send Tamar directly to Amnon is a way to bypass Absalom and his resistance to a union between the siblings. Like Lot in Genesis 19, David is willing to send his daughter out of his house to keep peace within it. And like Lot, he makes a crucial miscalculation. Lot and David believe that daughters are expendable. Both underestimate the destabilizing impact of sisters on their households.

Space and place are important in 2 Samuel 13 as they were in Genesis 19. At first, Genesis 19 distinguishes dangerous public space, the town square, from safe private space, Lot's home. By the end of the narrative, even private space is not safe. In 2 Samuel 13, space is differentiated by households—the house of David, the house of Amnon, and later, the house of Absalom. At different points within the narrative, Tamar enters within each of these households and falls under the custodial care of its specific master. At the start of the story, it appears that no space is safe for Tamar. David intentionally sends her from his home into Amnon's, where Amnon rapes her.

The narrative further differentiates space by rooms within Amnon's household. Once inside, Tamar moves deeper within Amnon's house into his bedroom. There, Amnon attacks her, and Tamar fights to protect herself:

> When she approached him to eat, he grabbed her and said: "Come, lie with me, my sister!" She said to him: "Don't, my brother, don't degrade me for this should not be done in Israel. Don't do this abomination! Where could I go with my disgrace? You would be like one of the violators in Israel. Speak to the king now. He would not withhold me from you." (2 Sam 13:11-13)

The familial relationships in this passage are clearly emphasized. Brother attacks sister, and sister responds to brother. Using the verb that connotes rape, Amnon grabs hold of Tamar[18] [ויחזק-בה]. He does not immediately sexually force himself upon her. Instead, he commands her to lie with him, as if her consent would render his actions less brutal. As I already noted, Amnon's command to Tamar to lie with him [שכבי עמי] echoes the command of the elder sister to the younger to lie with Lot in Gen 19:34 [שכבי עמו] and Potiphar's wife's command to Joseph in Gen 39:12 [שכבה עמי]. Like Lot's daughters and Potiphar's wife, Amnon is a sexual aggressor who seeks submission from a less powerful individual. By calling her "my sister," he makes his incestuous desire clear.[19]

Tamar does not consent. She fights back by attempting to convince Amnon not to act upon his desire. Her appeal is based on status, her own as well as his. Tamar begins by acknowledging her familial relationship with Amnon, perhaps hoping that it would deter him. She says, "Don't, my brother [אל-אחי]." Notably, her words echo Lot's[20] when he appeals to the Sodomites in Gen 19:7 [אל-נא אחי]. Tamar begs Amnon not to degrade her [אל-תעונני] or him by committing an abomination [אל-תעשה את-הנבלה הזאת]. Her words are a direct link to Dinah's story in Genesis 34 in which a similar abomination is committed [כי נבלה עשה בישראל] and a sister is degraded [ויענה]. Yet in Genesis 34, brothers do not commit the abomination. They avenge it. An allusion to this story suggests that Tamar appeals to Amnon as a *brother* and begs him to behave appropriately. Brothers should protect or avenge but not violate their sister's sexual purity. Fully understanding the consequences of her violation, Tamar asks Amnon: "Where could I go with my disgrace?" Her question must be taken literally and appeals to Amnon's compassion. Raped by her brother, Tamar has no husband and no hope of ever living in a husband's house. Where could she live as a ruined woman? In whose house does she belong after she is violated?

After appealing to Amnon's sense of propriety and sympathy, Tamar has one final tactic. She urges Amnon to speak to the king and claims he would allow Amnon to marry Tamar. In a narrative that carefully delineates familial relationships, Tamar strikingly uses David's title and not his name. By referring to David as the king, Tamar subtly reminds Amnon of her own status as the king's daughter. Amnon should treat the daughter of the king appropriately. Her suggestion that Amnon talk to David may also be a stalling tactic. Tamar may hope that Amnon would lose interest in her while awaiting the king's response. It is also possible that Tamar believes that David would approve their union, either because he considered a marriage between half-siblings to be legitimate or because when forced to choose, David would prefer incest over rape.

Unmoved and unconvinced, Amnon rapes Tamar. Instantaneously consumed by hatred, Amnon throws Tamar out of his house.

> He was unwilling to listen to her. He grabbed her, degraded her, and lay with her. Then Amnon hated her with a great hatred; for greater was the hatred that he felt for her than the love that he had felt for her. Amnon said to her: "Get up and go!" She said to him: "Don't! About this great calamity, sending me away is worse than the other that you did to me." But he was unwilling to listen to her. He called his servant that served him and said: "Send this away from me, outside, and lock the door behind her." (2 Sam 13:14-17)

Amnon's sudden and intense hatred for Tamar proves him to be a man of precarious passions and suggests that he never actually loved Tamar but only desired her.[21] Once he satisfies his desire, he throws her away. The root hate, שנא, appears in Deut 22:13 and Deut 24:3 to describe a husband's feelings toward a wife that he wants to divorce. It also appears as a divorce formula found in the fifth-century BCE Aramaic papyri from Elephantine as well as other documents from Syria and Mesopotamia.[22] The use of the root שנא not only reveals Amnon's volatile temper and erratic emotional life, it also has legal connotations indicating the formal dissolution of a marriage. By hating her, Amnon formally annuls his relationship with Tamar. Having slept with her, he effectively married her. Now, he divorces her.

Again Tamar masterfully fights back and appeals to Amnon's ego and his empathy. In one verse, she argues on behalf of Amnon, David, and herself. Tamar declares that if he sends her away, Amnon commits an even greater wrong—רעה—than the rape he already committed. Tamar takes the moral high ground with Amnon just as Lot does with the Sodomites in Gen 19:7.[23] Her appeal to Amnon informs him that he is guilty of a crime. It also lets him know that he can right the wrong he has already done by doing the right thing now. He should not further incriminate himself by sending her away. He should keep her as his wife for his own sake. Her use of the word רעה also links the narrative back to Nathan's prophecy that calamity—רעה—will rise from within David's house. As the fulfillment of that prophecy, Amnon's actions would introduce calamity into the house of David. Amnon should keep her as his wife for David's sake. Tamar also argues for herself. Her words "sending me away is worse than the other that you did *to me*,"[24] conveys that *she* is Amnon's victim and cannot be implicated in this crime.

Amnon proves impervious to Tamar's appeal. Filled with hatred, he can no longer even refer to her by name. This is a far cry from where he was at the start of the narrative when he admits to loving "Tamar, Absalom's sister, my brother." Now as he discards her, he calls her זאת—this one—as if absolving a familial relationship with her. Like David, Amnon sends Tamar away, but he does not remove her himself from his house. Instead, he orders a servant to remove her and to lock the door behind her. As in Genesis 19, a doorway appears in a sister story. In Genesis 19, Lot offers his daughters to the angry mob that surrounds his house, but the divine messengers protect the door to Lot's house and keep the sisters safe inside. In Lot's story, the door demarcates the inside from the outside and distinguishes a safer zone. Although Lot was willing to cast them outside, the messengers make it clear that Lot's daughters belong in Lot's house and not among the raging Sodomites. In 2 Samuel 13, Amnon rapes Tamar deep inside his home and then casts her outside as a violated and ruined woman. By closing the door behind her, Amnon makes it clear that Tamar does not belong in his home. Tamar's anguished plea to remain within Amnon's house reveals her fears that as a violated woman, she does not belong in any home.

Discarded, Tamar reacts:

She wore the long robe that the maiden daughters of the king wore. His servant cast her out and locked the door behind her. Tamar put dust on her head and tore the long robe that was upon her. She put her hands on her head and went about crying. (2 Sam 13:18-19)

Although the precise style of Tamar's garment remains unknown,[25] it functions as a marker of her identity and conveys two significant qualities of her character: that she is a maiden and that she is a princess. Although her sexual and marital status may be the most significant factors in this narrative,[26] Tamar's status as a princess is also important and is conveyed nonverbally through this garment.

As I mentioned previously, Tamar is never formally identified as "David's daughter" in the narrative. She exclusively and repeatedly is referred to as a sister—either Absalom's or Amnon's—and is connected to David only through her brothers, David's sons. This, I contend, is among the strongest arguments for reading Tamar's story as primarily a sister story, as opposed to a daughter story. Even when David sends for Tamar and commands her to go to her brother Amnon's house, he does not address her as "daughter." Tamar also presents herself as removed from David when she suggests that Amnon ask "the king" and not her father for her hand in marriage. Although she is never called one, the robe she wears marks her as a princess and is a visual reminder to Amnon that he violates one of the "maiden daughters of the king."

Violence against Tamar is violence against David. Amnon's rape and dismissal of Tamar, the king's daughter, should be considered a defiant act on par with Absalom's sleeping with David's concubines in 2 Sam 16:20-23. The rape of Tamar is really an attack on David's house. Like these concubines, Tamar lives in David's home and under his authority. By raping his sister and then discarding her, Amnon defies David's authority and weakens his house. This is another strong argument for identifying Tamar's story as a sister story. By relating the violation of a sister's natal household, 2 Samuel 13 follows the general contours of the typical sister story. In particular, it conforms closely to the incest narratives already discussed that relate the implosion of the natal household rather than its invasion and consequent weakening by rival patriarchs—the subject of the paired-sister stories. Either as objects or subjects of internally focused sororal desire, sisters contribute to the vulnerability of their natal households in the incest narratives. Tamar's story most resembles the story of wife-sister Sarah. In these stories, sororal agency and solidarity are not factors, as they were in the story of Lot's daughters. Tamar, like Sarah, is an object of her brother's plotting and desire.

Violated by her brother, Tamar leaves Amnon's house, but she does not go silently. She puts dust on her hair, tears her robe, and runs about shouting with her hands on her head. Her response mimics gestures of mourning that convey her deep sorrow for her ruin.[27] Although an innocent victim, the defiled Tamar has lost her position as a sexually pure princess eligible for marriage. She has become a disgraced abomination.

Tamar's reaction after she is cast out of Amnon's house not only communicates her distress, it also communicates publicly what has happened to her and its consequences. By tearing her robe, Tamar symbolically enacts the damage done to the king's house and forebodes the impending war with Absalom in which David's house will be ripped in two. Most significantly, Tamar's reaction indicts Amnon and incites Absalom. Her public gestures of mourning are an act of self-preservation. People know where she has been and with whom she has been. As Frymer-Kensky observes, people easily can read her reaction and figure out what has happened to her.[28] Fearing she may be accused later of not being a virgin, Tamar rips her rope and cries out. Frymer-Kensky comments on the specific use of the verb זעק, to cry out, and suggests that it has a special connotation. In the Bible, one who cries out expects to be heard and vindicated.[29] In this way, Tamar lets everyone know who took her virginity—especially Absalom.

Absalom hears his sister's cries and responds. He understands precisely what has happened to her and takes her into his home.

> Her brother Absalom said to her: "Has Aminon your brother been with you? Now, my sister, be quiet. He is your brother. Pay no attention to this matter." Tamar lived, a desolation, within the house of her brother Absalom. (2 Sam 13:20)

The pointed use of the familial terms in this passage pits the brothers against each other and distinguishes between the bad brother who raped his sister and the good brother who protects her. Absalom, the good brother, orders Tamar to be quiet [החרישי] and not to think about the matter.

His command is another echo of Dinah's story in Genesis 34 in which Jacob hears what has happened to Dinah and is silent [החרש] until his sons return. As I observe in my introduction, Jacob's silence could indicate an acceptance of events and a willingness to work with them. As a father, Jacob can negotiate with Shechem and his father Hamor to salvage the situation and to transform an improper marriage, or even a rape, into a proper one. Alternatively, Jacob's silence could be construed as patience as he waits for his sons to return home and avenge their sister's honor. Initially, it is difficult to discern whether Absalom commands acceptance or patience from Tamar. Does he ask her to accept her position as a ruined woman, or does he ask her to be patient until her ruin can be avenged?

Either way, Tamar's silence marks the end of *her* narrative. The woman who verbally fought her rapist both before and after the rape, the woman whose cries indicted one brother and incited another, never speaks again. She becomes a desolation, a שממה, within her brother's house. Tamar is not described as desolate; she becomes a desolation. Rarely in the Bible is the root שמם used to describe a person. Typically, the prophets use this root to describe a place that God devastates, as Jer 4:25-27 illustrates:

> I look: there is no human,
> All the birds of the sky have fled.
> I look: the farm land is desert,
> And all its towns are in ruin—
> Because of YHWH,
> Because of His blazing anger.
> For thus says YHWH:
> The whole land shall be a desolation [שממה].
> But I will not make an end of it.

Like the contaminated land of Israel, Tamar has become a desolate, barren site. Yet, unlike Israel in this passage, Tamar receives no hope of a brighter future. As she was at the beginning of the narrative, Tamar remains caught between two brothers. Violated by one brother and effectively imprisoned by the other, Tamar must live a compromised life. She can never marry nor have children. She can never become a mother in her husband's house. Instead, like dangerous sister Michal, Tamar is condemned to represent her father's troubled house and embody its distress.

Witnessing Tamar's desolation, David reacts:

> When King David heard these things, he grew angry. Absalom did not speak to Amnon either for evil or for good. Absalom hated Amnon because he degraded Tamar his sister. (2 Sam 13:21-22)

David's reaction to Tamar's ruin is vague when compared with Absalom's. Although David is angry, it is unclear at whom. He may be angry at Absalom for taking Tamar into his home and for denying any possible further negotiation with Amnon. In contrast to his father, Absalom's reaction is clear and direct. Just as Amnon hates Tamar, Absalom hates [שנא] Amnon for what he did to his sister. Unlike Dinah's brothers who condemn Shechem for violating a *daughter* of Jacob in Gen 34:7, Absalom makes clear that Amnon violated a sister. As a brother, Absalom does not have the capacity to accept his sister's defilement like a father can accept his daughter's. Whereas a father can negotiate a legitimate marriage for his daughter, a brother must avenge his violated sister.

Absalom convinces David to allow all the princes to go sheep-shearing with him. He asks specifically for Amnon and pressures David until he agrees. His initial reluctance to include Amnon among the princes indicates that David senses danger. But once again, he acquiesces to a son's request and sends [וישלח] Amnon with Absalom. David may feel powerless to appease Amnon and accepts the inevitable act of vengeance. Absalom commands his servants to give Amnon plenty of wine and then to kill him. Amnon dies with a heart happy from wine [כטוב לב-אמנון ביין]. Mention of Amnon's heart brings his story full circle and recalls his request for heart cakes that initially brought Tamar to him. In the end, appetite and vengeance kill Amnon.

Fully aware of what he has done, Absalom runs away and lives in exile while David mourns for Amnon. Upon his return, Absalom claims kingship for himself. He causes civil war within the house of David and sends King David into exile. The rape of Tamar functions as the narrative's catalyst for his treason. A dangerous, sexualized sister pits brother against brother and enables a son to rise up against his father. David's house, like Abraham's house, is not impervious to the dangerous sister. A sister can tear apart the Bible's most steadfast home [בית נאמן] and send its patriarch into exile. Ultimately, David and his household survive and thrive, but all those involved in the incestuous triangle do not. Amnon and Absalom die violent deaths while ruined Tamar suffers a kind of living death in her brother's house.

After she is brought into Absalom's house, Tamar the dangerous sister is never seen or heard from again. Yet her namesake lives on. In one of the most psychologically suggestive narrative details in the Bible, Absalom names his daughter Tamar in 2 Sam 14:27.[30] Perhaps the sister's life is redeemed through the birth of this daughter, and Tamar is granted a second life through her namesake niece. Yet by naming his daughter Tamar, Absalom further embeds Tamar in his home—into the next generation—and implies that she can never escape. Also, a brother who names his daughter after his sister—especially one who is the victim of brother-sister incest—is itself suggestive of incestuous desire and symbolically perpetuates the legacy of incest. By naming his daughter Tamar, Absalom demonstrates that incestuous unions do not advance a family forward. They do not introduce new blood (with new names) into a family and produce viable heirs. As we learned from Lot's example, children born from incest are off limits. Their births indicate the end of their family's line and the death of their households within Israel. Given this, Tamar's birth may be an omen that Absalom and his household are similarly doomed.

Like the other incest narratives, Tamar's story warns of the perils of incest and argues for a strict adherence to assuming one role within the family—whether father, husband, brother, wife, or sister—and for eradicating desires that could confuse these roles. These stories demonstrate that the patriarchal family is strongest when the boundaries that define the roles within the family are maintained. The particular focus on the sister in the incest narratives conveys the anxieties sisters induce both as objects and subjects of incestuous desire. As sexualized sisters, incestuous sisters destabilize their households, whether they initiate incest like Lot's daughters, are victims of incest like Tamar, or even are suggestive of incest like Sarah.

Although destabilizing figures, incestuous sisters, like paired sisters, serve the central concerns of the Bible and advance its narrative. They remove rival households such as Lot's, strengthen designated households like Abraham's, and weaken cursed households like David's. Despite the purposes they serve, incestuous sisters are not rewarded. Like paired sisters, they embody the fate of the vulnerable patriarchs and their households. Lot's daughters embody Lot's outsider status by gestating Israel's enemies. Sister Sarah embodies the vulnerability of Abraham's household while traveling in foreign territory. Perhaps more than any other sister, Tamar embodies the vulnerability and distress of her father's house. She is the fulfillment of Nathan's dire prophecy that calamity will arise from within David's house. Sister Tamar lives out the consequences of her father's crimes and tears his house apart.

Notes

1. Like the wife-sister narratives, Esther Fuchs considers the story of David and Bathsheba to conform to the adultery type-scene. See Fuchs, *Sexual Politics in the Biblical Narrative: Reading the Hebrew Bible as a Woman* (Sheffield: Sheffield Academic, 2003), 119.

2. Fuchs writes: "For both the rape laws and the narratives are based on the assumption that the real victim is the raped woman's father or brother." See ibid., 204.

3. See ibid., 213.

4. See ibid., 214.

5. Fuchs concludes: "The narrative focus shifts from sister to brother. The disappearance of the sister enables the brother to replace her as the primary victim of the injustice committed by the 'bad' brother. The disappearance of the sister also makes for a 'cleaner' transition to the brother(s)—the real hero(es) of both narratives. In order for the brother to effectively replace his sister as the wronged party, the latter must disappear as unobtrusively as possible." See ibid., 217.

6. Trible writes: "Between these two males stands the female who relates to each of them and also has her own identity. Sister to Absalom and object of desire to Amnon, this beautiful woman is Tamar. The circular arrangement of the verse centers upon her. . . . Two males surround a female." See Phyllis Trible, *Texts of Terror: Literary-Feminist Readings of Biblical Narratives* (Philadelphia: Fortress Press, 1984), 38.

7. The connection is even more pronounced in the slight alteration to Amnon's name—Aminon—found in verse 20.

8. Since Tamar and Judah's child is the progenitor of the Davidic line, both Tamars are connected to David's house. In significant ways, incest shapes the house of David.

9. William H. Propp suggests that 2 Samuel 13 raises the question whether marriage to one's half-sibling was considered incestuous and therefore forbidden. Despite the legal prohibitions, the narrative offers an ambiguous answer. See William H. Propp, "Kinship in 2 Samuel 13," *CBQ* 55 (1993): 43. Whereas Tamar seems open to the idea of marriage to a half-sibling, Absalom appears opposed. Amnon, Propp notes, has a more ambiguous perspective. See ibid., 46.

10. Propp draws a parallel between Amnon and Tamar and Abraham and Sarah and suggests that both couples are concerned with the purity of their line. See ibid., 44.

11. Frymer-Kensky writes: "Perhaps, we could speculate, the princesses of the realm were instructed in the creation of healing foods. This speculation accords with the well-known historical connection of women with healing. . . . If Tamar was instructed in medicinal herbs and rituals, then Amnon's request for her would seem legitimate, and David might be expected to comply without becoming suspicious or alarmed." See Tikva Frymer-Kensky, *Reading the Women of the Bible: A New Interpretation of Their Stories* (New York: Schocken, 2002), 158.

12. See ibid., 158.

13. In his commentary, Hans Wilhelm Hertzberg dismisses the notion that the cakes were heart shaped and suggests that they mean "what the heart desires." See Hertzberg, *I & II Samuel*, trans. J. S. Bowden (Philadelphia: Westminster, 1964), 323. Trible makes a similar observation. See Trible, *Texts of Terror*, 42.

14. 2 Sam 11:1.

15. 2 Sam 11:3-4.

16. 2 Sam 11:6.

17. 2 Sam 11:14.

18. See Deut 22:25.

19. Robert Alter similarly notes: "The dialogue in the story of Amnon and Tamar (2 Samuel 13) looks like a conscious allusion to the technique used in the episode of Joseph and Potiphar's wife. Amnon addresses to his half-sister exactly the same words with which Potiphar's wife accosts Joseph—'lie with me'—adding to them only one word, the thematically loaded 'sister' (2 Sam. 13.11)." See Alter, *The Art of Biblical Narrative* (New York: Basic, 1981), 73.

20. Although Lot is not related to the Sodomites, I suggest that his address indicates a desire to be included among them.

21. Phyllis Trible comments on the repeated use of the verb "שנא" in 2 Sam 13:15: "In using the word desire (*'hb*) to describe Amnon's feelings for Tamar (13:1,4), this line shows that all along the desire was lust, not love. Having gratified itself, lust deepens into hatred." See Trible, *Texts of Terror*, 47.

22. Bruce Wells considers the legal implications of the root שנא. See Wells, "Sex, Lies, and Virginal Rape: The Slandered Bride and False Accusation in Deuteronomy," *JBL* 124, no. 1 (2005): 57.

23. Lot begs the Sodomites not to behave badly [תרעו].

24. The root, שלח, to send, is another marker of divorce. When divorcing, a husband sends his wife from his home. See Deut 24:1-2.

25. The כתנת פסים appears only here and in the Joseph narrative in Genesis 37. Its style remains a mystery. The LXX is responsible for the perception of it as a coat of many colors by translating it as "an embroidered coat."

26. As I will mention in the story of Jephthah's daughter, virginity may be an assumption of maidenhood, but it is not a given. A maiden is an unmarried, adolescent girl who may or may not be a virgin.

27. Ezek 27:30-32 describes these as gestures of lament. David behaves similarly when he mourns Amnon's death in 2 Sam 13:31.

28. See Frymer-Kensky, *Reading the Women*, 165–66.

29. Ibid., 166.

30. Like sister Tamar daughter Tamar is described as beautiful. Jack Sasson suggests that daughter Tamar is a "vestigial" remnant of an alternate tale in which Amnon rapes Absalom's daughter. See Jack M. Sasson, "Absalom's Daughter: An Essay in Vestige Historiography," in *The Land That I Will Show You: Essays on the History and Archaeology of the Ancient Near East in Honour of J. Maxwell Miller*, ed. J. Andrew Dearman and M. Patrick Graham (Sheffield: Sheffield Academic, 2001), 189–90.

PART III

Sisterhoods

7

The Daughters of Adam, Moab, the Land, and Israel

In the previous parts, I identified a biblical sister story that is centered upon the vulnerable patriarchal home and that reflects the Bible's implicit gender ideology. Although there are ideal sisters like Rebecca and Miriam, who support their natal households, most of the Bible's sisters are dangerous. Dangerous sisters threaten their households by conspiring together, asserting agency or desire, or eliciting desire in others. They challenge patriarchal authority and societal norms like incest taboos that protect the patriarchal family. My analysis not only reveals the prominence of dangerous sisters, it reveals the important narrative role they play in weakening rival patriarchs, thereby enabling the Bible to focus on its designated family. My analysis also shows how dangerous sisters help preserve the Bible's patriarchal values by encouraging proper behavior. As destabilizing figures, dangerous sisters contribute to and reflect the vulnerability of their natal households. To protect the ideology that supports the patriarchal household, dangerous-sister stories warn women to control their desires, to remain within their proper familial roles, and not to defy patriarchal authority. They also warn men to be aware of dangerous sisters who can wreak havoc within even the most secure households.

I now broaden my focus and consider the Bible's sisterhoods—women's networks that are not necessarily defined by immediate kinship ties. In this part, I examine narratives that include groups of women that function as cohesive units. My goal is to understand how the Bible represents sisterhoods, and to consider how sisterhoods function within their narratives as well as within the Bible at large. As we will see, sisterhoods raise many of the same anxieties that actual sisters raise, and their narratives share common themes and concerns with the sister stories in the Bible. Yet, because sisterhoods extend beyond the family, sisterhood narratives cast wider nets than the sister stories. Their focus is more broadly on society and not on a particular family as in the sister stories. Whereas ideal sisters support their natal households in their narratives, ideal sisterhoods support Israelite society. Dangerous sisterhoods are destabilizing figures that threaten Israelite society. Marriage is a central concern of the sisterhood narratives as it is of the sister stories. Ideal sisterhoods ensure appropriate marriages that strengthen patriarchal Israelite society, whereas dangerous sisterhoods threaten those structures.

Given the prominence of dangerous sisters in the Bible, it is not surprising that dangerous sisterhoods appear frequently in the Bible, and I begin this chapter with their stories. Like the dangerous-sister stories, these narratives function as cautionary tales designed to encourage proper behavior and support patriarchal norms. They demonstrate the dangers of sororal solidarity and improper alliances though on a much broader scale than sister stories do. As we will see, dangerous sisterhoods weaken Israelite society and threaten its defining relationship with God.

More surprising, given the prominence of dangerous sisters, are the ideal sisterhoods that play significant roles within their narratives and within the Bible at large. In the next chapter, I examine the daughters of Jerusalem, an ideal sisterhood that appears in the Song of Songs. In the final chapter, I consider the ideal sisterhood formed between Ruth and Naomi—perhaps the Bible's most significant relationship—in the book of Ruth. Ruth and Naomi's ideal sisterhood, I argue, redeems dangerous sisters and sisterhoods and offers an essential paradigm of human relationship. My conclusion considers the theological implications of Ruth and Naomi's sisterhood and why sisterhoods may, in general, fare better than sisters in the Bible.

The groups of women who appear throughout the Bible are identified most often as daughters. In Gen 6:1-4, divine sons are attracted to בנות האדם, human daughters. In Gen 34:1, Dinah leaves home to see the daughters of the land, בנות הארץ. Moabite daughters, בנות מואב, seduce the Israelites in Num 25:1-5, and Jephthah's daughter spends her last two months alive among the daughters of Israel, בנות ישראל.

The daughters of Jerusalem, בנות ירושלם, appear throughout the Song of Songs. These daughters form sisterhoods—social networks of women that are not necessarily defined by immediate kinship ties. Living in small villages that consisted of several family compounds, it is likely that these young women were in fact distantly related to each other and comprised a clan.[1]

The frequent mention of these sisterhoods indicates that women were not confined to their individual households and natal families, but were part of larger cohorts in ancient Israel. Although there are only textual traces of them left in the Bible, based on epigraphic, archaeological, and ethnographic evidence, scholars, such as Carol Meyers, posit the existence of informal networks among Israelite women.[2] Despite the support for their existence, women's networks, as Aubrey Baadsgaard observes, "are rarely noted in public discourse or in historical writing, but nevertheless they provide critical social linkages among women."[3]

Meyers contends that gender was a determinative feature of life in ancient Israel. Although Israelite society depended on the labor of both men and women, gender defined the nature of their labor.[4] Samuel's grim prediction of what a king would require from Israel's sons and daughters illustrates how gender determines work:

> He said: This will be the practice of the king who will rule over you. He will take your sons and appoint them as his charioteers and horsemen, and they will run before his chariot. He will appoint them as his chiefs of thousands and of fifties; to plow his fields, reap his harvest, and make weapons and equipment for his chariots. He will take your daughters to be spice-mixers, cooks, and bakers. (1 Sam 8:12-13)

According to this text, a king would appoint Israel's sons as horsemen (making them plow and reap) and as soldiers (forcing them to construct weapons).

From this passage we learn that Israel's daughters performed tasks such as cooking and baking. Like women throughout the ancient world, Israelite women prepared the food and made the clothing for their households. The remains of communal ovens, grinders, and kneading troughs convince archaeologists like Jennie R. Ebeling that women performed these tasks communally. Ovens discovered outside of homes were larger and were often found alongside other food processing equipment, suggesting to Ebeling "that women worked on various household tasks in groups."[5] The skill, strength, and stamina required to do these household tasks demanded that women work in groups. Meyers notes the many steps involved in processing grain, which had to be soaked, milled, ground, and mixed before it could be set to rise. Meyers estimates that these steps would take at least two or more hours a day of a woman's time.[6] Indeed, the curse of Lev 26:26 that ten women would bake bread in one oven may have been the reality. In truth, Israelite women may have experienced this more as a blessing than as a curse.

Scholars consider the positive impact women's networks had for Israelite women and society. Cooperative labor could foster supportive relationships among the women who would share expertise and form alliances. Ebeling envisions Israel's women sharing wisdom and gossiping as they grind grain.[7] Women's networks potentially validated women's experience and expertise by providing a social space for women to appreciate and excel at their labor. Women, as Meyers suggests, would teach other women the technically complex skills required for cooking, producing cloth, or making baskets and ceramics.[8] Women's networks also could empower women by proving them essential to communal life and enabling them to exercise power within these networks—at least over other women. Given the technical expertise required to do the work that women regularly did, Meyers assumes there was a hierarchy within women's networks in which certain women enjoyed status and privilege over other women.[9]

Along with the social benefits afforded individual members, women's networks performed essential tasks that contributed to the stability of individual households, as well as to the society at large. Although not formally documented, Meyers asserts that Israelite women's networks established important alliances within and between villages and may have played a significant role in negotiating marriages.[10] They also may have engaged in the ritual activities of the community, particularly those related to child birth and mourning, as certain biblical texts suggest. For example, at the end of the book of Ruth, a network of female neighbors blesses and names Ruth's newborn son. The prophet Ezekiel condemns a network of female prophets that engages in activities that resemble birth rituals.[11] The specific mention of female mourners throughout the Bible suggests that there were formal, perhaps professional, networks of female mourners in ancient Israel.[12] In Jer 9:16-19, God summons the female lamenters to mourn over Zion's destruction. Jeremiah 49:3 commands the daughters of Rabbah, בנות רבה, to mourn over Ammon. Ezekiel 32:16 commands the daughters of the nations, בנות הגוים, to lament over Egypt. In 2 Sam 1:24, David commands the daughters of Israel, בנות ישראל to mourn for King Saul.

What is good for the individual woman and even good for Israelite society may not be considered good in the context of the Bible, which is invested in patriarchal authority. Although sisterhoods, defined by sororal solidarity, are essential for community life, they potentially challenge patriarchal authority. Ezekiel 16:45 relates the devastating effect of sororal solidarity when the women of Israel and Judah band together to defy their husbands and sons. As we will see, within the context of women's networks, male authority, even men themselves, could be dispensable. For Beverly Bow, this explains the Bible's discomfort with women's networks. Examining many of the same narratives I examine, Bow concludes that the Bible negatively depicts the interpersonal relationship among women to convey the "patriarchal message" that "women cannot or should not band together."[13] Rivalry among women serves the Bible's patriarchal interests and proves that Israelite society is better off when women do not cooperate with one another. Women who do cooperate in the Bible often do so to pursue evil purposes. From this, Bow draws the conclusion that "sisterhood is antithetical to patriarchy" and is "dangerous."[14]

Much of my study thus far supports Bow. I agree that sororal solidarity can threaten the home and, as we see in the sisterhood narratives, society. Yet, we also see that the sisterhood narratives present a more complicated picture of the interpersonal relationship among women than the sister narratives. Perhaps because of the crucial role women's networks played, the Bible also depicts significant ideal sisterhoods that support Israelite society and its patriarchal ideology. These ideal sisterhoods, if not redemptive, are stabilizing forces in their narrative context. Before turning to these ideal sisterhoods however, I consider four dangerous sisterhoods whose brief appearances have devastating narrative consequences.

DAUGHTERS OF HUMANITY

Although there are common elements between the Bible's sisterhood and its sister stories, one thing is clear: the stakes are higher with sisterhoods than they are with individual sisters. A dangerous sister threatens a household, but a dangerous sisterhood threatens society. This is evident in the Bible's first sisterhood story in Gen 6:1-4:

> When humanity began to increase upon the face of the earth, daughters were born to them. The divine sons saw the daughters of humanity, for they were beautiful and they took them as wives, any of them that they chose. YHWH said: "My spirit shall not abide in them forever for they are also flesh. Their lifetime will be 120 years." The Nephilim were on the earth in those days, and even after that, when the divine sons entered the daughters of humanity for whom they bore children. They were the heroes who long ago were men of renown.

Included among the primordial stories of Genesis 1–11, this story has the broadest focus of the sisterhood narratives and concerns itself with mortality and the setting of the human life span.[15] It is also concerned with appropriate marriage. The union between the divine sons and the daughters of humanity is arguably the Bible's most pronounced example of exogamous marriage. It is clear that from God's perspective, this is not a good thing.

Given the challenges the existence of these divine sons pose to biblical monotheism—suggesting that God cohabits with other divine beings who may be God's children—much attention has been paid to identifying these beings. Little attention, in comparison, has been paid to the daughters of humanity, who are oddly singled out in the first verse.[16] Although one assumes that human procreation resulted in both sons and daughters, only daughters are mentioned as a focus of attention and, as we will see, as an object of concern. They form a large sisterhood with a shared quality—they are attractive. The word used to describe the daughters is טבת. Carol M. Kaminski takes issue with translating the word as it often is as "beautiful" or "attractive." Her lexical study supports understanding טוב when used to describe people as denoting "an ethical or moral quality," and not physical beauty.[17] Despite Kaminski's analysis, I contend that attractive remains a fair translation. Whether because they are morally good or physically beautiful, the divine sons clearly are attracted to them and take them as wives.

The divine sons' aggressive behavior in Genesis 6 recalls Eve's behavior in Genesis 3, linking these narratives. Just as Eve sees the forbidden fruit is good [ותרא האשה כי טוב] (Gen 3:6) and takes it [ותקח], the divine sons see that the daughters are good and take them[18] as wives [ויראו בני-האלהים את-בנות האדם כי טובת הנה ויקחו להם נשים]. Like Eve, the divine sons transgress boundaries and take what is not rightfully theirs.[19] The linguistic similarities connecting these passages suggest that Genesis 6 continues Adam and Eve's troubled story and that the daughters of humanity bear the burden of their ancestors' legacy. God punishes Adam for passively obeying Eve. Admonished Eve must accept her husband's dominion. In Genesis 6, the daughters' passivity may reflect Adam's fatal flaw or Eve's punishment.

Either way, the daughters live out the consequences of Adam and Eve's indiscretions and, like dangerous sisters Michal and Tamar, reflect their ancestral parents' misfortunes and troubled households. A similar dynamic is evident in the Cain and Abel brother story that precedes this sisterhood story. Before Cain kills his brother Abel, God warns him that sin crouches at his door and desires him (Gen 4:7). God tells Cain that he has the ability to resist and overpower sin [ואליך תשוקתו ואתה תמשל-בו]. God's warning evokes Eve's punishment (Gen 3:16) of subservience [ואל-אישך תשוקתך והוא ימשל-בך], suggesting that brother Cain can reverse his mother's fate if he demonstrates restraint. The sisterhood is not granted the same opportunity. The daughters of humanity must submit to the divine sons' desires and to their fate.

Although passive, the daughters of humanity function as destabilizing figures in their narratives. Like Tamar, they are dangerous objects of desire though, as a sisterhood, they cast a wider shadow. God fears that unions between divine and human beings will mix the divine spirit with human flesh to create a dangerous hybrid that poses an immediate threat to God. As we know from God's fear that Adam and Eve will eat from the tree of life expressed in Gen 3:22, God does not want human beings to become too God-like. Both Gen 3:22 and 6:3 suggest that God fears human immortality.

Hoping to deter the divine sons so that they would not be attracted to human daughters and produce immortal offspring, God restricts the human life span to 120 years. But the divine sons are undeterred. They remain attracted to the human daughters and continue to mate with them. Although not immortal, their progeny are the dreaded Nephilim—men renowned for uncommon strength and size whom the Israelites meet and must defeat when they conquer the land.[20] Since imposing life limits proved ineffective, God resorts to more dramatic means to prevent divine-human breeding. God seeks to wipe out the dangerous sisterhood and the world it inhabits.

When viewed as an independent narrative, Gen 6:1-4 appears to be a non sequitur among the primordial stories. Closer examination reveals it is anchored firmly within its narrative context. Not only is the story of the daughters of humanity linked to Adam and Eve's story as I mentioned above, it is also deeply connected to the story that follows—the story of Noah and the flood.[21] The juxtaposition of these two narratives suggests that the story of the daughters of humanity serves as an introduction to the Bible's flood narrative and, in my reading, provides a catalyst for the devastation: a dangerous sisterhood. In Gen 6:5-7, God witnesses great, but unspecified human evil [וירא יהוה כי רבה רעת האדם], regrets having created humanity, and decides to wipe them off the face of the earth. Key words like אדם, רב,ראה,על פני האדם, link Gen 6:1-4 with the flood narrative and establish a shared focus on humanity, particularly its daughters, as a dangerous variable.

Although the divine sons are the sexual aggressors who transgress boundaries, God does not physically restrict them in Gen 6:1-4. Instead, God targets human beings and shortens their life span. In the immediate context of Gen 6:1-4, humanity refers specifically to the *daughters* of humanity. As I noted above, there is no mention of the *sons* of humanity. Only the daughters attract divine attention. God continues to target human beings—and, I argue, specifically the daughters of humanity who remain a cause for God's concern—at the start of the flood narrative. The great *human* evil [רבה רעת האדם] that God sees in Gen 6:5 recalls the population increase [האדם לרב]

in Gen 6:1 that results in the birth of the daughters of humanity. Evil in this context may not refer to immoral acts committed by humanity. Rather, it may refer to the calamity or misfortune that is humanity—meaning specifically the sisterhood. The daughters of humanity are the רעה, the calamity, that God sees, not unlike Tamar was David's calamity [רעה] as the fulfillment of Nathan's prophecy in 2 Sam 12:11.

Clearly, this sisterhood troubles God. As Kaminski observes, God remains focused on the daughters of humanity and directly overturns the divine sons' assessment of them. Although the divine sons consider them to be good [כי טבת הנה], God perceives them to be a threat [רבה רעת האדם] and wants them erased from the world.[22] God's promise in Gen 6:7 to wipe humanity off the face of the earth [אמחה את אדם...מעל פני האדמה] specifically echoes the birth announcement of the daughters of humanity in Genesis 6:1 [ויהי כי-החל האדם לרב על-פני האדמה ובנות ילדו להם]. As the flood narrative reveals, God is willing to throw the baby out with the bath water. By eradicating life off the face of the earth, God removes this dangerous sisterhood.

Not only does the flood remove the dangerous sisterhood, it also undoes the damage caused by them. As an enticing sisterhood, the daughters lure divine beings and provide an undesirable repository for the divine spirit. In Gen 6:3, God states clearly that God does not want the divine spirit [רוחי] residing in human flesh [בשר]. In its immediate literary context, human flesh means female flesh, referring to the daughters of humanity. After copulating with the divine sons, the daughters' bodies house the divine spirit. God again refers to the commingling of flesh and spirit when God announces plans to flood the world in Gen 6:17: "I am bringing a flood of water upon the earth to destroy all flesh [בשר] that has within it living spirit [רוח חיים] from under the heavens, all upon the earth will die." When viewed in the context of Gen 6:1-4, the flood comes specifically to destroy the daughters of humanity as the flesh that houses the divine spirit. God's success is apparent at the end of the flood when all flesh that once contained spirit [כל אשר נשמת רוח חיים באפיו] is dead,[23] and the divine spirit is released [24] to remove the floodwaters from the earth [ויעבר אלהים רוח על-הארץ]. Read together, Gen 6:1-4 and the flood narrative argue for maintaining categorical distinctions by marrying within one's kind.[25] The objective of these narratives is not unlike the objective of the incest narratives though with a distinctly broader focus. Whereas the incest narratives protect the categories and boundaries within a family, this sisterhood narrative protects the categories and boundaries within society. Divine sons should not marry human daughters. Ultimately, spirit triumphs over flesh, and the daughters of humanity perish in the flood. With this dangerous sisterhood removed, order is restored to the world.

DAUGHTERS OF MOAB

Numbers 25:1-5 is another story about an enticing and dangerous sisterhood that warns against exogamous marriage:

> When Israel dwelled in Shittim, the people began to behave promiscuously with the daughters of Moab. They invited the people to the sacrifices of their gods, and the people ate and bowed before their gods. Israel cleaved to Baal of Peor, and YHWH was angry with Israel. YHWH said to Moses: "Take all the heads of the people and impale them before YHWH in daylight so that YHWH's anger will abate from Israel." Moses said to the judges of Israel: "Each of you is to kill those from among his people who cling to Baal of Peor."

While wandering in the wilderness, Israel initiates a relationship with the Moabite women who respond positively.[26]

Unlike Genesis 6, this narrative does not clearly differentiate between the *daughters* of Moab and the *sons* of Israel. Instead, it uses the more inclusive term עם to describe the people and implies that all of Israel, men and women, were involved in the promiscuity. Yet only the Moabite *daughters* attract Israel's attention. Like the daughters of humanity, they form an enticing and dangerous sisterhood. What precisely Israel does with the Moabite sisterhood is unclear. Elsewhere the verb זני refers to sexual promiscuity, but it also figuratively describes religious or political betrayal.[27] In Ezekiel 16, the prophet uses the verb to indict Israel on all three counts of sexual, religious, and political betrayal. The specific mention of Moabite women in Numbers 25 suggests a sexual encounter. Yet the daughters' invitation does not mention any sexual activity. They invite [ותקראן] Israel to sacrifice, eat, and worship with them. In other words, they ask Israel to participate in the fundamental rituals of their cult.

The mention of Israel's promiscuity followed immediately by the Moabite invitation suggests that Israel began to intermarry with the Moabite women after having settled in Shittim. The events that follow, the apostasy with Baal Peor,[28] realize the specific fears of intermarriage expressed in Exod 34:15-16:

> You must not make a covenant with the inhabitants of the land for they will stray after [וזנו] their gods and sacrifice [וזבחו] to

their gods and invite you [וקרא], and you will eat [ואכלת מזבחו] their sacrifice. When you take their daughters for your sons, their daughters will stray after their gods and will cause your sons to stray after their gods.

Exodus warns against intermarriage with foreign women because it fears apostasy. Although married to Israelites, foreign women will continue to worship their gods—through sacrifice and cultic meals—and convince Israel to do the same.

Numbers 25:1-5 substantiates these fears and illustrates what happens when Israel marries foreign women: Israel participates in their cultic activities and worships their gods. Given the patrilineal structure of Israelite society, it is not surprising that women are cause for concern in both Exodus and Numbers. As Genesis 34 illustrates, intermarriage with foreign men is not an option and, therefore, not a threat. Unwilling to absorb even circumcised Hivite men into Israel and share their land and their property, Dinah's brothers kill them in revenge for Dinah's violation. But since inheritance passes through the male line, they have no problem taking Hivite wives for plunder.[29]

The incident at Shittim shows Israel's willingness to marry foreign women. It also shows what is at stake if they do. Marriage to the Moabite women threatens Israel's defining relationship with God. According to Deut 11:22, Israel should cling to God, ולדבקה-בו. Instead, it cleaves, ויצמד, to Baal Peor. To protect God's relationship with Israel, God rages against Israel and demands the deaths of those who showed allegiance to Baal Peor. God commands Moses to impale Israel's leaders. Those who witness the impalement should learn not to marry foreign women or to worship foreign gods.[30]

With the culprits killed and God's point made, the story should be over. Israel should understand the cost and consequences of exogamous marriage. Yet, just as the union between the divine sons and the daughters of humanity had a devastating aftermath, so, too, does this story. Numbers 25:1-5 precedes the gruesome story in Num 25:6-18 of the priest Phineas stabbing Zimri and Cozbi to death. Although the narrative narrows and shifts its focus from the Moabite sisterhood to a single Midianite woman, labeled a sister in verse 18, these stories are literarily linked. The deaths of Zimri and Cozbi end a plague that afflicted Israel after its apostasy with Baal Peor.[31] Numbers 25:18 even suggests that it was the Midianites and not the Moabites who are responsible for Israel's apostasy.[32]

What really connects these narratives is the theme of intermarriage. Zimri and Cozbi's story further refines the issue of intermarriage by introducing a different and perhaps less offensive marriage partner (after all, Moses marries the daughter of a Midianite priest in Exod 2:21) and by raising the issue of personal status. Cozbi is no commoner. She is the daughter of Zur, a Midianite chieftain. Marriage to a foreign woman of her status may be a wise political move precisely for the reasons that Hamor argues in Genesis 34. Intermarriage to dignitaries could bring security and financial benefits to Israel.

Phineas's brutal response makes it clear that this also is not a permissible marriage. The stories of the Moabite women and of Cozbi and Zimri work together to deter intermarriage and to condemn foreign women—even important ones.[33] They also illustrate how one bad situation can lead to a worse one. As Numbers 25 narrows its focus from the community to one couple, it seems to contain the threat of foreign women and apostasy. Yet the crime committed by Zimri and Cozbi is more direct and egregious than the crime committed by all of Israel. Zimri brings Cozbi to the tabernacle and has sex with her, as the text explicitly states, before Moses and the community and as the text implies, before God in his tabernacle.[34]

Given its proximity to the account and its audacity, Zimri's act appears to be a direct response to the incident of Baal Peor. Zimri intentionally and publicly defies Moses' authority and God's in a blatant act of political and religious rebellion. Although the text does not reveal Zimri's personal motivation, Helena Zlotnick Sivan suggests that Zimri, ironically as a descendant of Simeon, makes a misguided stance in favor of exogamous marriage. Zlotnick reads Numbers 25 as a companion story to Genesis 34. Both stories protect the borders of Israelite society by arguing against exogamy. Both explore the dangers of intermarriage for the individual (Dinah-Shechem and Zimri-Cozbi) and for the community (Israelite-Shechemite and Israelite-Moabite/Midianite).[35] In both stories, sister and sisterhood are destabilizing figures.

Just as violence restores order in Genesis 34 and in the flood narrative, violence restores order in Numbers 25. Reenacting the impalement of Israel's leaders, Phineas stabs Zimri and Cozbi to death.[36] As a reward for his zealotry, God grants Phineas and his descendents the covenant of fellowship, בריתי שלום, and the covenant of the eternal priesthood, ברית כהנת עולם. These restorative covenants link Numbers 25 directly to the flood narrative. After the flood, God establishes his covenant, בריתי, an eternal covenant, ברית עולם, with Noah and his descendents. Numbers 25 and the flood narrative share a narrative arc. Each begins with a dangerous sisterhood that destabilizes its world through intermarriage, purges this danger through violence, and closes by establishing a covenant with God. In both narratives, God establishes order by removing the offending and destabilizing sisterhoods. Numbers 25 proves to be an even more direct and pervasive assault on sisterhood than the flood narrative. Sword and plague remove the dangerous Moabite sisterhood and those associated with it from this narrative.[37] Having removed this dangerous foreign sisterhood, Numbers 25 then establishes the priestly line through the male descendants of Phineas.[38]

Israel's sisters and sisterhoods have no part in Israel's priesthood, which is passed exclusively through the male line.[39] The establishment of the priesthood at the end of this narrative serves as an added protection against dangerous sisterhoods, ensuring that Israelite sisterhoods, along with their foreign counterparts, do not threaten Israel's defining relationship with God. Through sacrifice and maintaining Israel's purity, as well as their own, the all-male priests—effectively a brotherhood—protect and sustain the relationship between God and Israel that the Moabite sisterhood threatened and to which the Israelite sisterhoods have no access. With the threat of all dangerous sisterhoods removed, Israel can cling to its God.

Daughters of the Land

Exogamy, violence, and covenant are also part of Genesis 34, which introduces another destabilizing sisterhood, the daughters of the land, בנות הארץ:

> Dinah, the daughter Leah bore for Jacob, went out to see the daughters of the land. Shechem, the son of Hamor the Hivite, chief of the land, saw her, took her, lay with her, and violated her. (Gen 34:1-2)

In the introduction, I considered Dinah to be the paradigmatic dangerous sister who threatens her natal household when she asserts her independence and leaves it. As Esther Fuchs observes, Dinah's initiative has devastating personal and familial consequences. Fuchs compares Dinah's story to the story of the concubine who, after leaving her husband's house for her father's, is gang-raped in Judges 19. For Fuchs, both stories demonstrate that "grave consequences" can happen to women who, on their own initiative, cross the threshold of their male custodian's house—whether a father or a husband.[40] In my reading, Dinah's story functions as a cautionary tale that supports patriarchal norms and authority by showing the dangers specifically wrought by the independent and sexualized sister.

Although Dinah is held solely accountable for her actions, the narrative provides her with a motive for leaving home—the enticing daughters of the land. It is Dinah's attraction to this sisterhood that initiates her victimization and transforms her into a dangerous sister. Her attraction to the daughters has serious consequences for her natal household that is made more vulnerable, as well as for all of Israel because Shechem's actions are described as an abomination in Israel [כי-נבלה עשה בישראל]. Genesis 34 is about dangerous sisters and dangerous sisterhoods. Read as a sister story, Genesis 34 is about Dinah's vulnerable natal house—the house of Jacob. Read as a sisterhood story, the stakes become higher. Genesis 34 is about protecting all of Israel's purity. Like Genesis 6 and Numbers 25, Genesis 34 argues for maintaining categorical distinctions by marrying within one's kind. In all three sisterhood narratives, dangerous sisterhoods function as seductive catalysts for violence.

Like the "daughters of humanity," the "daughters of the land" is a broad and vague term that appears in a previous chapter in Genesis. In Gen 27:46, Rebecca refers to the nubile Canaanite women whom she does not want Jacob to marry as "the daughters of the land." Fear of intermarriage with these daughters convinces Isaac to send Jacob to Rebecca's natal household to find an appropriate bride. In light of this, it makes sense that the daughters of the land in Genesis 34 are Canaanite young women. More specifically, given the narrative context, they could be young Hivite women, Shechem's clanswomen.

Although unexpressed, Dinah's motives for visiting these women may be social or political. Living with twelve brothers, she may seek female companionship for herself.[41] She also may be reaching out to the local women on behalf of her family and, more specifically, on behalf of her brothers. As Meyers observes, women's networks create valuable social alliances that strengthen communities by establishing good relations among them. Women's networks make good neighbors, and good neighbors often lead to good marriages.[42] By going out to see the daughters of the land, Dinah could function as an ambassador of her community, who actively seeks to form alliances with her neighbors—perhaps even marital alliances.

Her strategy may reflect her father's overall orientation toward his Canaanite neighbors[43] and, possibly, his openness to intermarriage. As I note in my introduction, Jacob's silence in response to Shechem's violation of Dinah indicates Jacob's willingness to negotiate marriage with the Canaanites. He waits for his sons to return from the field in order to do so. My understanding of Jacob's silence as an openness to intermarriage contrasts with Fuchs who argues that Jacob's silence conveys immediate, but not lasting restraint. Jacob controls his anger until his sons return from the field, at which point he channels his anger through them.[44] I contend that the way the events unfold in the narrative does not support Fuchs's reading. Later in the narrative, Shechem formally asks Jacob and his sons for Dinah's hand in marriage (Gen 34:11-12). Only Jacob's sons respond, במרמה, deceptively, (Gen 34:13). By not taking part in his sons' duplicitous negotiations, Jacob again indicates his willingness to negotiate honestly with Shechem and Hamor.

At the close of the narrative, Jacob's angry response to his sons' murderous rampage reveals how little he wants to upset his neighbors. Understanding the tenuous nature of his relationship with his neighbors and the vulnerability of his household, Jacob confronts Simeon and Levi, saying: "You have caused me trouble and made me stink among the inhabitants of the land, among the Canaanites and the Perizites" (Gen 34:30). Clearly, Jacob hopes to live peacefully among the Canaanites. Dinah's marriage to Shechem could have helped ensure this. Shechem and Hamor acknowledge this when they report to their clansmen in verse 21 that Jacob and his sons are peaceful men [האנשים האלה שלמים] since they have agreed to marriage with the Hivites. Wanting peace with his neighbors, Jacob appears open to intermarriage—a perspective his sons, and the narrative as a whole, do not share.

Jacob's concern for the inhabitants of the land, ישב הארץ, in his reprimand to his sons evokes the daughters of the land at the beginning of the narrative and helps explain Dinah's intentions for going out among them. Like Jacob, Dinah wants to establish positive ties with her neighbors. I contend that she seeks to do so through marriage. Just as the divine sons in Gen 6:2 see [ויראו] and then take the daughters of humanity in marriage, Dinah goes out to see [לראות] if the daughters of the land are worth taking in marriage. Tragically, the sister who sees is herself seen [וירא אתה שכם] and taken—first by Shechem, then by her brothers [ויקחו את דינה מבית שכם ויצאו] (Gen 34:26). The independent sister who went out to establish ties with her neighbors is brought back violated. When viewed as a sister story, Genesis 34 is primarily about sororal agency and desire and the anxieties induced by the independent and sexualized sister. When viewed as a sisterhood story, Genesis 34 is about sororal solidarity and the fear of intermarriage.

Despite Jacob and Dinah's openness to the Canaanites, Genesis 34 argues for definitive boundaries between Israel and its neighbors and aims to prohibit intermarriage. Dinah's brothers fight to protect the purity of Israel. They refuse to negotiate exogamous marriages, even with circumcised foreigners, on behalf of their sister and on behalf of all Israelite women.[45] By giving them the last words that challenge their father, the text privileges their position over Jacob's. Their rhetorical question "Should our sister be treated like a whore?" implies that Jacob has done just that. Jacob's willingness to negotiate marriage with the Hivites was an act that dishonored their sister and potentially all Israelite women.[46] In his sons' eyes, Jacob's willingness was, like Shechem's act, an abomination in Israel.

Like Genesis 6 and Numbers 25, Genesis 34 uses a sisterhood as a dangerous catalyst to initiate the narrative's violent events. All three narratives warn Israel against being seduced by, and forming alliances with, foreign sisterhoods. Yet Genesis 34 does more than warn Israel to stay away from foreign sisterhoods. It also protects Israelite sisterhoods from foreigners—even circumcised foreigners. The fate of one Israelite sister determines the fate of all Israelite sisters. When Dinah's brothers falsely negotiate with Shechem and Hamor, they mention the exchange of daughters only (Gen 34:16). Although they say they are willing to marry their daughters to the Hivites, their actions prove otherwise. Their massacre of the Hivite men makes it clear that Israelite daughters—in other words, Israelite sisterhoods—are off-limits to foreigners.

As a sister and a sisterhood story, Genesis 34 shows how Israel's families and society are strongest when its sisters and sisterhoods are contained within Israel. It supports a patriarchal society and ideology that seeks to protect and control its women. Just as Israelite sisters should not assert agency and leave their homes, Israelite sisterhoods should not leave their society. Along with Genesis 6 and Numbers 25, Genesis 34 supports endogamous marriages. Read alongside the incest narratives of part 2 that work to maintain appropriate sexual boundaries within a family, these sisterhood stories argue for the practice of qualified endogamy. Together, these sister and sisterhood stories ensure that Israel's young women marry outside their natal households but within Israel's broader kinship networks.

DAUGHTERS OF ISRAEL

Like Dinah, Jephthah's daughter leaves home to seek the company of other young women, a sisterhood, after being condemned to death by her father in Judges 11. Although this narrative is clearly about a daughter, I focus on the sisterhood that appears at its end and argue that it functions as a dangerous sisterhood. Notably, Judges 11 does not conform to the pattern identified in the other dangerous-sisterhood stories. First and foremost, the sisterhood in Judges 11 is Israelite and therefore does not introduce the threat of exogamous marriage into the narrative. Also, in this narrative, sisterhood is not a catalyst for violence. Instead, it appears at the end of the narrative and provides consolation for the violence soon to be enacted that was already initiated by a father. As we will see, sisterhood provides refuge from the violence of the patriarchal world and provides a young woman with a legacy apart from, and at the expense of, her natal family.

At the close of this tragic narrative, Jephthah's daughter seeks consolation among her friends before returning to her father's house to fulfill his vow. In Judg 11:30-31, Jephthah the Gileadite vowed to sacrifice the first thing to greet him if he returned home victorious from battle with the Ammonites:

> Jephthah vowed a vow to YHWH and said: "If you deliver the Ammonites into my hand that which comes out of the doors of my house to greet me when I return in peace from the Ammonites will belong to YHWH. I will offer it as a burnt offering."

Jephthah's words are simultaneously vague and specific and prove devastating.[47] Although he does not specify who or what will come out to greet him [היוצא], it is likely to be his daughter and not an animal since the custom was for young women to greet warriors when they returned from battle in song and dance.[48]

Like Dinah, Jephthah's daughter crosses the threshold that marks the safety of her home and therefore, as Fuchs suggests, must be held responsible for what happens next.[49] She independently goes out [ויצאת] to greet her father and, like Dinah, pays a price. When Jephthah sees his daughter, he tears his clothes as if already in mourning and laments in Judg 11:35: "You have brought me low and have become my troubler [עכרי]!" Jephthah's accusation that his daughter causes trouble echoes Jacob who accuses his sons of causing him trouble [עכרתם] among his Canaanite neighbors.

In Gen 34:31, Jacob's sons quickly deflect blame and reply that their violent actions were justified by the events. Similarly, Jephthah's daughter is a victim of events unfolding beyond her control. Like Jacob's sons, she is unwilling to assume blame and confronts her father. In Judg 11:36, daughter implicates father by declaring that it was Jephthah's vow that determined her fate: "Father, you opened your mouth to YHWH. Do to me according to what came out from your mouth [יצא מפיך]." Her use of the verb יצא asserts that it was the vow that *came out* of Jephthah's mouth and not the daughter that *came out* of her father's house that caused the trouble.[50]

Not only does Jephthah's daughter blame Jephthah, but she goes on to make demands of him:

> She said to her father: "Let this thing be done for me. Give me two months so that I can go down upon the mountains and weep over my maidenhood, I and my friends." He said: "Go!" He allowed her two months. She and her friends went and wept over her maidenhood upon the mountains. (Judg 11:37-38)

Although ultimately she succumbs to being a victim, in this moment Jephthah's daughter takes charge of her life and fate. In this way, she simultaneously submits to, yet defies, patriarchal authority. She demands a two-month reprieve to be with her female friends [רעותיה], her sisterhood. Unsurprisingly, she does not want to be with the father who has condemned her. Instead, she wants to mourn among her friends and weep over her maidenhood [בתוליה]—for her youth that will never mature.[51] She specifically and exclusively seeks female companionship. She does not make other reasonable requests, such as for more time so that she could marry and be with a man. Since Jephthah easily grants her two months, it makes sense that he would have granted her more time, especially if he would have reaped the benefits of accruing a bride-price. But Jephthah's daughter is only concerned with her own solace and not with supporting her father's house. The two-month reprieve is for her benefit [יעשה לי הדבר הזה] and not for her father's. She shows no interest in placating him.

In fact, her last wish to mourn her maidenhood among friends may be a way of throwing salt into her father's wounds and showing him precisely what his vow means. Maidens and friends appear together in Psalm 45, which commentators suggest was the psalm recited during a royal marriage.[52] Psalm 45:14-16 describes a princess accompanied by her maidens as she approaches the king to be married:

> The princess, clad in colorful garments, is led inside to the king.
> Maidens [בתולות] follow her; her friends [רעותיה] bring her.

This psalm indicates that friends accompanied brides on their wedding day—something we also consider in the context of the Song of Songs.[53] If this was the custom, then the presence of the daughter's friends contributes to the pathos of the moment. Instead of celebrating her marriage, they mourn her death. The painful irony of their presence is aimed directly at Jephthah who sacrifices his unmarried, only child. By inviting her friends to join her as she laments on the mountains, Jephthah's daughter forces her father to witness a distorted image of the wedding she will never have.

In this way, Judges 11, like the other sisterhood narratives, *is* about marriage. However, this sisterhood story is about a marriage that does not take place. Mourning with its friend, the sisterhood participates in a macabre wedding—one without a groom or, for that matter, any male participants. This wedding marks death and not fertility. After two months with her sisterhood, Jephthah's daughter returns to be killed by her father.

Although Jephthah's daughter dies, she is granted a legacy. Judges 11:40 records a commemorative ritual observed among the daughters of Israel [בנות ישראל]: "Yearly, the daughters of Israel went to commemorate [לתנות] the daughter of Jephthah the Gileadite for four days of the year." This verse provides the Bible's most overt mention of a woman's life-cycle ritual, though its form and even its tone remain a mystery. Deriving the root תני from "to repeat, narrate," the ritual seems to consist of young women who gather yearly for four days to tell the story of Jephthah's daughter. The ritual may have marked a young woman's transition into adolescence, perhaps in preparation for marriage.[54]

Ironically, the observance of the ritual provides Jephthah's daughter with a legacy denied her father and that perhaps comes at her father's expense. Generations of sisterhoods tell the story of a daughter killed by a foolish father. Although she remains nameless, her filial epitaph is more an indictment against her father than an erasure of her own identity. She is בת-יפתח, the daughter of one who opens his mouth. Jephthah may not be his proper name at all but rather an apt nickname of the man who could not keep his mouth shut. His actual name, like his legacy, is erased by his deadly vow. Nameless as well as heirless, Jephthah essentially dies with his daughter.

Jephthah's daughter is also nameless and heirless; however, unlike her father, she has a legacy that sisterhoods preserve for generations. As Phyllis Trible observes, sisterhood grants Jephthah's daughter immortality.[55] Her legacy is her story—a story that recounts her obedience, but is also a story that demonstrates her power to construct the last months of her life. It is also a story that condemns her foolish father. In the last months of her life, sisterhood provides solace to Jephthah's daughter, honoring her short life, and ensuring that, despite her father, she goes on living in the hearts and memories of all the daughters of Israel. Sisterhood ensures that Jephthah's daughter is the hero of her own narrative.

The portrayal of sisterhood in these narratives suggests that even though women's networks existed in, and may have contributed positively to, Israelite society, the Bible is suspicious of them. Sisterhoods can provide companionship to women and help construct broader communities among families or even peoples, but they do so often at the expense of patriarchal authority. Dinah's decision to leave home to visit with the daughters of the land weakens her father's house. Jephthah's daughter's choice to spend her last months alive in the company of other women secures her legacy at the expense of her father's.

Because women's networks foster interpersonal relationships among women, sisterhoods evoke anxieties about maintaining proper boundaries between communities. Dangerous sisterhoods such as the daughters of humanity, Moab, and the land help define the borders of Israel's community. Their stories function like the incest narratives though with a broader focus. Whereas incestuous-sister stories protect a family's boundaries, dangerous-sisterhood stories protect Israelite society's boundaries. Together, the dangerous-sisterhood and the incest narratives work to support qualified endogamous marriages that fall outside the immediate patriarchal household but within Israel's broader kinship network.

Indeed, the scope is broader and the stakes are higher with sisterhoods and their stories than they were with sisters. Whereas dangerous sisters destabilize households, dangerous sisterhoods reach far beyond the natal household to trespass the boundaries between the divine and the human and to entice Israel into apostasy. Devastatingly powerful, dangerous sisterhoods introduce chaos and cataclysm. It takes a flood, a plague, and a sword to remove dangerous sisterhoods and to restore order to the house of Israel and to the house of God.

Notes

1. See J. David Schloen, *The House of the Father as Fact and Symbol: Patrimonialism in Ugarit and the Ancient Near East* (Winona Lake, IN: Eisenbrauns, 2001), 151.

2. Meyers writes: "Decades of ethnographic research, informed by feminist anthropological sensitivities to the male biases of traditional cross-cultural research, have shown that women in peasant societies are invariably connected to each other in a series of informal relationships. Such relationships are designated 'women's networks'." See Carol Meyers, "Women of the Neighborhood (Ruth 4.17): Informal Female Networks in Ancient Israel," in *Ruth and Esther: A Feminist Companion to the Bible (Second Series)*, ed. Athalya Brenner (Sheffield: Sheffield Academic, 1991), 116.

3. See Aubrey Baadsgaard, "A Taste of Women's Sociality: Cooking as Cooperative Labor in Iron Age Syro-Palestine," in *The World of Women in the Ancient and Classical Near East*, ed. Beth Alpert Nakhai (New Castle upon Tyne: Cambridge Scholars, 2008), 19.

4. See Meyers, "Family in Early Israel," in *Families in Ancient Israel*, ed. Leo G. Perdue et al. (Louisville: Westminster John Knox, 1997), 23.

5. See Jennie R. Ebeling, *Women's Lives in Biblical Times* (London: T&T Clark, 2010), 51.

6. See Meyers, "Family in Early Israel," 25.

7. Ebeling, *Women's Lives in Biblical Times*, 50.

8. See Meyers, "Family in Early Israel," 25–26.

9. See Meyers, "'Women of the Neighborhood,'" 126.

10. Meyers notes: "The formal negotiation of marriage arrangements may be done by men, but the information obtained from women's networks is often decisive in selection of mates for offspring." See ibid., 118.

11. Nancy R. Bowen considers what the female prophets in Ezekiel 13 are doing in "The Daughters of Your People: Female Prophets in Ezekiel 13:17-23," *JBL* 118, no. 3 (1999): 427.

12. S. D. Goiten draws this conclusion in "Women as Creators of Biblical Genres," in *Prooftexts* 8, no. 1 (1988): 10.

13. See Beverly Bow, "Sisterhood? Women's Relationships with Women in the Hebrew Bible," in *Life and Culture in the Ancient Near East,* ed. Richard E. Averbeck, Mark W. Chavalas, David B. Weisberg (Bethesda, MD: CDL, 2003), 205.

14. See ibid., 214.

15. Considering Gen 6:1-4 to be a mythic remnant placed within the primordial narratives, scholars look for analogues among ancient Near Eastern myths. Ronald S. Hendel addresses the possible mythic analogues in "Of Demigods and the Deluge: Toward an Interpretation of Genesis 6:1-4," *JBL* 106, no. 1 (1987): 13–26.

16. See David J. A. Clines, "The Significance of the 'Sons of God' Episode (Genesis 6:1-4) in the Context of the 'Primeval History' (Genesis 1-11)," *JSOT* 13 (1979): 33–46 and Lyle Eslinger, "A Contextual Identification of the *bene ha'elohim* and *benoth ha'adam* in Genesis 6:1-4," *JSOT* 13 (1979): 65–73. Divine sons appear in Ps 29:1, 89:7; Job 1:6, 2:1, 38:7.

17. See Carol M. Kaminski, "Beautiful Women or 'False Judgment'? Interpreting Genesis 6.2 in the Context of the Primeval History," *JSOT* 32, no. 4 (2008): 470.

18. Kaminski also connects Gen 3:6 with Gen 6:2. See ibid., 467.

19. For Hendel, transgressing boundaries is the essential sin of the Primeval Cycle; he writes: "I suggest that the Primeval Cycle is characterized by a series of mythological transgressions of boundaries that result in a range of divine response which slowly build up the present order of the cosmos." See Hendel, "Of Demigods and the Deluge," 25.

20. In Num 13:33, the spies report seeing giant Nephilim in the land of Israel.

21. Hendel also notes a connection between these stories. See Hendel, "Of Demigods and the Deluge," 24.

22. Kaminski argues that the divine sons misjudged the daughters of humanity as good when they are in fact evil; she writes: "In view of this contrast in vv. 2 and 5, it seems that the sons of God are incorrect in their 'good' assessment of the women. In Gen. 6.2, the sons of God are, in effect, deeming 'good' those whose thoughts are 'only evil'."See Kaminski, "Beautiful Women of 'False Judgment'?" 472.

23. Gen 7:22.

24. Gen 8:1.

25. My reading resembles Hendel's. The flood comes to ensure that human and divine do not interbreed. Yet whereas I argue that God's target is the daughters of humanity, Hendel argues that God targets the Nephilim. See Hendel, "Of Demigods and the Deluge," 22–23.

26. The text presents Israel as initiator when it says "the people *began* to behave promiscuously with the daughters of Moab." Use of the root חלל, "to begin," in Num 25:1 may be a subtle link to Gen 6:1.

27. See Lev 20:5; Num 15:39; Deut 31:16; Ezek 16:26, 28.

28. Scholars debate whether Baal Peor is a specific divine name or an unspecified local deity associated with the site Peor mentioned in Num 23:28. For an overview of the discussion, see Baruch A. Levine, *Numbers 21–36* (New York: Doubleday, 2000), 283–85.

29. See Gen 34:29. Cohn remarks on the brothers seizing of the Hivite women: "Shechemite men cannot join the tribe even if they bear the tribal mark. On the other hand, the Hivite women captives can apparently be absorbed en masse without threatening the integrity of the first family." See Robert L. Cohn, "Negotiating (with) the Natives: Ancestors and Identity in Genesis," *HTR* 96, no. 2 (2003): 157–58.

30. According to Jan Jaynes Quesada, Numbers 25 reflects the particular ideology and concerns of Second Temple Judaism related to Israel's purity that also is articulated in the books of Ezra and Nehemiah. See Quesada, "Body Piercing: The Issue of Priestly Control over Acceptable Family Structure in the Book of Numbers," *BI* 10, no. 1 (2002): 32.

31. Quesada comments that "Numbers 25 presents the sequence as if it were inevitable." See ibid., 29.

32. The idiosyncrasies of the text suggest original multiple sources that have been given a narrative coherence. See Josebert Fleurant, "Phinehas Murdered Moses' Wife: An Analysis of Numbers 25," *JSOT* 35, no. 3 (2011): 285–94. Quesada addresses the shift from Moabite to Midianite women in "Body Piercing," 30.

33. Concurring with my reading, Quesada writes: "Apparently, the daughters of Moab, *en masse femmes fatales*, have provoked the punishing plague in the Israelite camp. To compound the disaster, a young Israelite man (a well-born youth in the tribe of Simeon) brings a Midianite woman (the daughter of a Midianite chieftain) into the devastated camp in the sight of Moses and the congregation. . . . In miniature, the Israelite man Zimri and his Midianite woman Cozbi dramatize the endangerment of several definitive boundaries." See Quesada, "Body Piercing," 29–30.

34. Like many commentators, my reading assumes that Pinheas kills Zimri and Cozbi while they are defiantly having sex before Moses, Israel, and God. Addressing the linguistic difficulties of the text, Harriet C. Lutzky offers a different reading. Lutzky argues that Cozbi might have been a Midianite priestess or prophetess, and she was engaged with Zimri in apostasy. See "The Name 'Cozbi' (Numbers XXV 15, 18)" in *VT* 47, no. 4 (1997): 546–49.

35. See Helena Zlotnick Sivan, "The Rape of Cozbi (Numbers XXV)," *VT* 51, no. 1 (2001): 73.

36. Quesada notes the phallic nature of the punishment. See Quesada, "Body Piercing," 30.

37. As I mention in my analysis of Genesis 19, Deut 23:4 removes the Moabites entirely from Israel's story by prohibiting marriage with them.

38. For Quesada, this is the point of the narrative—to ensure priestly control over the construction of the Israelite family. See Quesada, "Body Piercing," 24.

39. Sarah Shectman argues that women from priestly families, though not considered priests, enjoyed an elevated social status. See Shectman, "The Social Status of Priestly and Levite Women," in *Levites and Priests in Biblical History and Tradition*, ed. Mark Leuchter and Jeremy M. Hutton (Atlanta: Society of Biblical Literature, 2011), 98.

40. See Esther Fuchs, *Sexual Politics in the Biblical Narrative: Reading the Hebrew Bible as a Woman* (Sheffield: Sheffield Academic, 2000), 211.

41. Cohn offers this suggestion: "The introductory exposition describes one "daughter," Dinah, setting off to see the local "daughters." . . . Perhaps we are to imagine that, with twelve brothers at home, Dinah was simply looking for some female companionship." See Cohn, "Negotiating (with) the Natives," 155.

42. See Meyers, "Women of the Neighborhood," 118.

43. Camp also suggests that Dinah shares her father's openness toward their neighbors. See Claudia V. Camp, *Wise, Strange and Holy: The Strange Woman and the Making of the Bible* (Sheffield: Sheffield Academic, 2000), 284.

44. See Fuchs, *Sexual Politics*, 220.

45. As I already note in part 2, the Bible reflects tension around privileging endogamous or exogamous marriage. Camp argues that Genesis 34 reflects the Torah's priestly ideology, which is concerned generally with the purity of the patrilineal line and, specifically, with the purity of the priestly line—the line established through Levi's descendents. For Camp, Genesis 34 works initially to estrange Dinah through her exogamous marriage to Shechem to ensure that this priest's sister is not given a priest's status. It then reintegrates her, though with a compromised status, and insists on endogamous marriage, represented mythologically, according to Camp, through a marriage with Simeon and Levi. See Camp, *Wise, Strange, and Holy*, 293.

46. Camp notes the conflation of family honor with national honor in Genesis 34. See ibid., 283.

47. Alice Logan suggests that Jephthah makes a vague vow so that God, and not Jephthah, is responsible for what happens. See Alice Logan, "Rehabilitating Jephthah," *JBL* 128, no. 4 (2009): 678.

48. See Exod 15: 20; 1 Sam 18:6-7; Ps 68:12. For a discussion of the phenomenon, see S. D. Goitein, "Women as Creators of Biblical Genres," *Prooftexts* 8, no. 1 (1988): 5–7.

49. See Fuchs, *Sexual Politics*, 182.

50. My reading contradicts Fuchs who believes Jephthah's daughter echoes her father in order to affirm his words. See ibid., 187.

51. Maidenhood does not inherently mean virginity. The expression לא-ידעה איש, who has not known a man, which appears in verse 39 and elsewhere in conjunction with this term (Gen 24:16; Judg 21:12) modifies בתוליה and suggests that בתולה on its own refers to an adolescent girl who may or may not be a virgin. See Peggy L. Day, "From the Child Is Born the Woman: The Story of Jephthah's Daughter," in *Gender and Difference in Ancient Israel*, ed. Peggy L. Day (Minneapolis: Fortress Press, 1989), 59.

52. See Hans-Joachim Kraus, *Psalms 1-59*, trans. Hilton C. Oswald (Minneapolis: Fortress Press, 1993), 450–57.

53. For a description of marriage customs based on Psalm 45 and other biblical texts, see Philip J. King and Lawrence E. Stager, *Life in Biblical Israel* (Louisville: Westminster John Knox, 2001), 54–55.

54. See Day, "From the Child is Born the Woman," 66–67.

55. See Phyllis Trible, *Texts of Terror: Literary-Feminist Readings of Biblical Narratives* (Philadelphia: Fortress Press, 1984), 106–07.

8

The Daughters of Jerusalem

Like Genesis 34, the Song of Songs tells both a sister and a sisterhood story. When read as a sister story, the Song of Songs is about the sexualized sister who openly and actively pursues her lover. When read as a sisterhood story, as I do in this chapter, the Song of Songs is about sororal solidarity and the role women's networks play in a young girl's life. Throughout the Song, the Shulamite engages with the daughters of Jerusalem—a sisterhood comprised of the Shulamite's peers. Unlike the dangerous sisterhoods (with the exception of the friends of Jephthah's daughter) that I examined in the previous chapter, the daughters of Jerusalem do not function as a catalyst for disaster. Instead, we see that this ideal sisterhood protects the Shulamite from sexual violation and supports her emotional development. Above all, we see that sisterhood in the Song of Songs is a stabilizing force that upholds the Bible's patriarchal values and expectations.

As the Bible's only example of erotic love poetry, the Song mystifies scholars who seek to understand its place and purpose within the biblical canon. As David Carr observes, the Song offers a unique perspective on human sexuality, in which a young, unmarried, female lover—a sister—freely expresses and pursues her desire.[1] Centuries of interpretations attempt to make the Song's sexual dynamic conform to gender expectations and hierarchies. Jewish and Christian interpretations do this by perceiving the Song as a divine-human love song, in which the female lover assumes the human position and the male, the divine. The Shulamite's pursuit of her male lover, which challenges the Bible's typical sexual dynamic, reflects the accepted dynamic of the relationship between God and humanity. Like the Shulamite, human beings long for and seek God. Carr notes that this theological interpretation is unnecessary to explain the Song's inversion of gender and sexual expectations. He suggests that the Song could reflect an alternative view of sexuality—perhaps one that even reflects a woman's perspective.[2] If it does, the Song of Songs provides the most direct access into the social and emotional universe inhabited by biblical women. It preserves the voice of a sisterhood in the Bible.

At various points in the poems that constitute the Song,[3] the male lover refers to his female lover, the Shulamite, as "sister."[4] Although this term of endearment does not mark an actual familial relationship, it does evoke one to convey the intimacy, familiarity, and affection felt between the lovers.[5] This is evident toward the poem's end in Song 8:1 when the Shulamite expresses her wish that her lover could be her brother so that she could kiss him publicly and be with him in her mother's house:

If only it could be as with a brother,
As if you had nursed at my mother's breast:
When I find you outside, I could kiss you.
Indeed no one would despise me.

The Shulamite's words offer a rare glimpse into the dynamics of the brother-sister relationship, which is portrayed as intimate (they suck the same breast), physical (they kiss), and relatively non-hierarchical. This passage supports scholars like Ingo Kottsieper who argue that brothers had a particularly close emotional connection with their sisters, as I mention in my introduction.[6] The passage also provides support to scholars like Yael Almog who identify a latent incest fantasy in the Shulamite's request.[7]

Whether viewed as tender or illicit, a sister's relationship to her brother seemingly was not bound by the social behaviors that restricted other types of male-female relationships. As I have noted before, a sexually aggressive female is a destabilizing force in the Bible, which reflects Israel's patriarchal gender ideology. As Alice A. Keefe observes, "ancient Israelite women were not free agents . . . control of female sexuality was a cultural priority."[8] As the brutal punishment of Rebel Israel and Faithless Judah shows, women were not free to pursue men and initiate physical contact with them. Yet, sisters, this passage suggests, can pursue their brothers. If her beloved was her brother, the Shulamite could initiate contact with him and kiss him publicly. Sadly, the male lover is not one of her brothers. She must wait for him to initiate physical contact.

The Shulamite's real brothers appear at the start of the poem and seem to exercise a great deal of authority over her. In Song 1:6, the Shulamite complains to the daughters of Jerusalem about her suntanned skin:

Do not look at me for I am darkened, burnt by the sun.

My mother's sons were angry at me and made me guard the vineyards,
I did not guard my own vineyard.

The Shulamite's claim that she left her own vineyard untended to comply with her brothers' order, may imply that the brothers are responsible for the young lovers meeting. Perhaps if her brothers had not been angry with her and made her guard their vineyard instead of her own, she would not have caught her beloved's eye. There is no explanation for the brothers' anger, as J. Cheryl Exum notes. Exum suggests in her commentary that the cause of their anger is less significant than its consequence—the sending of the Shulamite into the vineyards.[9] By sending her to their vineyards, thereby leaving her own untended, the brothers place the Shulamite in a vulnerable position.

The Song uses horticultural imagery to describe the Shulamite. She is the lily, the rose, the fertile garden. She is the locked garden whose fruit trees and spices are sampled and enjoyed by her male lover. Like the locked garden in Song 5:1, the vineyard image in Song 1:6 may be a euphemism, as Ilana Pardes suggests, for the Shulamite's body,[10] or more specifically, her sexuality. Read in this way, the Song of Songs is about the sexualized sister and presents a shocking reversal of Genesis 34. In the Dinah narrative, brothers fail to preserve their sister's sexual purity and must avenge her violation. In the Song, the brothers place the Shulamite in a tenuous position physically, if not sexually, in which she is unable to tend to her own vineyard. They expose her to the sun and to other onlookers, like the daughters of Jerusalem, whom she begs to avert their gaze. They also may expose her to male attention. While tending her brothers' vineyards and neglecting her own, it is possible that she catches the eye of her male lover, who will continue to gaze at her through windows (Song 2:9), longing to see more (Song 2:14).

Although the Shulamite is described as a sister, the Song of Songs is primarily a sisterhood story. In the Song, the daughters of Jerusalem are central characters who engage directly with the two lovers. They are the only characters who speak in the Song besides the lovers. Other characters in the Song, like King Solomon and the city guards, do not dialogue with the lovers.[11] The unified perspective of the daughters of Jerusalem informs the Song and provides narrative cohesion.

Despite their distinct voice, scholars often view the daughters as a chorus who simply echo the Shulamite's emotions. In his commentary on the Song, Roland E. Murphy perceives the daughters to be "a foil for the woman's own reflections," who "are present solely to promote what the woman wishes to say."[12] Few scholars consider the daughters' unique voice and rhetorical function in the Song. In her commentary, Exum does address the rhetorical function of the daughters, though not their unique voice. For Exum, the daughters function as the lovers' audience and serve as a link between the Song's readers and its lovers. Exum contends that the invitation to the women of Jerusalem "to participate in the lovers' bliss is also an invitation to the reader." The daughters of Jerusalem invite readers into the lovers' world and show them how wonderful it is to be in love.[13]

Unlike Murphy, I contend that the daughters of Jerusalem have a unique voice and do not merely echo the Shulamite. Unlike Exum, I argue that the daughters of Jerusalem serve a specific narrative function and are not simply a rhetorical device. I contend that the daughters of Jerusalem comprise a sisterhood that plays an essential role in the lovers' courtship. The daughters of Jerusalem encourage the lovers while helping them to maintain an appropriate distance from one another. Sororal solidarity provides the Shulamite with safe physical and emotional space. We observe a pattern in the Song: When the lovers draw physically close to one another, the Shulamite turns to the daughters of Jerusalem and immerses herself in their company. By doing this, she simultaneously seeks the emotional support of her sisterhood while establishing a safe distance between herself and her lover. This distance prevents the lovers from consummating their relationship and protects the Shulamite's sexual purity, thereby upholding the Bible's patriarchal values and expectations.

Like the companions with whom Jephthah's daughter spends her last months, the daughters of Jerusalem are the Shulamite's peer group. Along with serving a crucial narrative purpose, their presence sheds light on the Song's intended life setting and even helps account for its inclusion in the Bible. As I mention in the previous chapter, Judges 11 and Psalm 45 suggest that young women accompanied a bride on her wedding day. Similarly, Song 3:11 invites the daughters of Zion, בנות ציון, to King Solomon's wedding day—perhaps to accompany his bride. The inclusion of the daughters of Jerusalem in the Song supports the theory proposed by some scholars that the Song was wedding liturgy, perhaps recited by young women as they accompanied a bride. Since the lovers are not portrayed as bride and groom, Exum expresses caution in accepting this theory.[14]

Carr concludes that possibly the Song was designed for entertainment, though not necessarily for a wedding. As I mention above, Carr also suggests that the Song may have been generated by and intended for women.[15] If the Song is wedding liturgy recited by women, the Song, like Judges 11, preserves a remnant of women's ritual and reveals the crucial role sisterhood played in marking women's lives. Even if the Song did not have this ritualistic function, it captures, as I demonstrate later, the significant role sisterhood played in supporting women's lives.

Because the daughters of Jerusalem encourage the lovers while keeping them physically apart, it is possible to perceive them as adhering to either of my paradigms—the dangerous or the ideal—depending on what one perceives as the objectives of the Song. If the goal of the Song is to unite the lovers physically, then the daughters of Jerusalem function as a dangerous sisterhood that prevents the lovers from consummating their relationship and the narrative from achieving its desired end. Indeed, they would be the threatening thistles around the lily that prevents the male lover from getting too close.

In my reading, the consummation of the young lovers' relationship is not the desired goal of the Song, nor does it take place. As I explain below, though verses, such as Song 5:1, indicate that the lovers have consummated their relationship, I read these verses metaphorically and think that they reflect the lovers' intense *desire* for consummation. As Pardes observes, sexual union in the Song "takes place only on a figurative level."[16] The Song, as Virginia Burrus and Stephen D. Moore observe, seeks to titillate, and not to satisfy desire.[17]

Like Pardes, Burrus, and Moore, I perceive the Song as conveying a flirtation between two young, unmarried lovers that the daughters of Jerusalem help sustain. The daughters thereby support the Song's overall objective and, I contend, the patriarchal values implicit within it.[18] The Song wants the lovers to engage with each other—but not to consummate their relationship. As Genesis 34 made clear, lovers are not free to satisfy their own desires. Consummation should follow proper marriage negotiations among the lovers' patriarchs.

The daughters function as an ideal sisterhood that keeps the lovers apart and prevents the unmarried Shulamite's sexual violation. The daughters of Jerusalem do what the Shulamite's brothers—and Dinah's brothers—cannot. They physically protect her and, by protecting her, protect her natal household.[19] In Genesis 34, a dangerous sisterhood corrupts a sister and sets in motion a series of events that destabilizes Jacob's house and by extension all of Israel. As Dinah's story shows, a sister's violation is also a violation against all of Israel[20] [נבלה עשה בישראל]. In the Song of Songs, an ideal sisterhood protects a sister and ensures that she remains pure. By protecting the Shulamite's honor and the honor of her household, the daughters of Jerusalem protect the honor of Israel. The daughters of Jerusalem make sure that the Shulamite does not suffer Dinah's fate and that no violation is committed against Israel.

Not only does this sisterhood protect the Shulamite, it also supports her and her relationship. In the insulating company of the daughters of Jerusalem, the Shulamite may confess her passion for and her fantasies about her lover. As we will see, their engagement helps the Shulamite develop her feelings for her lover and adds an emotional dimension that deepens the lovers' relationship. In this way, we see, in contrast to Murphy, that the daughters of Jerusalem do not simply echo the Shulamite's voice. Rather, they help the Shulamite find her voice, and they help her shape it. From this, we also see the positive impact sisterhood had on the lives of women by providing them emotional support and a means of expression.

To understand the role the daughters of Jerusalem play in the Song and their relationship with the Shulamite, we must consider the occasions when they are addressed or when they speak directly. Four times the Shulamite urges the daughters of Jerusalem and warns them. In some variation, she repeats the phrase that first appears in Song 2:7:

> I swear to you, daughters of Jerusalem,
> By the gazelles or the hinds of the field,
> Do not wake or rouse love until it is ready.[21]

The simple meaning of the Shulamite's oath remains elusive. It is unclear whether she warns the daughters about romantic love or erotic arousal, or whether she is speaking about love in general or about her own love and lover. Whether love or lust, the Shulamite expresses the need for restraint and commands the daughters of Jerusalem to exercise it. By considering each of the oaths in their narrative context, I identify a common trigger that causes the Shulamite to turn to the daughters for assistance at these moments. A threat of physical contact between the lovers, whether real or metaphorical, precedes all four adjurations. When her beloved seems too close, or when she imagines him touching her, the Shulamite retreats. Frightened, she addresses the daughters and elicits their help. She begs them to help her restrain love.

Before her first oath, the Shulamite describes her lover's embrace, "His left hand is under my head, while his right hand embraces me" (Song 2:6).[22] The use of the imperfect verb תחבקני, embraces me, could be read either as a future action or as descriptive of the moment, implying that the lovers are, in fact, embracing. The narrative context of this verse portrays the lovers apart from one another and not in the midst of physical contact or even in a position in which physical contact would be possible.

Immediately after the oath, Song 2:8-9 describes the male lover leaping like a gazelle over mountains, then standing behind walls and peering through windows. From this passage it appears that the lovers inhabit different worlds with barriers between them. The male lover freely inhabits the natural world, while the Shulamite is enclosed behind walls and windows. She is inside; he is outside. They are not together and lack easy access to one another. Given the lovers' physical distance described in these verses, the Shulamite must have imagined her beloved's embrace in Song 2:6. While imagining, she appears to be solely in the company of the daughters of Jerusalem, whom she is able to address immediately in Song 2:7.[23] It seems that within the safety of her peer group, she fantasizes her lover's embrace. But even this fantasy elicits anxiety. More comfortable imagining her beloved leaping over distant mountains than hugging her, the Shulamite entreats her peers. She wants them to help control her desire and to keep her lover at a safe actual or imagined distance.

A similar dynamic is evident in the second adjuration in Song 3:5. The chapter opens with the Shulamite searching for her lover through the city streets at night. Unable to find him, she encounters the city guards and asks if they have seen her beloved. Immediately she appears to find him:

> As soon as I passed, I found the one whom I love.
> I grabbed hold of him and would not let go
> Until I brought him into my mother's house,
> Into the room of the one who bore me. (Song 3:4)

Once again, the conjugation of verbs suggests that the lovers' game of cat and mouse is over. The Shulamite grabs her beloved and brings him into her mother's house. Lovers unite. One assumes love is consummated. Yet like the earlier embrace, this episode appears to be a fantasy.

Another nighttime search occurs in Song 5:2-7, which is also followed by an adjuration of the daughters of Jerusalem in Song 5:8. This second encounter challenges the reality of the first. If the Shulamite was able to bring her lover home, as she boasted in Chapter 3, he certainly does not stay for long since she must search for him again in Chapter 5. Also, later in Chapter 8, she expresses the desire that she bring her lover into her mother's house, as if he has never been there. As I mention above, she expresses the desire that her lover was "her brother" so that she can initiate physical contact with him and bring him home. If she had already done so, she would not long to do so.

Both searches occur at night after the Shulamite has gone to bed. Given the timing, location, and similar pattern of the episodes, the Shulamite's nighttime searches appear to be a recurring fantasy or even a dream.[24] Song 5:2 describes the Shulamite's dream-like state when she hears her beloved knock on her door: "I was sleeping, but my heart was awake." Responding to his knock, she opens the door to find him gone. Her dream quickly becomes a nightmare. The Shulamite once again searches the city streets for her lover where the city guards attack and strip her. Hurt and naked, she addresses the daughters of Jerusalem:

> I swear to you, daughters of Jerusalem,
> If you find my lover, what will you tell him?
> That I am love sick. (Song 5:8)

This time the Shulamite does not ask the daughters to exercise restraint over love. Yet by turning to them, the Shulamite turns away from her beloved or his image and exercises restraint. She no longer searches for him in the city streets. Instead, she asks the daughters of Jerusalem to serve as intermediaries and to convey a message to her lover.

In both dreams, she comes too close to her lover. In the first dream, the lovers unite in her mother's house. Terrified by the fantasy of consummation, the Shulamite retreats to her peer group and begs the daughters to help restrain her passions. In the second dream, the Shulamite feels her beloved's presence at her door and responds to his knock. The description of her lover in Song 5:4 as he waits to come in may be the most explicitly erotic passage of the Song: "My lover sent his hand [ידו] into the opening [החר] and my insides [ומעי] trembled over him." In her dream, the Shulamite seems ready and eager to receive her lover. She imagines his hand, a biblical euphemism for penis, reaching inside an opening. In response, she appears to have an orgasm.[25] Yet, once again, the fantasy triggers anxiety. As she wanders around the city searching for her beloved, she encounters the guards who strip her and beat her. The threat of physical contact with her lover, even imagined, feels like a violation to the Shulamite.[26] In her nightmare, the guards' blows are a distorted manifestation of her lover's touch. Her naked, beaten body reflects her feelings of vulnerability and violation.

At this moment, the Shulamite turns to the daughters to alleviate her anxiety and to protect her physically. She uses the daughters of Jerusalem to obtain the distance she wants between herself and her lover. The daughters respond directly to the Shulamite and begin a dialogue in Song 5:9:

> How is your lover different from another lover, most beautiful among the women?
> How is your lover different from another lover that you cause us to swear?

It is difficult to gauge the daughters' tone in this passage. Their questions may reflect genuine curiosity as they wonder what makes the Shulamite's beloved unique. They also may encourage the Shulamite to account for her passions, as well as her demands on the daughters, by asking her to enumerate what makes her lover so special. In response to their questions, the Shulamite describes her beloved's body, just as he described the Shulamite's body in Song 4:1-5.

These physical descriptions convey an erotic intimacy as the lovers focus on each body part. Although both lovers describe their beloveds' bodies, only the male lover speaks directly to his beloved, using the second person address in Song 4:1-2: "*Your* hair is like a flock of goats . . . *your* teeth are like a flock of sheep." In contrast, the Shulamite describes her lover to the daughters of Jerusalem, speaking of him in the third person. She describes "*his* head" and "*his* hair." Whereas the male lover speaks *to* his lover, the Shulamite speaks *about* her lover to her friends.[27]

This dynamic counters the Shulamite's image as a sexually aggressive female and conforms to the Bible's typical sexual dynamic in which men are aggressive while women are passive recipients of their attention and desire. Yet among her peers, the Shulamite freely articulates her passion. Within her sisterhood, she is able to describe his dripping, gleaming, and clearly arousing body. She concludes her description by proclaiming in Song 5:16: "This is my lover! This is my companion, O daughters of Jerusalem!"

The dialogue continues between the daughters of Jerusalem and the Shulamite in Song 6:1-2:

Where has your lover gone, most beautiful of women?
Where has your lover turned? Let us seek him with you.

My lover has gone down to his garden, to the beds of spices,
To shepherd among the gardens, to gather lilies.

The Shulamite's description of her beloved captivates the daughters, who are now eager to help her search for her lover. At this point, impressed by the Shulamite's description of her beloved, the daughters behave more like rivals than friends. They want to join the search, not to help their friend find her lover and serve as intermediaries, but instead to compete for his love. "Let *us* seek him *with* you," they suggest.

The Shulamite's response to their offer indicates that she perceives the daughters, not as helpful assistants but, as potential rivals. She informs the daughters that her lover shepherds in the gardens where he gathers lilies. Earlier in the Song, the Shulamite is the locked garden [גן נעול] that her lover enters.[28] She is the lone lily [שושנה] among all the thistles.[29] Now she is aware that her beloved shepherds in many gardens [גנים] and that the thistles now have become lilies [שושנים]. The Shulamite acknowledges that she has competition for her lover's attention.

Feeling threatened by the daughters, the Shulamite informs the daughters that, though her beloved shepherds among the lilies, he belongs exclusively to her. The Shulamite exclaims in Song 6:3: "I am my lover's and my lover is mine [אני לדודי ודודי לי], the one who shepherds among the lilies!" A few verses earlier, the Shulamite identifies her lover by saying "this is my lover." Now, in response to the daughters' interest in him, she claims him, saying "my lover is mine." Exum calls this "the refrain of mutual possession."[30]

The Shulamite again expresses a similar sentiment in Song 7:11, which offers an interesting point of comparison. Following her lover's description, in which he compares the Shulamite's breasts to grape clusters that he longs to harvest, the Shulamite says: "I am my lover's, for me is his desire [אני לדודי ועלי תשוקתו]." Recognizing echoes of Gen 3:16, Phyllis Trible argues that the verse overturns Adam and Eve's post-transgression gender dynamic. Whereas Eve is made sexually submissive to Adam in Gen 3:16, Song 7:11 allows for mutual desire.[31]

My reading of Song 7:11 differs from that of Trible. Although I agree that Song 6:3 conveys the mutuality of the lovers' relationship, I contend that Song 7:11 does not. Although the Shulamite admits that she belongs to her lover, she does not say that her beloved belongs to her. Instead, in Song 7:11 she focuses exclusively on his desire for her. The Shulamite knows he wants her. He has just told her directly. Secure in her beloved's affection, she does not mention other "lilies" competing for his attention. Without the threat of romantic rivals, the Shulamite has no need to claim him. At this moment, she sees herself solely as an object of his desire and declares: "for me is his desire." The comparison between Song 6:3 and 7:11 suggests that the presence of other women competing for her lover's affection adds a significant dimension to the lovers' relationship.

Further support for this reading is found in Song 2:16 where the refrain "I am my lover's and my lover is mine" also appears. In this passage, the refrain follows a description of vineyards that have been spoiled by foxes as well as an appeal to catch the foxes. Perceiving the foxes as threatening, Exum mentions that foxes can symbolize "amorous young men and women." She suggests that the foxes in this passage refer in general to young men who threaten young women's chastity.[32] I offer a different reading from Exum. Perhaps the foxes are not young men but young amorous women, like the daughters of

Jerusalem, who threaten the Shulamite's position with her beloved. Sensing competition from these "foxes," the Shulamite claims her beloved, referring to him, as she does in Song 6:3, as "the one who shepherds among the lilies." Once again, the Shulamite acknowledges that she has competition for his affection. When viewed as competition, the daughters of Jerusalem force the Shulamite to acknowledge her desire. They compel the Shulamite to claim him and to express the mutuality of their relationship. Sisterhood both forces her and enables her to say: "my lover is mine."

Although in my reading the lovers do not consummate their relationship, the Song reaches an emotional climax in its final chapter. The chapter begins with familiar feelings and typical behavior among the lovers. It opens with the Shulamite's wish that her beloved would be her brother so she could bring him home. This is followed by the Shulamite's description of her lover's embrace in Song 8:3. As it did earlier in Song 2:6, the description of physical intimacy between the lovers elicits anxiety.

Once again, the Shulamite turns to the daughters of Jerusalem and makes them swear not to arouse love [מה-תעירו ומה-תעררו] until it is time. At this point, the Song takes a dramatic turn. Despite her effort to disrupt the intimacy with her lover and to exercise restraint, the Shulamite herself arouses love:

> Who comes up from the wilderness, leaning upon her lover?
> Beneath the apple tree, I aroused you. There, your mother labored.
> There she labored and bore you. (Song 8:5)

Four times in the Song the Shulamite begged the daughters of Jerusalem not to arouse love [אם-תעירו ואם-תעוררו]. Now, underneath the apple tree, the Shulamite herself arouses [עוררתיך] her lover. Identified as the site where his mother gave birth, the location of the apple tree conveys the Shulamite's sexual intentions. Their union will be physical; it could produce a child.

As the Song draws to its close, the Shulamite either dismisses the daughters of Jerusalem as advocates for love or ignores them as barriers to love. Despite her recent appeal to them, she is ready to unite with her beloved emotionally *and* physically. She begs him: "Place me as a seal upon your heart, as a seal upon your arm" (Song 8:6). At last, the Shulamite asks to be inscribed internally upon her lover's heart and externally upon his arm. As a physical marker of an individual's identity, the image of the seal conveys a fusion of the physical with the emotional/psychic—of body and identity.[33] The Shulamite wants to be more than an object of her lover's desire. She wants to become a part of his body.

Her plea is followed by the Song's famous anthem about love in which the Shulamite compares love to death, Sheol, fire, and flood.

> For love is as strong as death, passion as hard as Sheol.
> Its flames are flames of fire, almighty flames.
> Floods are unable to quench love, nor will rivers drown it. (Song 8:6-7)

In this passage, the Shulamite proclaims the overwhelming power of love but does not surrender happily to its force. Her use of macabre imagery to describe love suggests that the Shulamite equates love with death.[34] In the context of the Song, the Shulamite's association is shocking. The Song's world is of springtime and vitality, not of death and destruction. The lovers reflect this world and blossom like spring flowers. They leap over hills like newborn deer and exude fragrance like ripe spice beds.

Although the lovers intimately participate in a world dedicated to the renewal of life, the Shulamite recognizes a fundamental similarity between love and death. Love and death share common and, at times, sinister qualities. They are strong, hard, and intense. Like fire and flood waters, both are consuming—even obliterating. Above all, love and death are inevitable. There is nothing anyone—not the Shulamite or the daughters of Jerusalem—can do to discourage or to prevent them. At the Song's close, the Shulamite accepts with dread the inevitability of her physical union with her beloved.

In response to the Shulamite's distressed resignation to love's death-like force, the daughters of Jerusalem make one final attempt to separate the lovers in Song 8:8-9:

> We have a little sister, she has no breasts.
> What should we do with our little sister on the day she is spoken for?
> If she is a wall, we will build upon it a silver tier.
> If she is a door, we will panel it in cedar.

The passage does not identify its speakers. Since they refer to the Shulamite as sister, it is possible to attribute these verses to the Shulamite's brothers. Yet the brothers have not spoken in the Song and to hear them now would be odd. Instead, it is the daughters of Jerusalem who speak.[35] By calling her "sister," the daughters assert their sisterhood with the Shulamite. The Shulamite may claim that she belongs to her lover, but the daughters claim that she belongs to them. And they make it clear that they will do everything necessary to protect one of their own.

The daughters of Jerusalem respond to the Shulamite's emotional distress as she accepts the inevitability of love and her lover. They are called into action. With physical union impending, the daughters promise to construct barriers to protect the Shulamite. They will build walls and cover doors to keep her lover away. Yet the daughters' action is futile as the Shulamite's response reveals in Song 8:10: "I am a wall but my breasts are like towers. Thus I appear in his eyes like one who pleases." There is no need for the daughters to build walls because the Shulamite is herself a wall. Throughout the Song, she functions as her own barrier to her beloved. For the most part, she resists her lover by appealing to the daughters of Jerusalem. In the end her efforts, and their efforts, are for naught. Love is too powerful. Walls are not effective barriers to fire, flood, death, or her beloved. Her lover sees through walls (Song 2:9), and her breasts rise above them.[36]

The Song does not record the lovers' seemingly imminent union. The game of cat and mouse between them continues to the end. Consummation, like death, is inevitable, but it has not happened yet due largely to the sisterhood's continued efforts. Sisterhood ensures that love is not consummated; the Shulamite is not violated. The Shulamite speaks the Song's final words in 8:14: "Flee my lover, become like a gazelle or a young deer upon the mountains of spices." The final verse of the Song evokes Song 2:8-9 in which the Shulamite describes her beloved leaping like a gazelle over mountains while she remains safe in her house. At the end of the Song, the Shulamite directly commands her lover to flee and to *become* like the gazelle. At this point, he appears to be near her, perhaps even in the same place. But she wants him back outside, far away from her.

Although closer to one another, the lovers still are not alone. The Shulamite remains in the company of her protective and supportive sisterhood as her lover's final words to her indicate in 8:13: "You who dwell in the gardens, companions listen to your voice. Let me hear it!" The Shulamite still dwells in the gardens.[37] Although her beloved is near her, she remains with companions [חברים], her sisterhood, where she feels most comfortable, and where she finds her voice. As the male lover says, her friends listen to her. The sisterhood hears the voice that he longs for, but still is unable to hear.

Unlike Genesis 34 and the other sisterhood stories, the Song of Songs is not about a dangerous sisterhood and the threat of intermarriage. It does not function as a cautionary tale that insulates Israel against foreigners and foreign gods. Instead, throughout the Song, the ideal sisterhood of the daughters of Jerusalem keeps the lovers at an appropriate distance and prevents the Shulamite's sexual violation. Although love is powerful and consummation may be inevitable, the daughters of Jerusalem ensure that it comes at the right time and in the right way. They succeed where the brothers of the Shulamite and the brothers of Dinah fail. Not only do the daughters of Jerusalem create a safe physical space for the Shulamite, they create a safe emotional space in which she can express desire.

Throughout this study, we have seen dangerous sisters assert desire only to become its tragic victims. In one way or another, Rachel, Leah, Michal, Rebel Israel, Faithless Judah, Lot's daughters, and Dinah are casualties of their own desire. Remarkably, the Song of Songs reveals that women can express desire when in the company of other women. The daughters of Jerusalem encourage the Shulamite to indulge her desire and to pursue her lover. They even express their own desire to join in the pursuit. Sisterhood also helps the Shulamite develop her emotions. Without the threat of rivals, the Shulamite would not have recognized the mutuality of the lovers' relationship and claimed her lover. Living in a patriarchal society, a young woman knows that she belongs to her suitor. Within a sisterhood, a young woman is free to say that he belongs to her.

Notes

1. See David Carr, "Gender and the Shaping of Desire in the Song of Songs and its Interpretation," *JBL* 119 no. 2 (2000): 242.

2. Carr draws parallels between the Song and Mediterranean and Middle Eastern love poems. See ibid., 243.

3. Scholars debate whether to consider the Song a poetic unit with literary coherence. My reading perceives poetic and narrative coherence, based largely on the dialogical nature of the poem that conveys the consistent point of view of its characters. J. Cheryl Exum argues similarly in her commentary on the Song. See Exum, *Song of Songs* (Louisville: Westminster John Knox, 2005), 4.

4. Song 4:9, 10, 12; 5:1, 2.

5. Madeline Gay McClenney-Sadler distinguishes between kinship terms used as a "term of address," as they appear in the Song, and those used as a "term of reference." Only terms of reference "indicate the status of one person relative to another." See Madeline Gay McClenney-Sadler, *Recovering the Daughter's Nakedness: A Formal Analysis of Israelite Kinship Terminology and the Internal Logic of Leviticus 18* (London: T&T Clark, 2007), 33.

6. See Ingo Kottsieper, "'We Have a Little Sister': Aspects of the Brother-Sister Relationship in Ancient Israel," in *Families and Family Relations: As Represented in Early Judaisms and Early Christianities: Texts and Fictions*, ed. Jan Willem Van Henten and Athalya Brenner (Leiden: Deo, 2000), 55.

7. See Yael Almog, "'Flowing Myrrh upon the Handles of the Bolt': Bodily Border, Social Norms and their Transgression in the Song of Songs," *BI* 18 (2010): 260–61.

8. Alice A. Keefe, *Woman's Body and the Social Body in Hosea*, (Sheffield: Sheffield Academic, 2001), 163.

9. See Exum, *Song*, 105.

10. See Ilana Pardes, *Countertraditions in the Bible: A Feminist Approach* (Cambridge MA: Harvard University Press, 1992), 140.

11. As I mention later, some commentators believe the brothers speak in Song 8:8-9, but I attribute these verses to the daughters of Jerusalem.

12. See Roland E. Murphy, *The Song of Songs* (Minneapolis: Fortress Press, 1990), 84–85.

13. See Exum, *Song*, 7.

14. See ibid., 79.

15. See Carr, "Gender and the Shaping of Desire," 242–44.

16. See Pardes, *Countertraditions in the Bible*, 125–26.

17. See Virginia Burrus and Stephen D. Moore, "Unsafe Sex: Feminism, Pornography, and the Song of Songs," *BI* 11, no. 1 (2003): 39–40. For a similar perspective, see Yael Almog, "'Flowing Myrrh upon the Handles of the Bolt,'" 253.

18. Pardes makes a similar observation: "Desire reigns in the Song, not fulfillment; and in this sense the Song adheres to the biblical worldview." See Pardes, *Countertraditions in the Bible*, 126.

19. The Shulamite refers specifically to her natal house as her *mother's* house in Song 3:4 and 8:2. Carol Meyers suggests that this rare term appears in the context of marriage negotiations. See Carol Meyers, "'To Her Mother's House': Considering a Counterpart to the Israelite *Bêt 'āb*," in *The Bible and the Politics of Exegesis: Essays in Honor of Norman K. Gottwald on His Sixty-Fifth Birthday*, ed. David Jobling, Peggy L. Day, and Gerald T. Sheppard (Cleveland: Pilgrim, 1991), 39–51.

20. Gen 34:7.

21. See also Song 3:5; 5:8; and 8:4.

22. The expression appears again before the final adjuration in Song 8:3.

23. Before imagining her lover's embrace, the Shulamite addresses a group in Song 2:5 and asks for raisin cakes and apples. Although the verbs are conjugated in the third-person-masculine plural, the daughters of Jerusalem are the obvious audience. See Exum, *Song*, 116.

24. Pardes writes: "There are two passages which are identifiable dreamlike sequences (3:1-5 and 5:2-8), but their mood colors the supposedly waking passages as well. Throughout the entire text there is constant oscillation between the incoherent movement of a dream and concrete reality, between wakefulness and imaginary wakefulness." See Pardes, *Countertraditions in the Bible*, 130.

25. See Isa 57:8, 10. חור literally means hole and "insides" are internal organs that can refer to the organs of procreation. See Gen 15:4; 2 Sam 7:12; 16:11. Pardes reads this passage as a "masturbatory fantasy." See Pardes, *Countertraditions in the Bible*, 132.

26. Burrus and Moore consider this episode to be a female fantasy of erotic violence. See Burrus and Moore, "Unsafe Sex," 48.

27. Fiona C. Black observes: "The woman describes her man in the third person, to a group of admiring, helpful, perhaps jealous women. The purpose of the description appears to be for the benefit of the daughters of Jerusalem (who have asked what he looks like), so that they might assist her in finding her lover. He, however, describes her to her face, always around statements that purport to extol her beauty (4:1; 6:4; 7:2), but appear, in the descriptions that follow, to be troubled, unflattering and ridiculous." See Black, "Beauty or the Beast? The Grotesque Body in the Song of Songs," *BI* 8, no. 3 (2000): 317–18.

28. Song 4:12; 5:1.

29. Song 2:2. The lover makes it clear that the thistles are other young women.

30. The Shulamite also claims her lover in Song 2:16. Exum comments on Song 6:2: "I am my lover's and my lover is mine," the refrain of mutual possession . . . expresses the lovers' total absorption in each other and leaves no room for company." See Exum, *Song*, 210.

31. See Phyllis Trible, *God and the Rhetoric of Sexuality* (Philadelphia: Fortress Press, 1978), 159–60.

32. See Exum, *Song*, 129–30.

33. As Exum observers: "(S)he longs to be as close to him, as intimately bound up with his identity, as his seal might be . . . If the seal is on the heart itself, perhaps there is, after all, a

suggestion that the woman wants to inscribe herself on the very core of her lover's being." See Exum, *Song*, 250.

34. The vocabulary in this passage alludes to mythic traditions of the underworld that are associated with the Canaanite gods Mot and Resheph. See Murphy, *Song of Songs*, 196–98.

35. My attribution agrees with Exum, who writes: "Whereas the woman's brothers are incidental, like the watchmen (3:3-4) or queens and concubines (6:8-9), the women of Jerusalem are not, and, as the only speakers in the poem besides the lovers, theirs could be the voice we hear here. . . . That the women of Jerusalem should speak now—at the very point when the poem has reached its climax in the affirmation of the strength of love (vv. 6-7)—is very much in keeping with the way they function elsewhere: to remind us, by their presence, that the poem is addressed to us." See Exum, *Song*, 257.

36. Pardes also recognizes the failure of the walls to protect the Shulamite. See Pardes, *Countertraditions in the Bible*, 141.

37. Above I argue that the word "gardens" is a euphemism for other young women.

9

Ruth and Naomi

Among the Bible's narratives concerned with having sons and selecting heirs, the book of Ruth tells an unconventional family story featuring women. As Ilana Pardes observes, the book of Ruth "violates" a number of biblical conventions, particularly the convention of featuring male protagonists.[1] Although named for only one woman,[2] female characters populate and are central figures in the story that chronicles the preservation of Elimelech's family and the birth of King David's ancestor. Ruth's notable focus on women has led scholars to consider whether it might have been authored by a woman. Epigraphic evidence, such as prayers and letters attributed to Sargon's daughter Enheduanna (c. 2300 BCE), supports the assumption that women wrote in the ancient world.[3] Because the Bible records that queens Jezebel (1 Kgs 21:8) and Esther (Est 9:29) wrote, it is not an unreasonable assumption that Ruth was authored by a woman.[4]

Even if not formally written by a woman, the book of Ruth may be an indirect product of women's culture and could consequently reflect women's experience. S. D. Goitein suggests that women composed stories and songs while they worked together.[5] In this way, Ruth may be a product of a women's network, as described in chapter 7. Unable to identify an author definitively, Carol Meyers urges scholars to focus less on the author's gender and more on the gender *perspective* of the book.[6] Meyers delineates six features of the book that support her argument that Ruth preserves a female perspective: a woman's story is being told; a wisdom association is present; women are agents in their own destiny; the agency of women affects others; the setting is domestic; and marriage is involved.[7] The presence of these features convinces Meyers that Ruth provides a rare glimpse into the lives and experiences of women.[8]

Meyers notes that the book of Ruth is not only about women; it is about their relationships.[9] Similarly, Pardes observes that Ruth is the only biblical book in which the word "love" defines a relationship between women.[10] The story focuses on the interpersonal relationship between Moabite Ruth and her Israelite mother-in-law Naomi. Bereft of husbands and sons while in Moab, Ruth and Naomi make their way back to Bethlehem to rebuild their family. Not bound by biology or familial obligation, Ruth and Naomi's relationship is the Bible's most developed and positively portrayed sisterhood.

In this chapter, I contend that an ideal sisterhood, one that is surprisingly modeled on the relationship between biological sisters, forms between Ruth and Naomi. This sisterhood secures the house of Elimelech and establishes the line of David. Many of the recurrent themes related to sisters and sisterhood appear in Ruth. Paired sisters, a vulnerable patriarchal house, Moabites, marriage, and even, as we will see, sororal desire and agency are all part of Ruth's story. My reading of the book of Ruth reveals how ideal sisterhoods support Israelite society, and how they redeem dangerous sisters and sisterhoods.

As Pardes notes, this sisterhood story rewrites the Bible's paradigmatic sister story—the story of Rachel and Leah.[11] When the people of Bethlehem pray that Ruth will be like Rachel and Leah (Ruth 4:11), who "together built the house of Israel," their prayer removes the rivalry that defined Rachel and Leah's relationship and provides these earlier sisters with closure to their story. These now ideal sisters may be imagined to have built the house of Israel, but Ruth and Naomi's sisterhood secures its future by enabling the birth of Obed, King David's grandfather. Although ultimately kinship determines dynasty, it is a sisterhood—a non-biological relationship among women—that establishes the Davidic dynasty. The book of Ruth demonstrates the power of sisterhood to alter individuals and to shape Israel's story and destiny.

Before considering Ruth and Naomi's relationship, I begin by looking at the more obvious sisterhood in the book, the sisterhood comprised of the women of Bethlehem. For Meyers, mention of the women of Bethlehem in Ruth provides textual evidence for the existence of women's networks in ancient Israel.[12] The women of Bethlehem first appear at the beginning of the narrative when Ruth and Naomi arrive from Moab sonless and widowed. Appearing again at its end to name Ruth's son, the women of Bethlehem neatly frame the narrative. Their engagement with Ruth and Naomi serves as an indicator of narrative progress. Ruth and Naomi's first encounter with the women of Bethlehem follows Ruth's declaration of allegiance to Naomi in Ruth 1:19-21:

> The two walked together until they came to Bethlehem. When they entered Bethlehem, the city buzzed around them. The women [of the city] said: "Is this Naomi?" She said to them: "Do not call me

Naomi, call me Mara, for Shaddai has made me very bitter. I left full, but YHWH has brought me back empty. Why do you call me Naomi when YHWH has witnessed against me and Shaddai has caused me misery?"

As I note earlier, it is not unusual for women like Jephthah's daughter to welcome guests or returning citizens to a city—particularly warriors who return from battle.[13] Yet the women of Bethlehem do not dance and celebrate with triumphant soldiers. Instead, they greet Naomi, returning defeated from Moab. Their question "Is this Naomi [הזאת נעמי]?" reverberates throughout the book and raises one of its central themes: identity. Over and over again, the book of Ruth raises the essential question of identity: Who are you? Later in the narrative, in Ruth 2:5 when Boaz first sees Ruth, he asks: "Whose young woman is this [למי הנערה הזאת]?" In Ruth 3:9, Boaz wakes to find Ruth lying at his feet and asks: "Who are you [מי-את]?" When Ruth returns home after her seduction of Boaz, Naomi asks: "Who are you, my daughter [מי-את בתי]?" (Ruth 3:16). Through the course of its narrative, the book of Ruth seeks to find out who Naomi is, who Ruth is, and, most important to my analysis, who Ruth is in relationship to Naomi.

As the first to raise the question of identity, the women of Bethlehem indicate that Naomi has been altered beyond recognition. She does not look like the same woman who left Bethlehem to go to Moab. Naomi's response confirms that she has changed—not just in looks but in spirit as well. Experience, it seems, has forced Naomi to rename herself. Her new name conveys her new reality. As Naomi explains, the woman who left Bethlehem was whole and content. Given the fact that she leaves Bethlehem because of famine and presumably hunger, Naomi's wholeness must be attributed to the wholeness of her immediate family. She returns empty and bitter without her husband and sons. Of course, she has Ruth, but Naomi does not acknowledge Ruth's presence to the women and does not seem filled by her.[14]

At this point in the narrative, Naomi's encounter with the women of Bethlehem is a clarifying and transformative moment for her. As Eunny P. Lee observes, "identity is dialogically formed." People define themselves "in dialogue with, and sometimes in struggle against, the things that others see in them."[15] Dialogue is a defining feature of the book of Ruth. Of the eighty-five verses in Ruth, fifty-six occur in dialogue. For Lee, these dialogues become "a vehicle for the deconstruction and reconstruction of identity and otherness."[16] Lee also notes the importance of recognition in identity formation, which aligns an individual's self-perception with the way others perceive the individual.[17] Sisterhood plays an important role in Naomi's identity formation. In dialogue with the women of Bethlehem, Naomi deconstructs and reconstructs her identity. Struggling to recognize her, the women of Bethlehem ask "Is this Naomi?" Wanting to be recognized for who she is, Naomi responds to their question and reconstructs her identity to match her new reality.[18] In dialogue with the women of Bethlehem, Naomi transforms and renames herself. Naomi, נעמי, pleasantness becomes Mara, מרא, bitterness.

Naomi's response reveals her depth of self-awareness while bearing a tone of defiance and accusation. Naomi clearly holds God accountable for her misery when she declares to the women of Bethlehem: "YHWH has witnessed against me, and Shaddai has caused me misery [ושדי הרע לי]" (Ruth 1:21). Naomi's words echo another biblical character who suffers. Diseased and bereft, righteous Job swears "By God who has deprived me of justice, by Shaddai who has embittered me [ושדי המר נפשי]!" (Job 27:2).

Feeling they suffer unjustly, both Job and Naomi hold God responsible.[19] Yet, whereas Job challenges God directly and demands justification,[20] Naomi challenges God indirectly. She addresses the women of Bethlehem and tells them that God brought her back empty, God afflicted her, and God made her miserable. As it did for the Shulamite in the Song of Songs, sisterhood provides a safe emotional space for Naomi. In the company of women, both the Shulamite and Naomi are free to express themselves in ways that challenge convention. To the daughters of Jerusalem, the Shulamite describes her lover and expresses desire for him. To the women of Bethlehem, Naomi expresses anger and challenges God.[21]

Having inspired Naomi to rename herself at the beginning of the book, the women of Bethlehem return at its end to name Ruth's child:

> Boaz took Ruth, and she became a wife to him. He entered her; and God made her conceive, and she bore a son. The women said to Naomi: "Blessed is God who has not withheld a redeemer from you today. May his name be called in Israel. May he sustain your life and provide for you in your old age. Your daughter-in-law who loves you, who bore him, she is better to you than seven sons." Naomi took the boy and placed him on her breast and she was his caretaker. The neighborhood women named him saying: "A son is born to Naomi." They named him Obed. He is the father of Jesse, father of David. (Ruth 4:13-17)

The presence of the women at the birth of Ruth's child supports scholars like Meyers who claim that women's networks performed rituals that marked and sanctified a woman's life.[22] Just as the friends of Jephthah's daughter attend her macabre anti-wedding in Judges 11, the women of Bethlehem are present for the birth of Ruth's child. Jennie R. Ebeling suggests that these women not only marked the birth of Ruth's child but that they also provided emotional support to this new mother and new member of their community.[23]

Not only do the women participate ritually in the birth by offering blessing and by naming the child, they also provide Ruth and Naomi with another opportunity for identity formation. With the birth of Ruth's child, the women recognize Ruth's valor, love, and loyalty. Although they appreciate all that Ruth has done for Naomi, they noticeably focus on Naomi in their blessing. Everything happens for Naomi's benefit. God does not deny *her* a redeemer. The child sustains *Naomi* in her old age. Naomi's daughter-in-law loves and is good to *her*. Their focus on Naomi effaces Ruth from the narrative as a distinct character, erasing Ruth's identity.

Esther Fuchs considers Ruth's disappearance at the end of the book to be a narrative death. According to Fuchs, having served her maternal function, Ruth no longer is of use and is effectively eliminated from the patriarchal narrative.[24] In the final scene, the women do not even refer to Ruth by name but identify her in relation to Naomi as "your daughter-in-law." Their reluctance to name Ruth is particularly noticeable, since, as we have seen, the women consistently appear invested in names and engaged in naming. As mentioned above, their initial engagement with Naomi provokes Naomi to adopt a new name and identity. Now, they appear at the close of the narrative to bless Naomi's redeemer and to pray that his name will resound in Israel.

This sisterhood formally names Ruth's baby Obed and appears to name Naomi as his mother.[25] The women proclaim: "A son is born to Naomi [וַתִּקְרֶאנָה לוֹ הַשְּׁכֵנוֹת שֵׁם לֵאמֹר יֻלַּד בֵּן לְנָעֳמִי]!" (Ruth 4:17). Athalya Brenner suggests that the baby's original name, according to one tradition, could have been Ben-Noam, son of Naomi.[26] The sisterhood's focus on Naomi in this final scene may be viewed, as Fuchs does, as an aggressive act against Ruth. The refusal to acknowledge Ruth may be the text's way of removing a birth mother from a patriarchal narrative, but it may also be the way it removes the problematic Moabite from David's ancestry.

Moabites, as we know from Genesis 19, descend from incest. Israelites are prohibited from marrying them in Deut 23:4. By naming Naomi the mother of this child, the women declare Israelite Naomi and not Moabite Ruth to be David's great-grandmother. Although such a reading is plausible considering the Bible's general attitude toward Moabites, clearly the women of Bethlehem honor Ruth for what she did for Naomi. Their blessing acknowledges Ruth's love as the pivotal force that transforms Naomi's life and secures her household. They recognize who she is and by doing so, they secure, rather than eliminate, Ruth's identity.

Given their appreciation of Ruth, it seems more likely that the women perform an act of kindness toward Ruth, not an act of aggression, in keeping with the kindness she has shown Naomi. They want to integrate Ruth and her child into Naomi's family and Israel rather than to delete them from their story.[27] By proclaiming a son is born to Naomi, the women of Bethlehem declare that Ruth's half-Moabite child is a full Israelite. It is *as if* he had been born to Naomi.

Strikingly, when the women of Bethlehem name the child, they reclaim Naomi's name, bringing the story to its close. As I discuss below, Ruth's identity and Naomi's are intertwined like those of biological sisters. By recognizing Ruth for who she is, the women also recognize who Naomi is. At the beginning of the story, the women of Bethlehem do not recognize the once-blessed woman who returns to Bethlehem bitter and bereft. Their confusion forces Naomi to rearticulate her identity. At its conclusion, with the birth of her grandchild, the women see that Naomi is no longer empty. They know precisely who she is. The women's recognition reconstructs Naomi's identity; Mara becomes Naomi once again.

Although the women of Bethlehem focus on Naomi, the relationship between Ruth and Naomi is central to the book. It is certainly the Bible's most developed depiction of a relationship among women and may also be its most developed depiction of any relationship, regardless of gender. Sisterhood, I argue, provides an illuminating model through which to understand it. What resembles a parent-child relationship at the start of the narrative comes to resemble a sororal relationship in its course. The relationship between Ruth and Naomi is not a biological relationship. As a widowed, Moabite daughter-in-law, Ruth has no biological connection to Naomi's family and no inherent rights within Israel.

As is clear from the start of the story, Ruth's relationship to Naomi is easily dissolved. After the deaths of her husband and her two sons, Naomi decides to leave Moab and return to Bethlehem. Initially, her daughters-in-law Ruth and Orpah go with her. Despite their company, Naomi acts singularly and independently. *She* gets up [וַתָּקָם], and *she* goes forth [וַתֵּצֵא] from Moab. As we have seen, the verb יָצָא appears throughout the sister stories to mark independent agency. In Gen 30:16, Leah goes forth to meet Jacob whom she purchased for the night from her sister. In Gen 34:1, her daughter Dinah goes forth to see the daughters of the land. In 2 Sam 6:20, Michal goes forth to greet David and to admonish him for his indiscretion before the ark. In varying degree, these sisters are punished for acting independently.

Acting like a dangerous sister, Naomi independently goes forth from Moab. Naomi's independence implies the independence of her daughters-in-law. She does not ask for, expect, or desire their company. Ruth and Orpah choose to accompany her. Naomi tries to convince her daughters-in-law to return to their natal households:

> Naomi said to her two daughters-in-law: "Go and return, each woman to her mother's house. May YHWH treat you as kindly as you have treated the dead and me. May YHWH grant you and may you find rest, each woman in the house of her husband." She kissed them, and they raised their voices and wept. They said to her: "Let us return with you to your people." Naomi said: "Return, my daughters. Why would you go with me? Do I have more sons in my womb that can be husbands for you? Return, my daughters. Go, for I am too old to be with a man. Even if I said I had hope that I would be with a man tonight and would bear sons, would you wait until they grew? Would you restrain yourselves from being with a man? Do not my daughters, for I am more bitter than you. The hand of YHWH has gone out against me." They raised their voices and wept again. Orpah kissed her mother-in-law, but Ruth clung to her. (Ruth 1:8-14)

Unlike Ruth, Orpah heeds Naomi and returns home.

Orpah's brief appearance in Ruth may raise questions about her purpose in the narrative. Orpah functions as a counterpart to Ruth. Like Rachel and Leah, Michal and Merav, Lot's daughters, and Israel and Judah, Ruth and Orpah function as a sister pair. Not defined by a genetic link, Ruth and Orpah form a sister-in-law pair. As I observe earlier, the literary convention of pairing sisters highlights their differences. One sister is older, more beautiful, more fertile, or more promiscuous than the other. Orpah's presence in the narrative similarly defines and distinguishes Ruth's character from Orpah's. Although both sisters-in-law are loyal, Orpah ultimately leaves Naomi while Ruth clings to her. Orpah's willingness to leave contrasts Ruth's steadfast allegiance and proves Ruth to be more loyal and loving to Naomi than Orpah.

Orpah's departure from the narrative creates a void that Naomi fills. Characters in Ruth appear in dyads—Elimelech and Naomi, their sons Mahlon and Chilion, Ruth and Orpah, and the potential redeemers Boaz and Ploni Almoni. Elimelech's death and Orpah's exit leave Naomi and Ruth without narrative partners. Without counterparts, Naomi and Ruth redefine their relationship to become each other's narrative partners. I suggest that they assume a sororal relationship—although one that is not defined by biology. In effect, they create a sisterhood. For this to happen, Naomi must first renounce her maternal position. By sending Ruth and Orpah back to their natal households, Naomi relinquishes her role as a maternal figure in what remains of her own household and in the lives of her daughters-in-law. Ruth and Orpah should return to their mothers' homes, she says, to begin new lives with new husbands.

The rarity of the designation "mother's house," as opposed to the expected "house of the father," has intrigued scholars like Meyers, who contend that the use of this term indicates maternal involvement in matrimonial negotiations.[28] In my reading of this passage, Naomi uses this term to convey to Ruth and Orpah that she no longer functions as their mother, and they must go back to their real mothers, who will help them find husbands. Not only is Naomi unwilling to behave like a mother and find husbands for Ruth and Orpah, but she is unable to. She tells Ruth and Orpah that she cannot provide them with husbands because she has no more sons in her womb. She is empty.

At this point in the narrative, Naomi's emptiness may be purely emotional. Bereft of husband and sons, she has no emotional resources to care for Ruth and Orpah. Naomi also may be describing her physical reality. Having reached a certain age, she surpassed her childbearing years. She may even have lost her sexual drive, which she suggests when she admits that she is too old to be with a man. Naomi cannot fulfill her role as a mother or even as a mother-in-law. Emotionally drained, she cannot care for Ruth and Orpah like a good mother and work to secure their marriages. Too old, she cannot be an effective mother-in-law who will bear sons that will perform the duties of levirate marriage and marry their sisters-in-law. Knowing this, Naomi dismisses her daughters-in-law and dissolves any formal, familial, or emotional relationship with them.[29]

Upset, but resigned, Orpah kisses Naomi and leaves while Ruth clings to her. Naomi tries once more to convince Ruth to follow Orpah:

> She said: "Your sister-in-law has returned to her people and to her gods; return, follow your sister-in-law." Ruth said: "Do not make me abandon you and return from following you. Where you go, I will

go. In the place you spend the night, I will spend the night with you.
Your people will be my people, your God, my God. In the place you
die, I will die and there be buried. Thus will God do to me and more
if death separates me and you." (Ruth 1:15-17)

Although Jewish tradition reads this passage as a declaration of Ruth's faith,
which becomes a paradigm of conversion, contemporary scholars read it as
marking a transformation in Ruth's status and not her faith.[30]

As Mark Smith observes, the Ruth passage contains idioms similar to those
found in 1 Kgs 22:1-4 and 2 Kgs 3:4-7 that describe treaties forged between
the kings of Israel and Judah and foreign powers.[31] Similar negotiations occur
in the Ruth passage, though set in the domestic sphere, which Smith believes
establishes a formal and familial relationship between two alien parties.[32] In
this passage, Ruth does more than argue with and declare her allegiance to
Naomi. By using formal treaty language, Ruth legally, though not biologically,
becomes part of Naomi's family. She reestablishes the ties that bound them
together while her husband was alive and that Naomi renounced. Essentially,
Ruth adopts Naomi and constructs a family with her.

I contend that sisterhood is the model with which Ruth and Naomi forge
their new relationship. Ruth's refusal in Ruth 1:14 to *follow* her sister-in-law
[שובי אחרי יבמתך] and her insistence in Ruth 1:16 on *following* Naomi
[אל-תפגעי-בי לעזבך לשוב מאחריך] indicate that Naomi functions as
Orpah's replacement and that she assumes her position in Ruth's life. Resonant
language further defines the nature of Ruth and Naomi's relationship. Ruth
clings to Naomi [דבקה] and refuses to abandon her [לעזבך]. The use of the
verbs דבק and עזב allude to the Bible's first family narrative. In Gen 2:22-23,
God constructs a woman from the body of Adam and brings her to him. Adam
then identifies her as "bone of my bone and flesh of my flesh" and calls her
"woman."

The story ends with a coda in Gen 2:24: "Therefore a man leaves [יעזב]
his father and his mother and clings [ודבק] to his wife, and they become
one flesh." This verse makes a bold statement about family dynamics in which
intergenerational strife is an inherent part. Sons abandon parents to become
husbands. It also makes a bold statement about the institution of marriage
by observing that a husband and wife become one flesh [לבשר אחד]. Flesh
[בשר] indicates a blood relative in Gen 37:27 and defines a familial relation in
Lev 18:6. Use of the word flesh in Genesis 2 suggests that marriage creates a
biological bond; an affinal relationship becomes consanguineous.[33] Marriage,
according to Gordon J. Wenham, establishes a blood line, thereby creating

vertical consanguineous relationships—those between parents and children—within a family. It also, he argues, creates "horizontal 'blood' relationships between the spouses."[34]

The intentional allusion to the Genesis passage supports my assertion that Ruth formally redefines her relationship with Naomi. Just as Adam clings to Eve and forges a new familial bond with her, Ruth clings to Naomi and forges a new familial bond with her. Naomi no longer functions as the parental figure in Ruth's life as she once did.

Although supporting my assertion that Ruth redefines her relationship with Naomi, the allusion to Genesis also challenges my reading that sisterhood becomes the model for their new relationship. Ruth's refusal to return to her mother's house enacts the family dynamic described in Gen 2:24. Like Adam, Ruth chooses her conjugal home over her natal home—her husband over her mother. Yet unable to cling to her dead husband, she clings instead to her husband's family and claims them as family. Ruth clings to Naomi like a husband clings to his wife. She seeks to establish a horizontal familial relationship and become one flesh with Naomi. This suggests that marriage more than sisterhood provides the model for the new relationship between Ruth and Naomi. Invested in finding the full gamut of sexual relationships in the Bible, some contemporary readers perceive Ruth and Naomi's relationship to be homosexual.[35] When seen in this way, Ruth's declaration of allegiance to Naomi functions as a commitment ceremony, and their relationship becomes a same-sex marriage.

Ruth and Naomi do move from a vertical to a horizontal relationship with one another. Certainly, marriage is a primary concern that structures the book's narrative and provides its drama. Ruth needs to find a husband to secure an heir and namesake for her husband's family. Yet marriage does more than determine the course of the narrative. Indeed, it provides a framework within which to understand the relationship between Ruth and Naomi—though not in the way it is typically understood. The type of marriage that drives the story and its characters is not same-sex marriage or even the typical heterosexual marriage. The book of Ruth is about levirate marriage, and levirate marriage is about siblings—brothers and sisters-in-law. In significant ways, the centrality of levirate marriage and the way it is construed makes the book of Ruth about sisterhood. This is the horizontal relationship established in the course of the narrative. Ruth and Naomi assume a sororal relationship to one another that resembles, in form and function, the fraternal relationship found in levirate marriage.

A widespread phenomenon in the ancient world, levirate marriage is the custom that is invoked when a man dies without an heir.[36] His brother is obligated to marry the widow in order to produce an heir that bears the name of the deceased.[37] At first glance, levirate marriage appears to share the central concern of the family narratives in the Bible—securing a male heir—as stated in Deut 25:6: "It will be that the firstborn she will bear will establish the name of his dead brother. His name will not be erased from Israel." Because it secures her place within her husband's family, it is also possible to view levirate marriage as being in the widow's best interests.[38] The active role the widow plays in the ritual outlined in Deut 25:5-10 indicates that levirate marriage is as much about protecting the widow as it is about preserving the patriline of her dead husband. The widow ensures her own security. If the designated brother refuses to fulfill his duty, the widow brings him before the elders at the gate and declares his refusal publicly. The elders then try to persuade the brother. If he still refuses, the widow removes his shoe, spits in his face, and declares: "Thus is done to a man who will not build up the house of his brother."[39]

Although the precise significance of the shoe ritual remains unknown,[40] the widow's actions are clearly meant to induce shame and work as a disincentive to a reluctant brother. The possibility of being shamed by your dead brother's widow encourages the fulfillment of one's levirate duties. Thus levirate marriage enables women actively to produce an heir and to protect themselves.

Unsurprisingly, women are central figures in the Bible's two narratives about levirate marriage—Genesis 38 and the book of Ruth. In Genesis 38, Tamar tricks her father-in-law Judah, who withheld his eligible son from Tamar, into performing the levirate duties himself. Similarly, Ruth and Naomi go to great lengths to pursue Boaz as a levir. In both of these stories, women trick and cajole men to protect their husbands' property and secure their own fates.

Levirate marriage, which is concerned with providing a biological heir, also reconstructs an existing kin relationship by having one brother assume the identity of another. The fusion of identities, which is central to the ritual, demands an element of pretending. A father sires his nephew and pretends not to be his son's biological father. To uphold levirate marriage, a man must be willing to forego his own identity, at least in relation to this child. He must be willing to assume his brother's identity. In this way, he must be willing to behave like a sister. Sisters, I have argued, are interchangeable figures within their patriarchal household. Without inheritance rights and destined for marriage, there is little that distinguishes them. In the family narratives of the

Bible, sisters are also interchangeable. Leah easily can stand in for Rachel and Michal for Merav. Two sisters can even share one husband. Jacob, Lot, and metaphorically God all marry two sisters. Within the institution of levirate marriage, brothers are interchangeable. One brother must stand in for another and forfeit his unique identity.

In the book of Ruth, Boaz ostensibly agrees to assume Mahlon's identity and to father his child. Despite Boaz's willingness to stand in for Mahlon, the final genealogy lists Boaz, and not Mahlon, as the father of Obed. Clearly, Boaz does not relinquish his identity as would be expected in levirate marriage. Given this, scholars debate whether the book of Ruth actually reflects the custom.[41] However, adapting the laws of levirate marriage as laid out in Deut 25:5-10, I contend that the levirate marriage is indeed a central motif of Ruth. Boaz does serve as levir. Yet, I also argue that, in significant ways, it is the identities of Ruth and Naomi—even more than the identities of Boaz and Mahlon—that are fused, even confused in the narrative. I argue that Ruth and Naomi fulfill the siblings' role in levirate marriage. They form a sisterhood. Like the brothers in levirate marriage, Ruth and Naomi come to share an identity, a spouse, and ultimately a child.

As I observe above, identity is a central theme in the book of Ruth. Determining Ruth and Naomi's identity—particularly in relation to each other—is a consistent focus of the book. As I noted, their identity is dialogically formed. The whole narrative can be seen as an attempt to answer Naomi's question to Ruth in 3:16: "Who are you?"[42] As we saw during the exchange with the women of Bethlehem, Naomi's identity is inextricably tied to her life's circumstance. When happy, she is Naomi. When bitter, she becomes Mara. Ruth's identity is particularly defined by her status as an outsider. She is the Moabite, the daughter-in-law, the one who comes from the fields of Moab.[43] Over time, Ruth and Naomi's relationship to each other transforms their identities. Ruth's love enables Naomi to integrate goodness [היא טובה] back into her life so that she can reclaim her name as Naomi. Naomi's acceptance of Ruth enables Ruth to lose the attributes that defined her otherness. Like Naomi, Ruth's designation changes to reflect who she is and how she is perceived. At the book's start, she is "Ruth, the Moabite, her daughter-in-law, the one who returned [השבה] with her from the fields of Moab."[44] At its conclusion, Ruth is no longer seen as the one who comes from outside. Instead, she becomes, האשה הבאה, "the woman who enters"—the one within.[45]

The sisterhood formed between Ruth and Naomi constructs an intimacy that more than transforms their individual identities. It fuses them. In the course of their narrative, Ruth and Naomi come to share an identity like brothers in a levirate marriage. Certainly, the declaration by the women of Bethlehem at the end of the story that a son was born to Naomi suggests the fusion of their identities. Yet, this fusion is also evident earlier in the narrative when Naomi instructs Ruth to seduce Boaz. In Ruth 3:3, Naomi commands Ruth to go down [וירדתי] to the threshing floor. Once there, Ruth must lie [ושכבתי] with Boaz who is eligible as Naomi's kinsman to perform the levirate duties. Without vocalization, the verbs should be read as they are written—in the first person singular—meaning "I will go down" and "I will lie down." The subject speaking is Naomi. Yet the verbs are vocalized, and therefore read, in the second person singular, identifying the subject to be Ruth. To address the discrepancy between how these verbs are written (in the first person) and how they are vocalized (in the second), scholars identify them as an archaic form of the second person feminine singular directed to Ruth. This understanding of the verbs removes the confusion about who is their subject. Naomi commands Ruth saying "You go down . . . you lie with Boaz."[46]

My reading embraces the discrepancy between the way the verbs are written and how they should be read and understood. The verbs remain conjugated in the first person but are intended and read as commands to Ruth. Although the verbs may be an archaic form, it seems unlikely since they appear in a string of verbs all conjugated in the second person singular [ורחצת וסכת ושמת...וירדתי]. More likely is that they are a product of scribal error and the idiosyncrasies of textual transmission that the text has chosen to preserve.

By writing the verbs one way and reading them another, I contend that the text intentionally preserves the confusion in the intended subjects of these verbs. Although narrative context supports Ruth as the subject and that is how the verbs should be read and understood, the text wants its readers to think about Naomi and to recognize the intimacy that has been formed between them. This is another moment of intentional ambiguity similar to the one we saw in Michal and Merav's story. Naomi's use of the first person to direct Ruth communicates their connection to one another. It also blurs their identities just as 2 Sam 21:8 blurs the identities of Michal and Merav and presents them as interchangeable figures.[47] Naomi's recorded use of the first person captures the empathy and gratitude she finally feels toward Ruth. This moment captures a shift in Naomi's identity that has been altered by her relationship with Ruth.

Ruth has earned Naomi's deep affection and loyalty. At the end of chapter 2, Ruth feeds Naomi with the barley from Boaz's field. Naomi has come a long way since she described her emptiness despite Ruth's presence (Ruth 1:21).

Feeling full at last, Naomi connects emotionally to the daughter-in-law who long ago declared allegiance to her. At last, Naomi recognizes Ruth as family when she informs her in Ruth 2:20 that Boaz is "*our* redeemer" and when she commands Ruth in verse 23 to cling [ותדבק] to Boaz, Naomi's—and now Ruth's—kinsman [קרוב לנו האיש]. This recognition marks a shift in Naomi's identity, drawing her closer to Ruth. Naomi is not only bound to Ruth by gratitude and obligation; they have become sisters. Like sisters, their fates and their identities have become fused.

Naomi's use of the first person as she directs Ruth shows that she is deeply present with Ruth during the seduction. It accentuates what Pardes considers to be Naomi's "vicarious involvement" in the seduction and "her sympathetic identification" with Ruth.[48] Naomi's fate is about to change along with Ruth's. By sleeping with Boaz, Ruth enacts the levirate marriage, securing her own home and future within Israel. Ruth also secures Naomi's home and future by providing her with a redeemer for her husband's land and the hope of grandchildren. The women of Bethlehem recognize this when they bless Naomi in Ruth 4:14, saying "Blessed is YHWH who has not withheld a redeemer from you today." When Boaz sleeps with Ruth, he effectively redeems both women. Just as two brothers share one wife and one identity in levirate marriage, Ruth and Naomi share one patriarch who will provide them with land, food, and support in their old age. They also share one identity. The confusion preserved in Naomi's command to Ruth to seduce Boaz conveys this. When Ruth goes down to the threshing floor, it is as if Naomi was there; it is as if Naomi and Ruth both marry Boaz.[49]

Like the brothers in levirate marriage, Ruth and Naomi functionally share a husband. They also, like the brothers, come to share a child. As I mention earlier, the book's closing image of Naomi tending her grandchild might convey Naomi's triumph at Ruth's expense. In this reading, by placing Ruth's child to her breast, Naomi would be claiming him. Supporting Naomi, the women of Bethlehem would be proclaiming her to be the child's real mother.

In my reading of this final scene, Naomi claims the child, but not at Ruth's expense. Her embrace of the baby follows the women's praise that Ruth is better than seven sons. Like a son, Ruth secures land and progeny for Naomi. By taking Ruth's son to her breast, Naomi recognizes what Ruth has done for her. Her embrace is a formal gesture that registers her own acceptance of Ruth and the baby and that asks for her community's acceptance. As אמנת, Naomi does not usurp Ruth's role as the baby's mother, she shares it.[50] Naomi will care for the child, protect him, and provide for him along with Ruth. As Pardes observes, the women agree to "joint motherhood."[51] In the book's final scene,

Naomi formally recognizes Ruth and her child as family and pledges to share the maternal responsibilities with Ruth.

By functionally sharing a spouse and a child, Ruth and Naomi assume the fraternal role in levirate marriage, though they are female and not biologically related. They construct a sisterhood, a fictive kin relationship, through which their identities and their fates fuse. Theirs is an ideal sisterhood that protects the house of Elimelech and strengthens Israelite society by ensuring the Davidic line. Their sisterhood enables vertical, consanguineous relationships to form that result in the birth of David and the establishment of the Davidic dynasty.

In remarkable ways, Ruth and Naomi's sisterhood is not only ideal; it is redemptive. Not only does their relationship provide Israel with an actual redeemer as imagined by the prophet Isaiah,[52] it overturns the expectations of sisters and sisterhood in the Bible. Their relationship secures a marriage, strengthens a vulnerable patriarchal house, and, at its end, reconciles paired sisters Rachel and Leah. It even redeems the most dangerous elements of the sister and sisterhood stories. Unlike dangerous sisters who assert agency and desire and suffer, Ruth and Naomi assert agency,[53] channel desire,[54] and are rewarded with a child.

Even Moabites find redemption in the book of Ruth.[55] As a Moabite, Ruth descends from Lot's incestuous daughters. In Numbers 25, her ancestors initiate one of the most egregious sins in Israel's history. Ruth's loyalty to Naomi challenges the image of the seductive Moabite women and reincorporates Lot's descendents into Israel's story. Unlike her ancestors, Ruth the Moabite does not threaten Israel or introduce foreign gods. Instead, she accepts Naomi's people and Naomi's God. Boaz's willingness to marry Ruth defies the Deuteronomic prohibition. Their union produces the Davidic line.

King David owes his life to Ruth and Naomi's relationship. Sisterhood is responsible for the Bible's most significant hero and its most stable dynasty. As stated unequivocally in Ruth 4:15, Ruth's love proves more valuable to Naomi than seven sons. This statement explodes like a bomb among the family narratives in the Bible in which sons are prayed for and fought over so that heirs can be born and families secured. In crucial ways, the book of Ruth is a typical family narrative, concerned with securing land and progeny. Yet, whereas brothers, fathers, and sons provide the central drama in most of the family stories in the Bible, sisterhood is the primary and defining relationship in the book of Ruth.

Ruth, the Moabite in-law, has no biological connection or familial obligation to Naomi. She follows Naomi even though Naomi renounces her maternal position and dissolves any familial obligation to her. In response to

Naomi's dismissal, Ruth reconstructs and redefines her relationship to Naomi. She adopts her as her sister. Through the course of the narrative, Naomi accepts Ruth as her sister. The book of Ruth demonstrates that love can override biology and that a loyal sisterhood can be worth more than seven sons.

Notes

1. See Pardes, *Countertraditions in the Bible: A Feminist Approach* (Cambridge, MA: Harvard University Press, 1992), 99.

2. The book of Esther is the only other book in the Bible named for a female character.

3. See Adrien J. Bledstein, "Female Companionships: If the Book of Ruth Were Written by a Woman," in *A Feminist Companion to Ruth,* ed. Athalya Brenner (Sheffield: Sheffield Academic, 1993), 116.

4. S. D. Goitein posits that Ruth was written by an "elderly prophetess-wise woman." See Goitein, "Women as Creators of Biblical Genres." *Prooftexts* 8, no. 1 (1988): 31. Fokkelien van Dijk-Hemmes argues for female authorship in "Ruth: A Product of Women's Culture?" in *Feminist Companion to Ruth,* 134–39.

5. See Goitein, "Women as Creators of Biblical Genres," 31.

6. Carol Meyers, "Returning Home: Ruth 1.8 and the Gendering of the Book of Ruth," in *Feminist Companion to Ruth,* 89.

7. Ibid., 109–10.

8. Ibid., 113–14.

9. See Meyers, "Women of the Neighborhood (Ruth 4.17): Informal Female Networks in Ancient Israel," in *Ruth and Esther: A Feminist Companion to the Bible (Second Series),* ed. Athalya Brenner (Sheffield: Sheffield Academic, 1991), 119–20.

10. Pardes, *Countertraditions,* 102.

11. Ibid., 101.

12. Meyers, "Women of the Neighborhood," 120.

13. See Exod 15:20; 1 Sam 18:6-7; Ps 68:12.

14. Trible offers a similar reading in *God and the Rhetoric of Sexuality* (Philadelphia: Fortress Press, 1978), 174.

15. Lee writes: "It is universally recognized—by developmental psychologists, social scientists, and philosophers alike—that identity is dialogically formed. People define their identity always in dialogue with, and sometimes in struggle against, the things that others see in them." See Eunny P. Lee, "Ruth the Moabite: Identity, Kinship, and Otherness," in *Engaging the Bible in a Gendered World: An Introduction to Feminist Biblical Interpretation in Honor of Katharine Doob Sakenfeld,* ed. Linda Day and Carolyn Pressler (Louisville: Westminster John Knox, 2006), 93.

16. Ibid.

17. Ibid.

18. Commenting on the repeated question of identity in Ruth, Lee writes: "But the questions also signal the potential for mutual transformation. Whether intended or not, they invite a dialogical reconstruction of identity to take place." See ibid.

19. Katharine Doob Sakenfeld comments on the intertextual relationship between the books of Job and Ruth. See Katharine Doob Sakenfeld, "Naomi's Cry: Reflections on Ruth 1:20-21," in *A God So Near: Essays on Old Testament Theology in Honor of Patrick D. Miller,* ed. Brent A. Strawn and Nancy R. Bowen (Winona Lake, IN: Eisenbrauns, 2003), 135.

20. See Job 10.

21. Peter W. Coxon also identifies a similarity in the narrative function of the daughters of Jerusalem in the Song of Songs and the women of Bethlehem; he writes: "[W]hen Ruth has been

won it is left to the people, the elders and the women of the neighborhood to chronicle the blessings of the family. In the manner of the anonymous chorus figures of the Song of Songs who help to delineate the romantic proceedings more sharply, the narrator here sharpens the profile of the Naomi-Ruth relationship as seen by the onlooker (and of course by intent the reader also)." See Peter W. Coxon, "Was Naomi a Scold? A Response to Fewell and Gunn," *JSOT* 45 (1989): 30.

22. See Meyers, "Women of the Neighborhood," 123–24.

23. See Ebeling, *Women's Lives in Biblical Times*, (London: T&T Clark, 2010), 103.

24. See Fuchs, *Sexual Politics in the Biblical Narrative: Reading the Hebrew Bible as a Woman* (Sheffield: Sheffield Academic, 2000), 86.

25. The women use the full naming formula, "to call the name," described by Phyllis Trible in "Depatriarchalizing in Biblical Interpretation," *JAAR* 41, no. 1 (1973): 38. The use of this formula suggests that the naming is a ritualized act.

26. See Athalya Brenner, "Naomi and Ruth," *VT* 33, no. 4 (1983): 386.

27. Similarly Lee argues that Ruth has been integrated into Naomi's family though with some degree of ambivalence that is reflected in this text. See Lee, "Ruth the Moabite," 100.

28. The phrase appears in Gen 24:28; Song 3:4; and 8:2. See Meyers, "Returning Home," 112.

29. Bledstein also suggests that Naomi formally renounces her relationship with Ruth. See Bledstein, "Female Companionships," 120.

30. Smith writes: "(M)uch of Jewish tradition has viewed Ruth's words as an expression of conversion. Scholars who address this view largely reject it." See Mark S. Smith, "'Your People Shall Be My People': Family and Covenant in Ruth 1:16-17," *CBQ* 69 (2007): 243. Agnethe Siquans similarly argues that Ruth and Naomi experience a change of legal status in the course of the narrative. See Siquans, "Foreignness and Poverty in the Book of Ruth: A Legal Way for a Poor Foreign Woman to Be Integrated into Israel," *JBL* 128, no. 3 (2009): 443–52.

31. See Smith, "Your People Shall Be My People," 248.

32. Smith observes: "Ruth expresses at the level of the family and clan what Jehoshaphat conveys at the level of international royal relations. The words of Jehoshaphat represent the treaty/covenant relationship on the royal level across family lines; Ruth's words represent the covenant relationship across family lines that have been sundered by the death of the male who had linked the lives of Ruth and Naomi." See ibid., 255.

33. Gen 2:22-23 makes explicit that Eve and Adam share flesh. Eve is made from Adam's flesh.

34. Not only do husband and wife have a consanguineous relationship, but they also have these relationships with a spouse's extended family. See Gordon J. Wenham, *The Book of Leviticus* (Grand Rapids, MI: Wm. B. Eerdmans Publishing Co., 1979), 255.

35. See Rebecca Alpert, "Finding Our Past: A Lesbian Interpretation of the Book of Ruth," in *Reading Ruth: Contemporary Women Reclaim a Sacred Story*, ed. Judith A. Kates and Gail Twersky Reimer, (New York: Ballantine, 1994), 91–96.

36. Levirate marriage was practiced among he Hittites, the Assyrians, and possibly in Ugarit. See Eryl W. Davies, "Inheritance Rights and the Hebrew Levirate Marriage, Part 1," *VT* 31, no. 2 (1981): 139. For a fuller study of levirate marriage, see Dvora E. Weisberg, *Levirate Marriage and the Family in Ancient Judaism* (Hanover: University Press of New England, 2009).

37. The laws of levirate marriage appear in Deut 25:5-10. Besides Ruth and Deuteronomy, the only other biblical reference to levirate marriage is the story of Tamar and Judah in Genesis 38.

38. Unlike other ancient Near Eastern societies, Israel did not enable the widow to inherit her husband's property. Davies concludes: "Moreover, it is probable that a further purpose was served by the levirate custom in Israel, namely the protection and security of the widow, and the most obvious way for this to have been accomplished would have been through marriage." Davies, "Inheritance Rights," 142–43.

39. Deut 25:9.

40. For a discussion of the meaning of the shoe ritual, see Calum M. Carmichael, "A Ceremonial Crux: Removing a Man's Sandal as a Female Gesture of Contempt," *JBL* 96, no. 3 (1977): 321–36.

41. Josh Ketchum acknowledges the difficulties in identifying the marriage of Ruth and Boaz as a levirate marriage; he writes: "[I]t is clearly evident that these laws are not exactly applied in Ruth as set forth in the Pentateuch. For example, a specific levirate marriage as laid forth in Deut 25:5-10 is not what takes place in Ruth; however, it seems that the same foundational goals and customs are at work. The marriage of Boaz and Ruth is never called a levirate marriage, leading some to argue that it is not levirate marriage." See Josh Ketchum, "The Go'el Custom in Ruth: A Comparative Study," *Restoration Quarterly* 52, no. 4 (2010): 237.

42. Lee writes: "The question of who Ruth is for Naomi will not be fully answered for Naomi until the story's end, when the women of Bethlehem declare that "your daughter-in-law who loves you . . . is more to you than seven sons" (4:15)." See Lee, "Ruth the Moabite," 99.

43. Ruth refers to herself in Ruth 2:10 as a נכריה, a foreigner, as Siquans observes: "Ruth recognizes and acknowledges her status as a foreigner and wonders why Boaz ever takes notice of her." See Siquans, "Foreignness and Poverty," 448.

44. Ruth 1:22.

45. Ruth 4:11. Lee also notes Ruth's transformation. See Lee, "Ruth the Moabite," 99.

46. Tamara Cohn Eskenazi and Tikva Frymer-Kensky comment on the discrepancy between the written and read verbs: "But some scholars consider this to be an archaic second-person feminine form, meaning "you will go down," in the singular. Such usage would be consistent with the other archaic verb forms that characterize the speech register of Naomi and of Boaz . . . both of whom are from an older generation." See Tamara Cohn Eskenazi and Tikva Frymer-Kensky, *The JPS Bible Commentary: Ruth* (Philadelphia: The Jewish Publication Society, 2011), 52.

47. Second Samuel 21:8 refers to Michal and Adriel's five sons as opposed to the more logical Merav and Adriel's sons.

48. See Pardes, *Countertraditions*, 104–5.

49. Pardes writes: "Hence, as the Book of Ruth revises the story of Rachel and Leah, the rivalry between the younger and the elder co-wives gives way to a harmonious sharing of the same man." See ibid., 105.

50. The word אמן is used to describe a caregiver. See Num 11:12; Isa 49:23; and Est 2:7.

51. Pardes suggests that neither Ruth nor Naomi names the baby as a way of assuring their shared maternal roles. See Pardes, *Countertraditions*, 106.

52. Isa 11:1-10 describes the Davidic king who will be Israel's redeemer.

53. Naomi decides to return to Bethlehem. Ruth chooses to go with her.

54. Together, they plan and enact Boaz's seduction.

55. Nehama Aschkenasy observes a similar "redemptive" narrative progression from Genesis 19 to 38 to Ruth; she writes: "Thus we move from incestuous relations to covenantal marriage, from illicit sexual encounters . . . to a marriage ceremony conducted in public with the blessings of judges and the entire people." See Aschkenasy, "Reading Ruth through a Bakhtinian Lens: The Carnivalesque in a Biblical Tale," *JBL* 126, no. 3 (2007): 449.

10

Conclusion

Although anticipating the birth of sons and securing a son's legacy provides much drama, sisters and sisterhoods also have an integral role to play in the family narratives in the Bible. My study shows that sisters and sisterhoods are a defined typology in the Bible, and it reveals common features and concerns that shape their narratives. Just as there is a typical brother story, there is a typical sister story in the Bible. At their core, both types of stories work to protect the Bible's designated family and to ensure Israel's future.

Defined by rivalry, brothers fight to secure heirs and to protect property. Younger brothers Isaac, Jacob, and Joseph defy the norms of primogeniture to become their fathers' primary heirs. Their struggles with their older brothers help prove that they are the rightful successors. Human grit and divine will, not convention, determines legacy.

Without the right of inheritance, sisters do not engage directly in efforts to secure it. Instead, they protect their families through their loyalty and obedience. Their stories manifest the implicit gender ideology of the Bible that supports patriarchal authority and protects patrilineal inheritance. Many sister stories are concerned with brokering marriages, like Rebecca's to Isaac, which enrich and strengthen a sister's natal household. Most of the marriages brokered in the sister stories of the Bible do not conform to this model. More often, rival patriarchs and inappropriate unions threaten and, ultimately, weaken a sister's natal household. Marriage is a prominent feature in biblical narratives about sisterhood as well. Reflecting a broader focus, sisterhood stories are concerned with securing marriages that strengthen Israelite society. The threat of exogamous marriage, as opposed to the threat of specific rival patriarchs, pervades these stories.

Whereas the Bible's brother stories are about continuity, its sister and sisterhood stories are about stability. Although the ideal sister or sisterhood provides stability in the home or Israelite community, sisters and sisterhoods are often destabilizing figures within the Bible's patrilineal, patrilocal, and patriarchal context. Paradigmatic ideal sisters, like Rebecca and young Miriam, who support their natal households, are outnumbered by dangerous sisters like Rachel, Michal, Lot's daughters, and Tamar, who weaken their natal households. My study reveals that sisters and sisterhoods pose a particular threat to patriarchal norms and authority as depicted in the Bible. For reasons that I suggest below, dangerous sisters are particularly prominent in the Bible. Their stories reveal unique anxieties associated with sisters, which are also evident, though modified, in the sisterhood stories. Fears of sororal agency, desire, and solidarity underlie the Bible's sister and sisterhood stories. Sisters and sisterhoods become dangerous when they assert independent agency, when they elicit or exercise desire, or when they conspire together.

Fears of female agency and desire are unsurprising in a text like the Bible, which reflects a patriarchal society in which women are subject to men, and their sexuality is controlled and protected by the men in their lives. Similar fears are evident in all the Bible's stories about women—whether a mother, a wife, a daughter, or a sister—though, I argue, these fears are manifest differently depending on the specific role the woman plays in the narrative. Therefore, by studying the Bible's sisters and sisterhood stories, we can deepen our understanding of the Bible's gender ideology and expand our understanding of the roles women play in its narratives.

What differentiates a sister story from other stories about women is the way the fears of female agency and desire play out within the less hierarchical sibling context or—as is the case of sisterhoods—within a peer context. By definition, a sister story is a sibling story that focuses either on the brother-sister relationship or the sister-sister relationship. Each relationship raises unique anxieties. As the stories of Dinah, Sarah, and Tamar show, the brother-sister relationship reflects anxieties associated with the sexualized sister. Ideally, a brother should protect his sister's sexuality and prevent her violation. A brother, like Laban, may negotiate marriage on behalf of a sister, but once a sister becomes sexualized in the Bible's patrilocal context, she no longer needs to engage narratively with him. As Rebecca did, she leaves her father's house for her husband's and becomes a wife and a mother who engages with a husband and sons. Dinah's story illustrates well the problems posed by the unmarried, sexualized sister. Having failed to protect their sister's sexuality—essentially having failed as brothers—Dinah's brothers no longer know how to relate to her. Their question in Gen 34:31: "Should our sister be treated like a whore?" conveys their genuine distress and confusion.

As the incest narratives show, the sexualized sister can be an object of her brother's desire. According to the sexual prohibitions found in Leviticus 18 and 20 and Deuteronomy 27, the brother-sister relationship should remain asexual. Despite these prohibitions, Abraham is said to have married his half-sister. Princess Tamar implies that King David would be open to a similar union. The number of incest narratives involving sisters is notable and suggests that either the Bible indulges in the fantasy of, or expresses an anxiety induced by, incest. My reading considers these narratives to be a reflection of the anxiety induced by, as opposed to the fantasy of, incest.

Within each of these narratives, incestuous unions weaken the sister's natal household. Lot's daughters remove Lot from Israel's story and destiny. Amnon's rape of Tamar fulfills Nathan's curse on David. It is the calamity that arises from within David's house that serves as his punishment for sleeping with Bathsheba and killing her husband Uriah. In her role as sister, Sarah compromises Abraham's house and reflects his vulnerability. Like the incest prohibitions, these narratives encourage clear boundaries within the family to ensure the stability of the family. A daughter should not become her father's wife. A brother should not marry his sister.

Whereas the brother-sister relationship reflects anxieties related to sororal desire and the sexualized sister, the sister-sister relationship reflects anxieties related to sororal solidarity and the independent sister. Like brothers, sisters are often paired in their narratives. Yet, unlike brother stories, sister stories are not bound by the trope of sibling rivalry. Since primogeniture is not an issue for them, sisters are interchangeable within their families and narratives. Neither blessing nor inheritance is granted to the firstborn sister. As a result, Leah easily can stand in for Rachel and Michal for Merav. Either sister is worth one hundred Philistine foreskins. Because sisters do not fight for inheritance, they are free to engage with each other in a greater variety of ways than brothers. Sisters can be rivals, but they also can function as narrative partners, as Rachel and Leah's story illustrates. Although rivalry defines their relationship, there are moments in their story when the sisters conspire together.

Sororal solidarity proves dangerous. Rachel and Leah conspire at two crucial moments in their story—to barter their husband's sexuality and to consent to leaving their father's home. Both moments of conspiracy challenge patriarchal authority. When negotiating over the mandrakes, Rachel and Leah overturn patriarchal norms and assert control over their husband's sexuality. Together, they agree to leave their father's house and denounce their place within it and, by extension, Laban's authority over them. Lot's daughters, another sister pair, conspire together and overturn patriarchal authority. Their rape of Lot proves him to be an ineffective patriarch and removes him from Israel's narrative. Rebel Israel and Faithless Judah also demonstrate sororal solidarity at the expense of patriarchal authority. Younger sister Judah learns her promiscuous behavior by watching Israel. Sin spreads as sister teaches sister to defy patriarchal authority and to despise their husbands and sons. These stories reveal the Bible's fear of sororal solidarity and its investment in sororal rivalry. They argue rhetorically for keeping women apart by revealing the benefits of rivalry and the detriments of solidarity, once again to ensure the stability of the household. Sororal solidarity destroys Lot's house, whereas sororal rivalry builds Jacob's.

Interestingly, the sisterhood stories present a more complicated picture of sororal solidarity. Sororal solidarity creates loyal fellowship among women. Although dangerous sisterhoods like the daughters of Moab entice Israel to apostasy, ideal sisterhoods like the daughters of Jerusalem in the Song of Songs protect a young woman's sexual purity and prevent an abomination from occurring in Israel. Most remarkable of all, Ruth and Naomi's sisterhood ensures the birth of King David. Below, I consider why the sisterhood stories convey less anxiety about sororal solidarity than do the sister stories.

Dangerous sisters may destabilize their families by introducing rival patriarchs or by invoking incestuous desire. They may conspire to defy patriarchal authority and overturn its norms. Given this, dangerous sisters do not experience happy endings in the patriarchal world of the Bible. As Ezek 23:48 makes clear, a defiant woman must be punished so that other women may learn from her example. Similar to Ezekiel's graphic images of the punishment of Israel and Judah, dangerous-sister stories function as cautionary tales. Dinah's independence ruins her. Rachel's selfish desire for more children effectively kills her. Michal's love for David dooms her. Even when the sister is the object of her brother's subversive desires, she is punished. Tamar does nothing wrong, yet she is condemned to a life of desolation. Arguably, Sarah is granted a happy ending to her story. She gives birth to Isaac immediately after returning from Gerar where she assumed the role of Abraham's sister. Notably, however, Isaac's birth occurs after Sarah resumes her position as Abraham's wife and no longer functions as a sister in the narrative. Wife Sarah, and not sister Sarah, is granted a happy ending. Also, Sarah's happiness is tempered by her bitter struggle with Hagar, which comprises the last story in her narrative. Sarah does not enjoy life much beyond her role as a dangerous sister.

The fates of these dangerous sisters could suggest that sisters are expendable and unwelcome members of the biblical family narratives. Yet my study reveals that although sisters are destabilizing figures, they play a crucial role in the family narratives in the Bible. Rachel, Leah, Michal, Merav, Lot's daughters, and Tamar fulfill a similar and significant narrative function that advances the overall narrative. These dangerous sisters weaken the houses of their fathers—Laban, Saul, Lot, and David. With the exception of David and his household, the biblical narrative requires that these patriarchs and their homes be weakened. Lot is a rival to Abraham, Laban to Jacob, and Saul to David. To secure the positions of the designated patriarchs, the Bible employs dangerous sisters to remove their rivals. In their unique way, sister stories work to secure heirs and legacy by destabilizing their natal households. Lot's daughters remove Lot as Abraham's viable heir. Rachel and Leah build Jacob's house at Laban's expense. Michal and Merav help David rise to power at Saul's expense.

Dinah, Sarah, Tamar, Rebel Israel, and Faithless Israel also destabilize their natal households. Yet these dangerous sisters serve a different narrative and rhetorical purpose. They do not remove rival patriarchs from the narrative so that it can focus on the designated patriarchs. Rather, they weaken the homes of the designated patriarchs and function either as a punishment of, or a deterrent to, improper behavior. Their stories serve as warnings that encourage appropriate behavior. By instigating civil war within David's home and kingdom, dangerous sister Tamar punishes David for decimating Uriah's household. As a wife-sister, Sarah reflects and contributes to the vulnerability of Abraham's house and deters incestuous feelings between a brother and a sister. Dinah's actions make Jacob vulnerable among his Canaanite neighbors, showing that even designated patriarchs are not immune to, and must be wary of, the dangerous sister. Prophets Jeremiah and Ezekiel also rely upon the rhetorical power of dangerous sisters. Their portrayal of Israel and Judah as promiscuous sisters married to God capitalizes on the anxieties sisters raise and proves their potency as a rhetorical device employed to reform Israel's wayward behavior.

Although reflecting a broader perspective, sisterhood stories share common features and concerns with sister stories. My study of the sisterhoods in the Bible supports recent scholarship that posits the existence and significance of women's networks in Israelite society. Scholars believe these networks trained women for the labor required of them, such as baking and weaving, and helped them perform their tasks. They also provided women with social and emotional support. Scholars assert that sisterhoods valued and validated women's experience and expertise. They enabled women to enjoy a status denied them in Israel's patriarchal society and may have produced and performed rituals that marked and enriched a woman's life. They also contributed to Israelite society by socially connecting communities and perhaps by negotiating marriages between them.

I identify the groups of women, often designated as daughters throughout the Bible, as sisterhoods—women's networks that were not defined by immediate kinship ties. My reading of the role these sisterhoods assume in their narratives affirms scholars' assumptions that sisterhoods supported women socially and emotionally and contributed to Israelite society. Sisterhoods, like the daughters of Jerusalem in the Song of Songs, protected young women from sexual violation while providing safe spaces for women to express their feelings and even to shape their identities. When feeling emotionally and sexually vulnerable, the Shulamite seeks the company of her sisterhood, the daughters of Jerusalem, in order to put a comfortable distance between herself and her lover. Safe within her sisterhood, the Shulamite is able and encouraged to express desire for her lover. Similarly, the women of Bethlehem provide a safe space for Naomi to express her emotions and to define her identity. In their company, Naomi is able to claim her identity as Mara, the embittered one, and later to reclaim her identity as Naomi, the pleasant one. Present for the birth of Ruth's child, the women of Bethlehem also appear to serve a ritual purpose in Ruth and Naomi's lives by blessing and naming the child.

Like sister stories, sisterhood stories are concerned with security. Whereas sister stories are concerned with the security of the household, sisterhood stories are concerned with the security of Israelite society. Dangerous sisterhoods threaten the stability of Israelite society. Their stories manifest fears of sororal desire, agency, and solidarity in which exogamous marriage is an insidious theme. They warn against sexual liaisons with dangerous, foreign women who either passively attract or actively lure Israel.[1]

Just as the incest narratives encourage maintaining family boundaries, dangerous-sisterhood stories encourage maintaining national/religious boundaries. Divine sons should not marry human daughters; Israelites should not marry Moabite or Canaanite women. If Israelites cross these boundaries, they risk their property and, more importantly, their defining relationship with God.

Numbers 25 serves as a paradigmatic dangerous-sisterhood story, manifesting core anxieties and demonstrating what is at stake if Israel intermarries with its neighbors. Seduced by the dangerous Moabite sisterhood, Israel commits religious infidelity and clings to the women's god Baal Peor and not to Israel's god YHWH. It takes sword and plague to remove the sisterhood and its effects and to restore order to Israel.

Naturally, sororal solidarity is a major concern of the sisterhood narratives, as it was of the sister stories. If conspiring sisters weaken households, then larger groups of women weaken society. As the prophet Ezekiel observes, sisterhoods can threaten patriarchal authority directly. In Ezek 16:45, the prophet describes how Israel's women ally together and reject their husbands.

Sisterhood also poses a less direct threat by creating an autonomous realm in which women can express themselves and exhibit behavior not typical of women within a patriarchal society. As the Song of Songs illustrates, a young, unmarried woman feels free to express sexual desire while in the company of other women. The book of Ruth tells the story of two biologically unrelated women who secure property and progeny and shows how far sisterhood can go beyond the patriarchal norms of the Bible's family narratives.

In the story of Jephthah's daughter, sisterhood creates a realm defiantly void of men. Condemned to death, Jephthah's daughter asks her father for two months of life and chooses to spend those months with her friends, a sisterhood, and not with her father. She does not ask her father for more time so that she can marry. Instead, she chooses to mourn the wedding she will never have with the friends who would have celebrated with her. Not only does sisterhood provide Jephthah's daughter with solace, it also institutes a yearly ritual in her honor that provides her with a legacy denied to her father.

If sisterhood provides women with the opportunity to express themselves and to exercise autonomy, at times at the expense of patriarchal authority, then it makes sense that most, if not all, of the Bible's sisterhoods would be dangerous. At best, their narratives would serve as warnings that support patriarchal norms and that encourage appropriate behavior. Indeed, dangerous-sisterhood stories like Genesis 6, Genesis 34, and Numbers 25, protect Israel's religious and cultural borders by warning against exogamous marriage.

Yet, as we have seen, not all of the Bible's sisterhoods are dangerous. The daughters of Jerusalem and the women of Bethlehem offer a positive model of sisterhood that supports the women in their narratives but does not threaten the Bible's patriarchal objectives. In general, my study of the Bible's sisters and sisterhoods reveals that sisterhoods fare better than sisters. The Bible appears particularly invested in its dangerous sisters. Not only do their stories outnumber their ideal counterparts, they advance the biblical narrative by securing its designated patriarchs.

Although time and again dangerous sisters make sure that the right patriarch succeeds, remarkably it is a sisterhood that ensures the birth of one of the Bible's most legendary figures—King David. Naturally, no one can account for the discrepancy between the way the Bible depicts sisters and sisterhood. The more positive depictions of sisterhood may reflect the roles sisterhoods played in Israelite society. The biblical writers may have understood the value of women's networks and sought to support them through these narratives. Or perhaps, on a deeper level, they were more comfortable with sisterhoods than with sisters. Biological sisters who conspire and assert agency and desire, or become objects of desire, pose an immediate threat to patriarchal authority and to their families and, therefore, are seen as more dangerous. Certainly sisterhoods pose similar challenges to patriarchal authority and can inflict even greater damage than sisters. Whereas dangerous sisters upend their natal households, dangerous sisterhoods upend Israelite society.

Yet the Bible's positive depictions of sisterhood suggest that actual Israelite women were free to express desire and assert independence when in the company of other women. Sisterhood supported women socially and emotionally. It enabled women to assert themselves and to express themselves without being a direct threat to patriarchal authority and society. Sisterhood provided women with an appropriate outlet for the expression of desire, agency, and solidarity in the Bible. As it does in the Song of Songs, sisterhood shielded the family from the more immediate threat posed by the dangerous sister.

Not only does sisterhood support Israel's women, the book of Ruth shows that it also determines Israel's destiny. At the start of the book, Ruth and Naomi dissolve their parent-child relationship with one another. In the course of the narrative, they reconstitute their relationship as a sisterhood that is modeled on the fraternal relationship in levirate marriage. Like brothers in levirate marriage, Ruth and Naomi fuse identities and come to share a spouse and a child. The sisterhood that forms between them is arguably the most significant relationship in the Bible because it leads to King David and the Davidic dynasty. The book of Ruth seems intentionally to redeem Moabites and to elevate sisterhood as an ideal model of human relationship.

Although it is possible that the book of Ruth preserves some historical truth and that King David, in fact, descends from Ruth the Moabite, it is my assumption that the narrative and its characters were carefully constructed.[2] It could have offered a more stereotypical birth narrative in which God and a husband intervene and transform a barren wife into a mother. Instead, Ruth tells the story of two biologically unrelated women who secure their family's legacy and establish the Davidic dynasty. The choice to make Ruth a Moabite accentuates her "otherness" in relation to Naomi and highlights the fact that Ruth and Naomi construct a relationship. They *choose* to be in relation to each other.

Ruth and Naomi's elective sisterhood stands in tension with the biologically determined dynasty it produces and, I suggest, offers a different paradigm of family. In the Davidic dynasty, biology determines succession and destiny. God promises David a successor and an eternal dynasty saying:

> When your days are over and you lie with your ancestors, I will raise up your seed that comes from your loins after you and establish his kingship. He will build a house for my name, and I will establish his royal throne forever. (2 Sam 7:12-13)

In the books of Samuel and Kings, King David's sons and grandsons fight to establish the most secure dynasty in Israel's history. In the book of Ruth, sisterhood overrides biology. A Moabite woman proves more valuable than seven Israelite sons. In Ruth, sisterhood provides an alternative paradigm of family that celebrates love and loyalty over lineage and legacy.

The book of Ruth remains a compelling mystery. Despite generations of inquiry, commentators have not offered a definitive explanation for why David's story begins with Ruth and Naomi's or how the book of Ruth impacts the status of the Davidic line.[3] Some recognize a subversive ideology in a book that features women and celebrates the other.[4] Others see a conventional ideology in a book that provides an heir and protects the patriline.[5] In my reading, Ruth is an unconventional family narrative in which sisterhood drives the narrative and not fathers, sons, brothers, or even mothers. I contend that the book of Ruth intentionally uses elective sisterhood as a counterbalance to genetic dynasty. Once David's ancestor is born, biology takes over. Yet it is sisterhood that sets the dynastic wheels in motion. The association of sisterhood with David's story asserts that biology does not always determine destiny. Families are made as well as born.

In the book of Ruth, sisterhood shapes Israel's story. It also reflects it. Ruth's qualities of kindness, generosity, and loyalty, encapsulated in the word חסד, are often seen as reflecting God's qualities. Ruth's loyalty to Naomi, and the acts she performs to support her, are recognized in the book as her[6] חסד. Like Ruth, God extends חסד toward Israel and supports Israel.[7] Ruth may manifest divine qualities, but I believe that it is her choice to cling to Naomi that makes her most God-like. As an elective relationship between two women not bound to each other by biology or obligation, Ruth and Naomi's sisterhood may offer the Bible's best paradigm for the divine-human relationship. Just as Ruth chooses Naomi, God chooses Israel. Like Ruth's relationship to Naomi, the relationship between God and Israel is loving and intimate and modeled on a familial relationship.[8] There is no rational explanation for God's relationship to Israel. God chooses Israel because God loves Israel as Deut 7:7-8 conveys:

> YHWH did not desire you and choose you because you are the most numerous among all the nations—indeed you are the smallest among the nations. Rather it is because YHWH loved you [מאהבת יהוה] and honored the oath he swore to your ancestors that YHWH brought you with a strong arm and freed you from the house of slavery and from the hand of Pharaoh, king of Egypt.

Whereas sisterhood defines Ruth and Naomi's elected relationship to one another, God's relationship to Israel alternates between a spousal and an adoptive-parental relationship. Although the marriage metaphor looms large throughout the prophets, Ezekiel 16 captures both types of relationships. At the beginning of the chapter, God adopts the abandoned baby Israel.[9] Once she matures, God renews his commitment and marries her. Whether God adopts or marries Israel, love—and not biology—is the determining factor in creating God's family. Because God loves Israel, God commits to Israel and establishes David's eternal dynasty as an act[10] of חסד. In the Bible's greater narrative, a story of love precedes a story of legacy. The book of Ruth encapsulates this narrative. It is a love story that makes way for a legacy story. Ruth's devotion to Naomi and their sisterhood ensures the birth of David's ancestor.

Whether ideal or dangerous, sisters and sisterhoods are significant figures in the Bible. My study shows that they have their own stories and their own essential role to play within Israel's story. Sisters and sisterhoods remove rival patriarchs, build the house of Israel, and establish the Davidic monarchy. Their stories ensure the stability and purity of the Israelite family and society and help Israel remain loyal to God. They even offer a paradigm for God's relationship to Israel. The time has come to bring sisters and sisterhoods from the margins of the Bible's narratives and to recognize them as vital figures. It is time to heed the prophet Hosea who commands:

אמרו לאחיכם עמי ולאחותיכם רחמה

Call your brothers "My People" and your sisters "Mercifully Accepted!"[11]

Notes

1. Claudia V. Camp notes the association of foreignness with foreign women in the book of Numbers and considers it part of a priestly rhetorical strategy. See Camp, *Wise, Strange and Holy: The Strange Woman and the Making of the Bible* (Sheffield: Sheffield Academic, 2000), 225.

2. For a discussion of the historicity of King David, see Hershel Shanks, ed., *Ancient Israel: A Short History from Abraham to the Roman Destruction of the Temple* (Englewood Cliffs, NJ: Prentice Hall, 1980), 85–108; and Israel Finkelstein and Neil Asher Silberman, *The Bible Unearthed: Archaeology's New Vision of Ancient Israel and the Origin of its Sacred Texts* (New York: Free Press, 2001), 128–45.

3. Tamar Frankiel acknowledges the on-going and important questions the book of Ruth raises, particularly for religious Jews. See Frankiel, "Ruth and the Messiah," in *Reading Ruth: Contemporary Women Reclaim a Sacred Story, ed. Judith A. Kates and Gail Twersky Reimer* (New York: Ballantine, 1994), 324.

4. See Ilana Pardes, *Countertraditions in the Bible: A Feminist Approach* (Cambridge, MA: Harvard University Press, 1992), 99.

5. See Esther Fuchs, *Sexual Politics in the Biblical Narrative: Reading the Hebrew Bible as a Woman* (Sheffield: Sheffield Academic, 2000), 89.

6. See Ruth 1:8; 2:20; and 3:10.

7. God extends חסד to Israel in Exod 20:6; and Deut 7:9. Tamara Cohn Eskenazi comments on the use of the term in Ruth: "The term *hesed* appears only three times in the book (1:8; 2:20, and 3:10), but its meaning is woven into the book's entire fabric. . . . In refusing to abandon Naomi, Ruth embodies *hesed* (1:8; 1:16-17). Ruth's loyalty to her mother-in-law inspires wealthy Boaz, who extends generosity toward Ruth, stretching himself beyond the call of duty (2:8-12)." See Tamara Cohn Eskenazi and Tikva Frymer-Kensky, *The JPS Bible Commentary: Ruth* (Philadelphia: The Jewish Publication Society, 2011), l.

8. Love defines Ruth's relationship with Naomi (Ruth 4:15) as it does God's with Israel. See Deut 6:5; 7:8; and 10:12.

9. Exod 4:22, 2 Sam 7:14, and Jer 3:19 also evoke the image of adoption.

10. See 2 Sam 7:15-16.

11. Hos 2:3.

Bibliography

Almog, Yael. "'Flowing Myrrh upon the Handles of the Bolt': Bodily Border, Social Norms and Their Transgression in the Song of Songs." *BI* 18 (2010): 251–63.

Alpert, Rebecca. "Finding Our Past: A Lesbian Interpretation of the Book of Ruth." In *Reading Ruth: Contemporary Women Reclaim a Sacred Story*, edited by Judith A. Kates and Gail Twersky Reimer, 91–96. New York: Ballantine, 1994.

Alter, Robert. *The Art of Biblical Narrative*. New York: Basic, 1981.

Aschkenasy, Nehama. "Reading Ruth through a Bakhtinian Lens: The Carnivalesque in a Biblical Tale." *JBL* 126, no. 3 (2007): 437–53.

———. *Woman at the Window: Biblical Tales of Oppression and Escape*. Detroit: Wayne State University Press, 1998.

Baadsgaard, Aubrey. "A Taste of Women's Sociality: Cooking as Cooperative Labor in Iron Age Syro-Palestine." In *The World of Women in the Ancient and Classical Near East*, edited by Beth Alpert Nakhai, 13–44. Newcastle upon Tyne: Cambridge Scholars, 2008.

Baumann, Gerlinde. *Love and Violence: Marriage as Metaphor for the Relationship between YHWH and Israel in the Prophetic Books*. Collegeville, MN: Liturgical, 2003.

Ben-Barak, Zafrira. "The Legal Background to the Restoration of Michal to David." In *Telling Queen Michal's Story: An Experiment in Comparative Interpretation*, edited by David J. A. Clines and Tamara C. Eskenazi, 74–90. Sheffield: Sheffield Academic, 1991.

Berquist, Jon L. *Controlling Corporeality: The Body and the Household in Ancient Israel*. New Brunswick, NJ: Rutgers University Press, 2002.

Black, Fiona C. "Beauty or the Beast: The Grotesque Body in the Song of Songs." *BI* 8, no. 3 (2000): 302–23.

Bledstein, Adrien J. "Female Companionships: If the Book of Ruth Were Written by a Woman . . ." In *A Feminist Companion to Ruth*, edited by Athalya Brenner, 116–33. Sheffield: Sheffield Academic, 1993.

Blenkinsopp, Joseph. "The Family in First Temple Israel." In *Families in Ancient Israel (Family Religion and Culture)*, edited by Leo G. Perdue, Joseph

Blenkinsopp, John J. Collins, and Carol L. Meyers, 48–103. Louisville: Westminster John Knox, 1997.

Block, Daniel I. "Marriage and Family in Ancient Israel." In *Marriage and Family in the Biblical World,* edited by Ken M. Campbell, 33–102. Downers Grove, IL: InterVarsity, 2003.

Boase, Elizabeth. "Life in the Shadows: The Role and Function of Isaac in Genesis: Synchronic and Diachronic Readings." *VT* 51, no. 3 (2001), 312–35.

Bow, Beverly. "Sisterhood? Women's Relationships with Women in the Hebrew Bible." In *Life and Culture in the Ancient Near East,* edited by Richard E. Averbeck, Mark W. Chavalas, and David B. Weisberg, 205–15. Bethesda, MD: CDL, 2003.

Bowen, Nancy R. "The Daughters of Your People: Female Prophets in Ezekiel 13:17-23." *JBL* 118, no. 3 (1999): 417–33.

Brenner, Athalya. "Female Social Behaviour: Two Descriptive Patterns within the 'Birth of the Hero' Paradigm." In *A Feminist Companion to Genesis,* edited by Athalya Brenner, 204–21. Sheffield: Sheffield Academic, 1993.

———. "Naomi and Ruth." *VT* 33, no. 4 (1983): 385–97.

Bronner, Leila Leah. *Stories of Biblical Mothers: Maternal Power in the Hebrew Bible.* Dallas: University Press of America, 2004.

Burrus, Virginia, and Stephen D. Moore. "Unsafe Sex: Feminism, Pornography, and the Song of Songs." *BI* 11, no. 1 (2003): 24–52.

Camp, Claudia V. *Wise, Strange and Holy: The Strange Woman and the Making of the Bible.* Sheffield: Sheffield Academic, 2000.

Carmichael, Calum M. "A Ceremonial Crux: Removing a Man's Sandal as a Female Gesture of Contempt." *JBL* 96, no. 3 (1977): 321–36.

———. *Law, Legend, and Incest in the Bible: Leviticus 18–20.* Ithaca: Cornell University Press, 1997.

Carr, David. "Gender and the Shaping of Desire in the Song of Songs and Its Interpretation." *JBL* 119, no. 2 (2000): 233–48.

Carroll, Robert P. "Whorusalamin: A Tale of Three Cities as Three Sisters." In *On Reading Prophetic Texts: Gender-Specific and Related Studies in Memory of Fokkelien Van Dijk-Hemmes,* edited by Bob Becking and Meindert Dijkstra, 67–82. Leiden: Brill, 1996.

Clines, David J. A. "The Significance of the 'Sons of God' Episode (Genesis 1–4) in the Context of the 'Primeval History' (Genesis 1–11)." *JSOT* 13 (1979): 33–46.

———. "The Story of Michal, Wife of David, in Its Sequential Unfolding." In *Telling Queen Michal's Story: An Experiment in Comparative Interpretation,* edited by David J. A. Clines and Tamara C. Eskenazi, 129–40. Sheffield: Sheffield Academic, 1991.

Cohn, Robert L. "Negotiating (with) the Natives: Ancestors and Identity in Genesis." *HTR* 96, no. 2 (2003): 147–66.

Cox, Benjamin D., and Susan Ackerman, "Rachel's Tomb." *JBL* 128, no. 1 (2009): 135–48.

Coxon, Peter W. "Was Naomi a Scold? A Response to Fewell and Gunn." *JSOT* 45 (1989): 25–37.

Davies, Eryl W. "Inheritance Rights and the Hebrew Levirate Marriage: Part 1." *VT* 31, no. 2 (1981): 138–44.

Day, Peggy L. "From the Child is Born the Woman: The Story of Jephthah's Daughter." In *Gender and Difference in Ancient Israel,* edited by Peggy L. Day, 58–74. Minneapolis: Fortress Press, 1989.

Dever, William G. *Did God Have a Wife? Archaeology and Folk Religion in Ancient Israel.* Grand Rapids, MI: William B. Eerdmans, 2005.

Doyle, Brian. "'Knock, Knock, Knockin' on Sodom's Door': The Function of פתח/דלת in Genesis 18–19." *JSOT* 28, no. 4 (2004): 431–48.

Ebeling, Jennie R. *Women's Lives in Biblical Times.* London: T&T Clark, 2010.

Eskenazi, Tamara Cohn and Tikva Frymer-Kensky. *The JPS Bible Commentary: Ruth.* Philadelphia: The Jewish Publication Society, 2011.

Eslinger, Lyle. "A Contextual Identification of the *bene ha'elohim* and *benoth ha'adam* in Genesis 6:1-4." *JSOT* 13 (1979): 65–73.

Exum, J. Cheryl. *Fragmented Women: Feminist (Sub)versions of Biblical Narratives.* Valley Forge, PA: Trinity, 1993.

———. *Song of Songs.* Louisville: Westminster John Knox, 2005.

———. *Tragedy and Biblical Narrative.* Cambridge: Cambridge University Press, 1992.

Finkelstein, Israel, and Neil Asher Silberman. *The Bible Unearthed: Archaeology's New Vision of Ancient Israel and the Origin of Its Sacred Texts.* New York: Free Press, 2001.

Fleurant, Josebert. "Phinehas Murdered Moses' Wife: An Analysis of Numbers 25." *JSOT* 35, no. 3 (2011): 285–94.

Frankiel, Tamar. "Ruth and the Messiah." In *Reading Ruth: Contemporary Women Reclaim a Sacred Story,* edited by Judith A. Kates and Gail Twersky Reimer, 321–35. New York: Ballantine, 1994.

Frymer-Kensky, Tikva. *Reading the Women of the Bible: A New Interpretation of Their Stories*. New York: Schocken, 2002.

Fuchs, Esther. *Sexual Politics in the Biblical Narrative: Reading the Hebrew Bible as a Woman*. Sheffield: Sheffield Academic, 2000.

Goitein, S. D. "Women as Creators of Biblical Genres." *Prooftexts* 8, no. 1 (1988): 1–33.

Greenspahn, Frederick E. *When Brothers Dwell Together: The Preeminence of Younger Siblings in the Hebrew Bible*. Oxford: Oxford University Press, 1994.

Greenstein, Edward L. "An Equivocal Reading of the Sale of Joseph." In *Literary Interpretations of Biblical Narratives, Volume II*, edited by Kenneth R. R. Gros Louis with James S. Ackerman, 114–25. Nashville: Abingdon, 1982.

Hendel, Ronald S. "Of Demigods and the Deluge: Toward an Interpretation of Genesis 6:1-4." *JBL* 106, no. 1 (1987): 13–26.

Hepner, Gershon. "Abraham's Incestuous Marriage with Sarah: A Violation of the Holiness Code." *VT* 53, no. 2 (2003): 143–55.

Hertzberg, Hans Wilhelm. *I & II Samuel*. Translated by J. S. Bowden. OTL. Philadelphia: Westminster, 1964.

Holladay, William L. *Jeremiah I*. Hermeneia. Philadelphia: Fortress Press, 1986.

Holt, Else K. "King Nebuchadrezzar of Babylon, My Servant, and the Cup of Wrath: Jeremiah's Fantasies and the Hope of Violence." In *Jeremiah (Dis)placed: New Directions in Writing/Reading Jeremiah*, edited by A. R. Pete Diamond and Louis Stulman, 209–18. London: T&T Clark, 2011.

Huebner, Sabine R. "'Brother-Sister' Marriage in Roman Egypt: A Curiosity of Humankind or a Widespread Family Strategy?" *The Journal of Roman Studies* 97 (2007): 21–49.

Jay, Nancy. "Sacrifice, Descent and the Patriarchs." *VT* 38, no. 1 (1988): 52–70.

Kaminski, Carol M. "Beautiful Women or 'False Judgment'? Interpreting Genesis 6.2 in the Context of the Primeval History." *JSOT* 32, no. 4 (2008): 457–73.

Keefe, Alice A. *Woman's Body and the Social Body in Hosea*. Sheffield: Sheffield Academic, 2001.

Ketchum, Josh. "The Go'el Custom in Ruth: A Comparative Study." *Restoration Quarterly* 52, no. 4 (2010): 237–45.

King, Philip J., and Lawrence E. Stager. *Life in Biblical Israel*. Louisville: Westminster John Knox, 2001.

Kottsieper, Ingo. "'We Have a Little Sister': Aspects of the Brother-Sister Relationship in Ancient Israel." In *Families and Family Relations: As Represented in Early Juadaisms and Early Christianities: Texts and Fictions,* edited by Jan Willem Van Henten and Athalya Brenner, 49–80. Leiden: Deo, 2000.

Kraus, Hans-Joachim. *Psalms 1–59.* Translated by Hilton C. Oswald. Minneapolis: Fortress Press, 1993.

Kunin, Seth Daniel. *The Logic of Incest: A Structuralist Analysis of Hebrew Mythology.* Sheffield: Sheffield Academic, 1995.

Lapsley, Jacqueline E. "Shame and Self-Knowledge: The Positive Role of Shame in Ezekiel's View of the Moral Self." In *The Book of Ezekiel: Theological and Anthropological Perspectives,* edited by Margaret S. Odell and John T. Strong, 143–73. Atlanta: Society of Biblical Literature, 2000.

Lee, Eunny P. "Ruth the Moabite: Identity, Kinship, and Otherness." In *Engaging the Bible in a Gendered World: An Introduction to Feminist Biblical Interpretation in Honor of Katharine Doob Sakenfeld,* edited by Linda Day and Carolyn Pressler, 89–101. Louisville: Westminster John Knox, 2006.

Levenson, Jon D. *The Death and Resurrection of the Beloved Son: The Transformation of Child Sacrifice in Judaism and Christianity.* New Haven: Yale University Press, 1993.

Levenson, Jon D., and Baruch Halpern, "The Political Import of David's Marriages." *JBL* 99, no. 4 (1980): 507–18.

Levine, Baruch A. *Numbers 21–36,* AB. New York: Doubleday, 2000.

Logan, Alice. "Rehabilitating Jephthah." *JBL* 128, no. 4 (2009): 665–85.

Low, Katherine B. "The Sexual Abuse of Lot's Daughters: Reconceptualizing Kinship for the Sake of Our Daughters." *JFSR* 26, no. 2 (2010): 37–54.

Lutzky, Harriet C. "The Name 'Cozbi' (Numbers XXV 15, 18)." *VT* 47, no. 4 (1997): 546–49.

Macwilliam, Stuart. "Ideologies of Male Beauty and the Hebrew Bible." *BI* 17 (2009): 265–87.

Maier, Christl M. *Daughter Zion, Mother Zion: Gender, Space, and the Sacred in Ancient Israel.* Minneapolis: Fortress Press, 2008.

McCarter, Kyle P. *1 Samuel.* AB 8. New York: Doubleday, 1980.

McClenney-Sadler, Madeline Gay. *Recovering the Daughter's Nakedness: A Formal Analysis of Israelite Kinship Terminology and the Internal Logic of Leviticus 18.* London: T&T Clark, 2007.

Melnyk, Janet L. R. "When Israel Was A child: Ancient Near Eastern Adoption Formulas and the Relationship between God and Israel." In *History and Interpretation: Essays in Honour of John H. Hayes,* edited by M. Patrick Graham, William P. Brown, and Jeffrey K. Kuan, 245–59. Sheffield: JSOT Press, 1993.

Meyers, Carol. *Discovering Eve: Ancient Israelite Women in Context.* New York: Oxford University Press, 1988.

———. "The Family in Early Israel." In *Families in Ancient Israel (Family Religion and Culture),* edited by Leo G. Perdue, Joseph Blenkinsopp, John J. Collins, and Carol L. Meyers, 1–47. Louisville: Westminster John Knox, 1997.

———. "'To Her Mother's House'" Considering a Counterpart to the Israelite *Bêt 'āb.* In *The Bible and the Politics of Exegesis: Essays in Honor of Norman K. Gottwald on His Sixty-Fifth Birthday,* edited by David Jobling, Peggy L. Day, and Gerald T. Sheppard, 39–51. Cleveland: Pilgrim, 1991.

———. "Returning Home: Ruth 1.8 and the Gendering of the Book of Ruth." In *A Feminist Companion to Ruth,* edited by Athalya Brenner, 85–114. Sheffield: Sheffield Academic, 1993.

———. " 'Women of the Neighborhood' (Ruth 4.17): Informal Female Networks in Ancient Israel." In *Ruth and Esther: A Feminist Companion to the Bible (Second Series),* edited by Athalya Brenner, 110–27. Sheffield: Sheffield Academic, 1991.

Milgrom, Jacob. *Leviticus 17–22.* AB 3. New York: Doubleday, 2000.

Miscall, Peter D. "Michal and her Sisters." In *Telling Queen Michal's Story: An Experiment in Comparative Interpretation,* edited by David J. A. Clines and Tamara C. Eskenazi, 246–60. Sheffield: Sheffield Academic, 1991.

Murphy, Roland E. *The Song of Songs.* Hermeneia. Minneapolis: Fortress Press, 1990.

Olyan, Saul M. *Disability in the Hebrew Bible: Interpreting Mental and Physical Differences.* Cambridge: Cambridge University Press, 2008.

Pardes, Ilana. *Countertraditions in the Bible: A Feminist Approach.* Cambridge, MA: Harvard University Press, 1992.

Propp, William H. "Kinship in 2 Samuel 13." *CBQ* 55 (1993): 39–53.

Quesada, Jan Jaynes. "Body Piercing: The Issue of Priestly Control over Acceptable Family Structure in the Book of Numbers." *BI* 10, no. 1 (2002): 24–35.

Rashkow, Ilona N. *Taboo or not Taboo: Sexuality and Family in the Hebrew Bible.* Minneapolis, Fortress Press, 2000.

Sakenfeld, Katharine Doob. "Naomi's Cry: Reflections on Ruth 1:20–21." In *A God So Near: Essays on Old Testament Theology in Honor of Patrick D. Miller,* edited by Brent A. Strawn and Nancy R. Bowen, 129–43. Winona Lake, IN: Eisenbrauns, 2003.

Sasson, Jack M. "Absalom's Daughter: An Essay in Vestige Historiography." In *The Land that I Will Show You: Essays on the History and Archaeology of the Ancient Near East in Honour of J. Maxwell Miller,* edited by J. Andrew Dearman and M. Patrick Graham, 179–96. Sheffield: Sheffield Academic, 2001.

Schloen, J. David. *The House of the Father as Fact and Symbol: Patrimonialism in Ugarit and the Ancient Near East.* Winona Lake, IN: Eisenbrauns, 2001.

Setel, T. Drorah. "Prophets and Pornography: Female Sexual Imagery in Hosea." In *Feminist Interpretation of the Bible,* edited by Letty M. Russell, 86–95. Philadelphia: Westminster Press, 1985.

Shanks, Herschel, ed. *Ancient Israel: A Short History from Abraham to the Roman Destruction of the Temple.* Englewood Cliffs, NJ: Prentice Hall, 1988.

Shectman, Sarah. "The Social Status of Priestly and Levite Women." In *Levites and Priests in Biblical History and Tradition,* edited by Mark Leuchter and Jeremy M. Hutton, 83–99. Atlanta: Society of Biblical Literature, 2011.

Shields, Mary E. "Circumcision of the Prostitute: Gender, Sexuality, and the Call to Repentance in Jeremiah 3.1–4.4." In *Prophets and Daniel: A Feminist Companion to the Bible (Second Series),* edited by Athalya Brenner, 121–33. (London: Sheffield Academic, 2001.

———. *Circumscribing the Prostitute: The Rhetorics of Intertextuality, Metaphor, and Gender in Jeremiah 3.1–4.4.* London: T&T Clark, 2004.

Siquans, Agnethe, "Foreignness and Poverty in the Book of Ruth: A Legal Way for a Poor Foreign Woman to be Integrated into Israel." *JBL* 128, no. 3 (2009): 443–52.

Smith, Mark S. "'Your People Shall Be My People': Family and Covenant in Ruth 1:16–17." *CBQ* 69 (2007): 242–58.

Steinberg, Naomi. *Kinship and Marriage in Genesis: A Household Economics Perspective.* Minneapolis: Fortress Press, 1993.

Tosato, Angelo. "The Law of Leviticus 18:18: A Reexamination." *CBQ* 46 (1984): 199–214.

Trible, Phyllis. "Depatriarchalizing in Biblical Interpretation." *JAAR* 41 (1973): 30–48.

———. *God and the Rhetoric of Sexuality.* Philadelphia: Fortress Press, 1978.

———. *Texts of Terror: Literary-Feminist Readings of Biblical Narratives.* Philadelphia: Fortress, 1984.

Valler, Shulamite. "King David and 'His' Women: Biblical Stories and Talmudic Discussions." In *A Feminist Companion to Samuel and Kings,* edited by Athalya Brenner, 129–42. Sheffield: Sheffield Academic, 1994.

Van der Toorn, Karel. *Family Religion in Babylonia, Syria and Israel: Continuity and Change in the Forms of Religious Life.* Leiden: E. J. Brill, 1996.

———. *Scribal Culture and the Making of the Hebrew Bible*. Cambridge, MA: Harvard University Press, 2007.

Van Dijk-Hemmes, Fokkelien. "The Metaphorization of Woman in Prophetic Speech: An Analysis of Ezekiel 23." *VT* 43, no. 2 (1993): 162–70.

———. "Ruth: A Product of Women's Culture?" In *A Feminist Companion to Ruth*, edited by Athalya Brenner, 134–39. Sheffield: Sheffield Academic, 1993.

———. "Sarai's Exile: A Gender-Motivated Reading of Genesis 12:10–13:2." In *A Feminist Companion to Genesis*, edited by Athalya Brenner, 222–34. Sheffield: Sheffield Academic, 1997.

Weems, Renita J. *Battered Love: Marriage, Sex, and Violence in the Hebrew Prophets*. Minneapolis: Fortress Press, 1995.

Weisberg, Dvora E. *Levirate Marriage and the Family in Ancient Judaism*. Hanover, NH: University Press of New England, 2009.

Wells, Bruce. "Sex, Lies, and Virginal Rape: The Slandered Bride and False Accusation in Deuteronomy." *JBL* 124, no. 1 (2005): 41–72.

Wenham, Gordon J. *The Book of Leviticus*. Grand Rapids, MI: William B. Eerdmans, 1979.

White, Ellen. "Michal the Misinterpreted." *JSOT* 31, no. 4 (2007): 451–64.

Yee, Gale A. *Poor Banished Children of Eve: Woman as Evil in the Hebrew Bible*. Minneapolis: Fortress Press, 2003.

Index of Names and Subjects

Index of Biblical References

CPSIA information can be obtained at www.ICGtesting.com
Printed in the USA
LVOW05s0626171213

365574LV00006B/8/P